THE CONNECTED CONDITION

The Connected Condition

Romanticism and the Dream of Communication

YOHEI IGARASHI

STANFORD UNIVERSITY PRESS
Stanford, California

STANFORD UNIVERSITY PRESS
Stanford, California

Printed in the United States of America on acid-free, archival-quality paper

Library of Congress Cataloging-in-Publication Data
Names: Igarashi, Yohei, 1979– author.
Title: The connected condition : Romanticism and the dream of communication / Yohei Igarashi.
Description: Stanford, California : Stanford University Press, 2019. | Series: Text technologies | Includes bibliographical references and index.
Identifiers: LCCN 2019005195 (print) | LCCN 2019006187 (ebook) | ISBN 9781503610736 | ISBN 9781503610040 | ISBN 9781503610040 (cloth : alk. paper)
Subjects: LCSH: English poetry—18th century—History and criticism. | Communication—England—History—18th century. | Romanticism—England.
Classification: LCC PR571 (ebook) | LCC PR571 .I35 2019 (print) | DDC 821/.170936—dc23
LC record available at https://lccn.loc.gov/2019005195

Cover design: Kevin Barrett Kane

Cover image: From Coleridge's notebook entry 2:2406, from January 1805 (Add MS 47518, f130v). © The British Library Board. Reprinted with permission of the British Library.

Text design: Kevin Barrett Kane

Typeset at Stanford University Press in 10/15 Spectral

Dedicated to the memory of Ryoji Takeyama

An inventive Age
Has wrought, if not with speed of magic, yet
To most strange issues.

William Wordsworth, *The Excursion*

We all have to swim for ourselves in a verbal medium of mixed quality.

I. A. Richards, *Basic in Teaching: East and West*

CONTENTS

THE CONNECTED CONDITION

The Age of Romanticism, on the verge of the
electronic age.

Walter J. Ong, *Orality and Literacy*

INTRODUCTION

THE DREAM OF COMMUNICATION

The Connected Condition

How can Romantic poetry, motivated by the poet's intense yearning to impart his thoughts and feelings, be so often obscure and the cause of readerly misunderstanding? Can a poet compose a verbal artwork, carefully and lovingly put together, and send it out into the world at the same time that he is adopting a stance against communication? And if a poet both does and does not want to "reach out and touch someone"—as the song in old AT&T television commercials went—how might that influence the language of her poem, and account for the form it takes . . . or its deformity? Perhaps we are accustomed to all this. Poetry gets a pass: it is exempt from the obligation to get something across, at least in the usual manner. Even so, is there not a flickering expectation every time we begin reading a new work that it might "speak" to us? And if it is the case that certain rules of communication are suspended for poetry, when and how did this kind of understanding of poetry come about?

The Connected Condition addresses such paradoxes and questions, and others besides, by suggesting that major Romantic poets and hallmarks of Romantic poetic style respond to the advent of a modern culture of communication. There are other ways to take on the questions above— other ways to look at any single one of them or at the whole set as a general problem—and the approach this book takes is just one. But it has come to seem to me that it is one worth sharing, and one that might resonate, especially nowadays.

For much of this book derives from a certain feeling, or in Keats's phrase, "the feel of": the feel of being a slow reader and writer on Romantic poetry while inhabiting a time when most other forms of communication are designed to be faster than ever.[1] Connectedness is a given. But just as constant as "always on" connection is the feeling that constant connection should maybe not be a given—and that the connected condition is also maybe the connected syndrome. One senses that the idea of communication itself is synonymous with conveying information, and conveying it as quickly as possible to as many people as possible. Scholars of media studies consider the workings and effects of the viral, "spreadable" content that reaches us through the digital networks that mediate and pervade our lives.[2] But this view of communication—the "spreading" of "content" of whatever sort in the most efficient, effective manner—has an even more fundamental hold on our everyday lives, so thoroughly commonsensical as to be nearly invisible, and therefore all the more powerful. I conform to it in writing these sentences: I am trying to get something across clearly (and I have just mentioned "sharing" and hoping that my claims will "resonate") and without detaining you unduly—without being like Coleridge's Ancient Mariner. You too conform to it, in large measure, every time you talk and write. But communication seems to, and can, involve so much more: it is endlessly complex, diversely and unpredictably instantiated, often frustrated and frustrating, and yet successful enough, enough of the time. One can communicate an ambivalent wanting and not wanting to communicate effectively, and poetry can be very good at that. There is the feel of a gross reduction when communication is imagined only as the transfer of information, the shorter and swifter the better.

Romantic poets felt this condition too. But they felt an early version of it: I mean that they early on or presciently felt something emerging, but also that what they were registering—though it will evolve into our world of communication—was very different too. Thomas De Quincey's essay "The English Mail-Coach, or the Glory of Motion" (1849) is a good case in point. De Quincey looks back at the establishment of a national mail coach system in Great Britain in 1784, of delivering mail by this infrastructure rather than by couriers on foot or individual horseback riders. And although he is writing during the time of railways, it seemed to him that the advent of the mail coach during the time we call Romanticism was when a new world was first coming into being. News and correspondence were "running day and night" and at a "velocity, at that time unprecedented."[3] With the "rapid transmission of intelligence" coordinated by the mail coach system—an echo of the "rapid communication of intelligence" that Wordsworth refers to more fretfully in his "Preface" to *Lyrical Ballads* (1800)—information could now flow across "all nations and languages."[4] The system is so innovative in its organization and efficiency that De Quincey almost cannot describe it other than by recourse to a series of metaphors likening the infrastructure to an orchestra, a nervous system, and a circulatory system. The constant, wide flow of information between capitals and provinces is like the "flowing and ebbing of the sea."[5] De Quincey's world sounds like a preview of our own interconnected planet. Still, it is only a preview: he marvels that the quickest mail coach, charging ahead on recently improved roads, could cover in "fifty minutes . . . eleven miles"—so, about thirteen miles per hour.[6] Historians guess a slightly slower rate, estimating that mail coaches, and thus the information carried by them, traveled at around six miles per hour in the 1780s, going up to ten miles per hour by around 1830.[7] In any case, what the Romantic poets sensed as under way has striking similarities to our own connected condition and equally striking differences. One of the aims of this book is to maintain a balance between historical resonances with explanatory value and historical remoteness, between sympathetic identification across the span of time and the strange specificity of the past.

The Romantic connected condition has the feel of familiarity and un-familiarity at once. There was the practice of swiftly taking handwritten notes in shorthand, the period's imperfect but primary technology for recording spoken language in real time. Stenography was the era's audio recording equipment, its speech recognition software for converting talk into text. The Romantic poets saw the rise of sophisticated systems for collecting and processing information. In the age of Wordsworth, the stream-lined, large-scale management of data (or, as data were then described, "particulars") relied on standardized blank paper forms, that much abused documentary subgenre of bureaucracy, itself too unthinkingly abused by both sides. This is before Big Data (prior to) and also Before Big Data (a precursor to)—alternatively, Big Particulars, a term that better draws out the element of oxymoron, and the thorny problems introduced when aggregating, scaling up. The Romantic poets knew well the early expectations surrounding quick telegraphic communication across previously unthinkable distances, and they pondered the ramifications: what is the fate of dense literary language, and the slow reading that usually goes with it, in an era of instantaneous communication? They also felt, before us, a familiar facet of networked life: being extremely and always connected and yet somehow alone. And as this problem became a foundational problem for the emerging discourse of sociology, they reacted to these debates with their own poetic insights.

This book suggests that Romantic poets responded to their connected condition by engaging the *dream of communication*. The dream of communication is the powerful fantasy that has driven the modern communications order, as well as its norms, practices, and infrastructures. The fantasy is of a transfer of thoughts, feelings, and information between individuals made as efficient as possible, and of perfectible media that could facilitate the quickest and clearest communication. This desire leads to certain norms of communication (for example, "perspicuity" of writing); but these norms, being also ideals, have a way of going unmet, further intensifying the wish for perfectible communication and the perceived necessity of the norm—and so on.[8] Norms of communication serve as the basis for communications practices, media, and infrastructures, which take the form they do in significant part because of the ideals they presuppose and the tenacious wish at their root; in turn, communications practices, media, and infrastructures continually reinforce and reproduce certain norms and the underlying desire. In the context of this book's primary concerns and texts, I am imagining something along the lines of the accompanying diagram (allowing for further refinement), going from the ground up.

The Dream of Communication

Practices, media, and infrastructures of communication
(e.g., shorthand practices, bureaucracy, telegraphy)

Norms and standards of communication
(e.g., "perspicuity," "precision"; shorthand characters;
standardized questions on paper forms)

The fantasy of perfectible contact
(the desire for it and its frustration)

The dream of communication was an area of particular expertise and concern for Romantic poets: after all, these poets were first and foremost literary writers and members of "the dreamer tribe," not technologists, even though many of them gave considerable thought to non-literary technologies like shorthand scripts, optical and perhaps electric telegraphy, and administrative forms, and knew more about them than one might at first expect from their literary writings.[9] The chapters that follow do not link poets directly to technical media but to broader social fantasies and anxieties about communication—that is, my analyses relate writers to technologies only through the mediation of the dream of communication—because their poetry met medial and communicative issues most intensely and intricately at the registers of desires about communication and the norms that gave social expression to them.[10] The poets featured in this book—Samuel Taylor Coleridge, William Wordsworth, Percy Shelley, and John Keats—share a great attraction and skepticism toward the wish for mediated forms of communication made more effective so as to feel like unmediated contact. Imagining their own artistic medium of poetic language in relation to this dream, these writers internalized fantasies and norms about speedy, transparent communication even as they tried out contrarian literary strategies: darkening the poetic medium, prolonging literary reading, being cryptic, and ironizing information-centric views of communication. The Romantic writers bent to social desiderata about communication as much as, and at the same time that, they tried to bend them.

The communications practices taken up in this book are not registered exclusively by poetic genres. It is well known, for example, that Charles Dickens was trained and interested in shorthand (a technology taken up in Chapter 1), a topic that appears in his novels.[11] And writing in the personal essay genre, Charles Lamb recounts his fiscal-bureaucratic work (the kind of work examined in Chapter 2), whether it is his feeling that he "had grown to [his] desk . . . and the wood had entered into [his] soul" or his anxiety dreams about "imaginary false entries, errors in my accounts."[12] Yet *The Connected Condition* chooses to focus on poets and poetry for several reasons. I have already brought up one reason above: poetry, and particularly Romantic poetry, is an especially good place to study the contradictory wish both to communicate and not to communicate—to adhere to then recently installed norms like clarity and brevity in communication, and yet to be obscure, perplexing, and overlong.[13] Furthermore, as Celeste Langan and Maureen N. McLane suggest in their pioneering essay "The Medium of Romantic poetry," poets of the period composed their works with a heightened awareness of poetry as a communicative medium, along with attendant "phantasies of media transparency and immediacy."[14] Consider this anecdote about Wordsworth's reaction upon learning of Coleridge's death, in 1834:

> Wordsworth, as a poet, regretted that German metaphysics had so much captivated the taste of Coleridge, for he was frequently not intelligible on the subject; whereas, if his energy and his originality had

been more exerted in *the channel of poetry*, an instrument of which he had so perfect a mastery, Wordsworth thought he might have done more permanently to enrich the literature, and to influence the thought of the nation, than any man of the age.[15] (Emphasis mine)

This is the kind of "self-consciousness about the problem of poetry's medium and the status of its mediation" noticed by Langan and McLane, a self-consciousness appearing here under the signature of "channel"—a "Romantic Poetry Channel," as it were, through which the poets tried to communicate, and of which some of them gained "mastery." At the conclusion of "The Medium of Romantic Poetry," Langan and McLane ask what lies on the other side of such fantasies of immediacy, and this book offers one answer: the poets' desire to controvert while adhering to the immediacy and transparency fantasies driving communication and information systems of their time, including poetry itself. A final reason for this book's decision to focus on poetry is that there exist good studies of the novel in the context of information technologies. These studies tend to examine the novel for the very reason that novelistic prose, unlike poetry, is closer to referential, informational language. Richard Menke explains this rationale well: "in contrast to the era's poetry, fiction minimizes the formal markers that might separate it from a larger world of everyday printed information," thus inviting an examination of how novelistic prose compares to other, kindred information systems.[16] In contrast to such work, and hoping to offer a complementary account, this book seeks precisely to relate the intensified literary qualities for which Romantic poetry is known—from Coleridgean symbols to Shelleyan difficulty—to the seemingly quite different communicative ideals of contemporaneous information practices. Then it becomes possible to reimagine Romantic poeticity as shaped not only by, say, the stylistic tendencies of earlier literary historical periods or by other kinds of contemporaneous pressures, but also by the modern world of communication—a world we have inherited from them.

To view Romanticism in this way is to propose a series of different timelines and thence to see both Romanticism and the history of communication in a new light. It means locating the origins of modern communication fantasies before the emergence of electronic media technologies in the later nineteenth century. In *Speaking into the Air: A History of the Idea of Communication*, John Durham Peters argues that although our communication problems may be a timeless aspect of the human condition, there is, with communication as with many other ideas, "something historical and contingent about ... something transhistorical and given."[17] For Peters, our yearnings for contact, particularly co-present contact, were given their now familiar articulations in large part by the mediated interactions offered by modern electrical technologies like the electrical telegraph, telephone, and radio: "interpersonal relations gradually became redescribed in the technical terms of transmission at a distance" associated with later nineteenth-century technical media.[18] We might still say, "It was all perfectly friendly, but there just wasn't a connection." Yet before these Victorian inventions, and beginning in the later seventeenth century, the dream of communication centered on language as a medium, and then increasingly also on the medium that would give inventions like the telegraph and phonograph their "-graph"s and their logics: *writing*.[19] During the eighteenth century, according to Clifford Siskin, the long-standing technology of writing gained renewed conspicuousness as a technology because of an increased volume of printed matter and writing's function in the modern specialization of work.[20] In the context of the history of communication, writing in this epoch was also the epicenter of the dream of communication in the way that later media—say, the telephone or social media—would also come to be. Inscription was the multi-medial hub where speech, handwriting, and print, but also language, poetic language, and the like all interacted, where hopes and anxieties about communication were directed, and where these longings were worked through and sometimes implemented as societal norms.

Walter J. Ong's understanding of "the Age of Romanticism" as "on the verge of the electronic age" is therefore worth underscoring.[21] His deliberately anachronistic definition, describing one epoch by way of the one typically thought to succeed it, reveals something important about how the "Age of Romanticism" is not quite, and yet on many counts anticipates, the "electronic age." Significant pre-electric expressions of the dream of communication suffused the British social and literary imagination beginning in the mid- and later eighteenth century: the New Rhetoric's codification and teaching of stylistic standards like clarity, brevity, precision, and "purity" in written communications; the promise of pre-electric telegraphy, of instantaneous contact at a distance; the pursuit of a transcription method that could keep up with speech and thereby save the human voice for transmission through time and space; the proliferation of utilitarian written subgenres, like the printed blank form, aimed at the efficient recording, processing, and communication of information; and the possibility of connection via the poetic medium in increasingly differentiated, anomic societies. *The Connected Condition* suggests that within the domain of writing practices and text technologies, poets were especially sensitive to the dream of communication. This was also their turf, their business. They kept returning to the problem of how, in Wordsworth's words, feelings and pleasure might or might not be "forcibly communicated" through poetry, how thoughts and feelings might or might not be expressed to that unknowable "being to whom we address ourselves."[22] It is very true that we oftentimes speak about personal relations in terms of later nineteenth-century technologies. But it is also true that, in Andrew Piper's words, Romantic-era communications "offer insights into where and when some of the most salient issues surrounding communication today emerged."[23] Notions like "TL;DR"—contemporary internet speak, probably already passé, both for the complaint "too long; didn't read" and for its cure in the form of the briefest summary—and "instant messages" and "direct messages" are arguably outgrowths of Romantic-era communication premises, promises, and practices.

The Romantics also lived in—perhaps better to say, lived with and lived through—an information society or an information state.[24] According to James R. Beniger's influential account, the "Information Society"—our information society—came about in the middle of the nineteenth century in response to the need created by the industrial revolution for rationalized feedback systems. "Means of bureaucratic organization, the new infrastructures of transportation and telecommunications, and system-wide communication via the new mass media" amounted to the "control revolution" that ushered in the information age.[25] Yet one of the more unexpected things I found in writing this book was the degree to which bureaucratic organization, systems for amassing and processing information, and infrastructural connectedness—in short, something approaching, but not entirely, an information society—were being put into place, and were in fact quite developed, in the later eighteenth and early nineteenth centuries. Whenever Romantic literature comes up—in scholarship, course descriptions, anthologies, the odd conversation—the same few revolutions are always invoked (for example, the French Revolution, Burke's "revolution in sentiments, manners, and moral opinions," a revolution in poetic language), but one almost never hears mention of the control revolution.[26] This should not be the case. We have previously seen De Quincey portraying something like a modern information network. Wordsworth too witnessed the establishment of "easier links connecting place with place" (like Beniger's "new infrastructures of transportation"), the workings of the British fiscal-bureaucratic system from his position within the government Stamp Office, and the "systematizations" occurring across all sectors of society.[27]

Closely related to the above, the Romantic movement is also the *first* efficiency movement. I mean partly that Romantic-era developments seem to presage the better known "efficiency movement" or "efficiency craze" that ensued from Frederick Winslow Taylor's *The Principles of Scientific Management* (1911) and its revolutionizing of labor in the twentieth century. Toward a science by which enterprises could achieve a "state of maximum efficiency," Taylor conducted meticulous studies of, for example, the labor of pig iron handlers and managers at the Bethlehem Steel Company in the 1890s.[28] Yet there are precedents around the time of Romanticism: Josiah Wedgwood's "clocking-in system" and other rationalizing methods of factory and time discipline in his potteries (this being the Wedgwood dynasty that would go on to patronize Coleridge), the Bentham brothers' utilitarian schemes for streamlined organizations, and arguably even Wordsworth's description in his "Preface" of the "uniformity of . . . occupations" of factory laborers.[29] But beyond these Romantic-era forebodings of scientific management, I mean that "the first efficiency movement" is also a very good way to understand the norms and practices entailed by the dream of communication: first, efficiency (as in, our first priority is efficiency). A calculation close to Jeremy Bentham's motto for efficient administration, "official aptitude maximized, expense minimized"—that is, something close to the formula of big output and frugal input—came stubbornly to shape communications practices too.[30] Manifestations of this spirit in the realm of communication have impacted the forms, genres, and media of contact ever since, including those of poetry. The formula of efficient communication tacitly works on the narrator of Wordsworth's "Michael," who is anxious about being long-winded, about engaging in "a waste of words." But we recall too that the narrator of "Michael" heedlessly goes on with his digression, describing "minutely" the significance of the lamp in Michael's cottage.[31] As Wordsworth and his poetic peers accommodated the rule of efficiency in communication, they also knew better than most that the efficiency obsession inevitably breeds—is inextricable from—inefficiency, repetition and tautology, and information overload.[32]

From the perspective of "artifactual" histories of communications media and technologies, the Romantic period can be construed as a relatively tame time.[33] There is no arrival of the printing press or the phonograph or television or the Internet. The approach taken by scholars interested in such matters has been to study decidedly literary media (literary books, ballads), and/or to foreground the proliferation of older media (writing, print, books), and/or to focus on the dynamic between literary writers and the radically expanded and more complex audiences with which the Romantics famously had conflicted relations.[34] Together these approaches have generated a large body of excellent scholarship, without which this book would not have an understanding of the Romantic media ecology to take as a point of departure. For the last couple of decades, one useful way of organizing such concerns—literary media, proliferations, and the problem of Romantic-era audiences—has been the concept of "print culture." But recently, there has been a welcome effort to rethink the print culture paradigm. Such efforts remind us, for example, of the persistence of manuscript culture, or that print had been around for a very long time before the later eighteenth century, or that the concepts of print and print culture are vaguer than our routine reliance on them as analytics allows us to pause and consider.[35]

The Connected Condition is informed by these recent responses to print culture (for example, in the treatment of handwriting in discussions of shorthand and blank forms), and it pivots from the print culture paradigm—and from studies that place at their center proliferations or Romantic audiences—for more fundamental reasons. For one thing, this book takes much inspiration from scholarship on the history of communication and from media studies, where shorthand, standardized blank forms, "alone togetherness," and telegraphy are more significant objects of study than the literary media on which Romantic literary scholars tend to concentrate. If we begin to examine further how Romantic writing was shaped not only by the media of its own production and circulation but also by the logics of the broader scriptural economy and infrastructures of connection, then that would be all for the good.[36] A useful analogy might be made with contemporary works of fiction: Elif Batuman's *The Idiot* (2017), to name a recent, favorite work of mine, ruminates on the tempos and tensions associated with early university email systems and the correspondence carried out through them. The novel is not at all concerned with printed paperback books like *The Idiot* itself. In the same way, the Romantics dealt with text technologies as well as communications practices and infrastructures other than those captured by print culture. Second, and along the same lines, this book depends on changes in magnitude other than the proliferation of print: for example, the dramatic development of British fiscal bureaucracy and its paper- and parchment-work, or different degrees and kinds of societal connectedness (what Émile Durkheim calls "material density" and "moral density").[37] Finally, there is certainly a version of the dream of communication at work in Romantic writers' vexed relationships with the reading public, whether those of their own time or imaginary, future publics. In the context of this book, however, the term *dream of communication* indicates quite precisely a different, and far less studied, set of fantasies: larger social desiderata about efficient communication that define the Romantic connected condition and which, for better or for worse, persevere into our own time.

Thus from the perspective taken by this book—which sees the period from the complex of fantasies, standards, and practices that can be grasped as the dream of communication—very different things come into view and present themselves for study: a Romanticism "on the verge of the electronic age," contemporary with the emergence of an information society, and embodying the first efficiency movement. With this switch in perspective, Romanticism need not be a quiet moment in the history of media and communication; nor is our only recourse, given these circumstances, the study of literary media, proliferations of old media, or new kinds of audiences, each guided by the concept of print culture. Rather, a considerable epistemic stretch of the modern history of communication is premised on what can be grasped as a fundamentally Romantic-poetic dream—that, in Keats's words, "pouring forth thy soul abroad" is maybe desirable and might be possible.

The Dream of Communication

The term *communication* in this book's subtitle (*"The Dream of Communication"*) perhaps has the look and ring of a throwback. Part of this effect is surely due to the recent discursive preponderance of *media*: our world is one of ceaseless media coverage, social media, digital media, mediatization, and so on. Although the media concept did not come about until the later nineteenth century with the emergence of electronic technical media, scholars now routinely and justifiably impute media, multimedia phenomena, remediations, as well as media awarenesses and practices to prior historical periods. There are medieval old media; in one recent account, the "deep time of the media" goes back to antiquity.[38] And media are not only for all time, but everywhere, even places one might never have thought to look—the air we breathe and the clouds in the sky. John Durham Peters reminds us that it is not so easy to disentangle media technologies from their environments, and offers the idea of "elemental media," including "water, fire, sky, earth"—an idea that is forward thinking but also reminiscent of how earlier epochs debated the suitability of different natural media (stone, wood, linen, leather) for legal documents needing to withstand tampering and time.[39] In the context of literary study too, there may be an atavistic air around *communication*. Those in literary studies are likelier to have an easier rapport with colleagues in Media Studies Departments—through bridging areas of interest like the history of the book or any number of cultural studies topics—than with those in Communication Departments. *Communication* can sound as if it belongs to another era, conjuring the kinds of keywords from the first great era of communication research and theory in the 1920s: propaganda, crowds, mass opinion, public opinion.[40] Or it can sound hopelessly broad, seemingly corresponding to the history of human civilization.

This book nevertheless emphasizes communication. One reason is quite pragmatic: there are several top-notch, recommendable studies on media and Romanticism, to which I have already alluded. They have informed my thinking throughout, while also suggesting the potential value of the approach this book takes, which is primarily to look above and below the medial level to see what we might learn. Looking at the higher order problem of communication allows one to traverse questions about classical rhetoric and New Rhetorical theories of communication, later eighteenth-century concerns about personal connection, informational-administrative genres, note-taking and recordkeeping practices, and other matters that are better grouped together under the heading of communication, although they all necessarily involve thinking about media too. At the same time, this book looks below the medial level—below print and the book, for example—to focus on desires and standards pertaining to contact. For example, Wordsworth worked extensively with paper tax forms, yet his literary writing responds most acutely not to paperwork itself but to the societal drive for efficient inscription, whose formal instantiation across written genres—whether in a poem or tax form—I discuss as *bureaucratic form*. Or, to put this somewhat differently: the *forms* of blank forms and shorthand techniques are not quite covered by "print," "print culture," or the "book": forms and notes are often measured in "sheets," involve mixtures of handwriting, print, non-alphabetical marks and characters, tables, and blank fields, and are molded by the criteria of brevity, speed (speed of processing, filling out, transcription), and ease (forms that are easy to fill out, shorthand script that is easy for the transcriber to decipher later). There is something to be learned about the Romantic media situation, and ours, by focusing not only on the middle—that is, the level of media—but all around it, especially the communication concept that subsumes it, and the communication compulsion that consumes it.

In communication theory, there is a well-known distinction between two views of communication. James W. Carey, with American culture in mind, contrasts a "transmission" view of communication and a "ritual" one. The transmission view is "the commonest in our culture and perhaps in all industrial cultures . . . [and] is defined by terms such as 'imparting,' 'sending,' 'transmitting,' or 'giving information to others,'" explains Carey. This view emphasizes that communication is "a process whereby messages are transmitted and distributed in space." The second view, "the ritual view," is associated with ideas like "'sharing,' 'participation,' 'association,' 'fellowship,'" and is "directed not toward the extension of messages in space but toward the maintenance of society in time; not the act of imparting information but the representation of shared beliefs."[41] The first view foregrounds the sending of something through space, and takes a more or less utilitarian stance; the second view foregrounds passing something down through time, the idea of tradition or the continual reproduction of society. Yet, as we will see, Romantic poets are already thinking about such questions concerning communication. At times they rely on, and at other times they resist, the simplified, utilitarian understanding of communication as "transmission"—the efficient sending and receiving of information— at the very moment when the industrial culture Carey describes was coming into being in Britain. Similarly, as we will see, they have much to say about the ritual or tradition-oriented view, whether it is Shelley's sociological concerns about the social bonds imagined to guarantee "the maintenance of society in time," or, in a more literary context, Keats's ongoing ritualistic dialogue with his literary precursors or his allegorization of a troubled form of communication-in-time via the succession of Titans by Olympians in *Hyperion* (1819–1820).

There are also good reasons for thinking about communication fantasies—for foregrounding not only communication but also the *dream* of communication. The first is that such fantasies reveal the imaginative horizons of communication during a particular age, and therefore why communications practices and technologies take the forms that they do. Carolyn Marvin, in her landmark *When Old Technologies Were New: Thinking about Electric Communication in the Late Nineteenth Century* cautions that "artifactual approaches foster the belief that social processes connected to media logically and historically begin with the instrument," and explains the value of considering "media fantasies." Fantasies and dreams reveal "what thoughts were possible, what thoughts could not be entertained yet or anymore" about communication. To give an example: from antiquity through much of the nineteenth century, recording the human voice in real time kindled the dream of handwriting fleet enough to keep pace with speech; the idea of recording the human voice by any means other than inscription of one kind or another was not imaginable, hence the profusion of competing stenographic systems, each one obsessively trying to devise the shortest and easiest way symbolically to represent the English language.[42] I would add to Marvin's account that this imagination-centric approach to the history of communication is also—was already—the Romantic-poetic approach: not only because communicative norms and desires were these poets' purview too, but because of the insightful, idiosyncratic responsiveness to the connected condition with which they can be credited. Keats, as we will see, registers not optical or electric telegraphic technologies per se, but the cultural fantasy about rapid contact that attended telegraphy.

Second, the dream of communication points to the paradoxical power of desires. Communication desires—along with the standards that try to help realize them—often project an impossible or contradictory ideal. The wish is for a medium that is so transparent—able to transfer messages with the greatest celerity and clarity—that it is no medium; yet it allows for a connection and is perforce a medium.[43] Geoffrey Hartman, in a remarkable essay, "I. A. Richards and the Dream of Communication," notes that "a desire for communication" can be "so strong, so idealistic and hence so frustrated," but the desire's frustration, in turn, only strengthens the compulsion to communicate.[44] I would add that the flummoxing of communication fantasies also strengthens the standards that attempt to codify what counts as good communication—and that too is often flummoxed in a way that circles back to intensify the desire and now the standard too. I alluded previously to Romantic poets' recognition that the drive for efficiency invites—even guarantees—inefficiencies. An additional example from a later period captures in a nutshell this cyclical aspect of the dream of communication. As his students recall, William Strunk, in his Cornell lectures that would lead to his famous manual of stylistic standards, *The Elements of Style* (1920), insisted, "Omit needless words! Omit needless words! Omit needless words!"[45] The stronger the wish for perfectible written communication, the more the obscurities creep in (the repetition of "needless" makes one wonder all the more what kinds of words count as "needless," and whether the repetition of "needless" is also needless), and the wish to purge communication of superfluities leads to a stark rule of brevity which all but guarantees superfluity (in this case, redundancy). And this makes imperatives like Strunk's all the more imperative: Omit needless words!

One final, crucial dimension of the dream of communication, of particular relevance for the subsequent chapter on Wordsworth and bureaucracy: the dream in the dream of communication also points to a certain technocratic, systematic, rationalist ideology and its way of defining progress. This aspect of the dream of communication is like the "desire" that James. C. Scott associates with what he calls "high modernist ideology."[46] Though Scott's examples—Soviet collectivization, villagization in Tanzania—are remote from those of this book, his definition of "high modernist ideology" is very relevant. This ideology encompasses "a strong, one might even say muscle-bound, version of the self-confidence about scientific and technical progress . . . the growing satisfaction of human needs, the mastery of nature (including human nature), and above all, the rational design of social order."[47] The same characteristics are applicable to the Romantic and post-Romantic myth of controllable communication, which is arguably another part of "high modernist ideology." And just as applicable to this book are Scott's explanations of why state schemes based on this rage for order fail, why this kind of desire gets dashed: designs based on this ideology are "necessarily schematic," premised on a set of radical simplifications of human complexities.[48] The positing of perfectible contact does not always come from the state, but the visions associated with it almost always resemble what Scott calls "seeing like a state": that is, seeing through a reductive modeling, a "series of typifications that are always some distance from the full reality." The connected condition is a "condition" in the other sense—that is, not only the "reality," but a syndrome—because of the presumption that communication can be sped up and systematized through various kinds of typifications and reductions that are at some distance from the full reality.[49]

The Stylistic Standards of the New Rhetoric:
The Case for Easy Writing

As I have begun to suggest, there is a relatively coherent modern communications order, fueled by the fantasy of faster, clearer, better contact, and of media that might make this finally possible. This wish and the standards it entails are a constant beneath highly variable kinds of media as well as through media transitions. Media can change, but the need and the norms of communication are remarkably consistent. I do not pretend to offer anything like a history of communication, but I would like to notice some crucial developments for the dream of communication as it bears directly on the Romantics and then us. Key premises—the terms, the visual imagery, the supposed goal—of the fantasy of efficient communication began to arise in intertwined discourses and projects in the later seventeenth century. As Kevis Goodman has shown, the proposals of the new science for language reform, the science of optics, and universal language projects (most famously that described in John Wilkins's *Essay Towards a Real Character and a Philosophical Language* [1668]), studied, took apart, and attempted to perfect and purify the English language, so that it might become a transparent medium of communication.[50] Moreover, as Goodman points out, all of these endeavors are best understood not as a reflection of the Restoration-era faith in the transparency of language so much as a compulsion that produced more schemes: "the desire for what Wilkins and others called a 'noise'-free, pure system of words or signs . . .

was just that: a desire."[51] Universal language schemes—from Wilkins up to and through twentieth-century successors, most famously C. K. Ogden's and I. A. Richards's Basic English—do not come up with perfect, universal languages so much as they reproduce, and perhaps intensify, the idée fixe that is the dream of communication.[52]

Closely related to these universal language projects was Locke's semiotic theory, put forth in *An Essay Concerning Human Understanding* (1689). As several excellent histories of communication show, the concept of communication familiar to us—the "imparting, conveying, or exchange of ideas, knowledge, information"—derives from Locke's *Essay*.[53] Before Locke, "communication" had a range of different semantic emphases, particularly a set of meanings suggested by the root word, *communis* (common): coming together, sharing, meeting, giving someone an object, and so forth, all denoting a kind of physical sharing, and closer to the ritual kind of communication outlined by Carey than the transmission kind.[54] Yet it is with Locke's treatise that the concept of communication comes predominantly "to drift from physical to mental sharing" and, in tandem with that drift, to shift from a semantic emphasis on communality to a one-way transmission of ideas.[55] If Locke defines communication as "the chief End of Language," that goal is continually frustrated by the "imperfection of words."[56] As is well known, because of Locke's presupposition of the arbitrariness or conventionality of the word-idea relation, words signify "nothing, but the Ideas in the Mind of him that uses them."[57] Given that language is the "chief End" and medium of communication, and yet communication is always impeded by the "imperfection of words," Locke goes on to propose a series of "remedies" for language, to make the medium clearer, less like a mist: "[Words] interpose themselves so much between our Understandings, and the Truth, which it would contemplate and apprehend, that like the *Medium* through which visible Objects pass, their Obscurity and Disorder does not seldom cast a mist before our Eyes, and impose upon our Understandings."[58] Elsewhere he writes that the "Obscurity of Terms . . . [is] like a Mist before Peoples Eyes."[59] As John Guillory puts it, the *Essay*'s desire somehow to cure the imperfection of language gives rise to the insight that "the medium makes communication possible but also possible to fail," and in many ways Locke thereby sets the stage for the impossible ideal of communication in modernity: "the desire for an immediate transfer of thoughts and feelings."[60]

Locke's treatise considers communication in the context of spoken linguistic communication, in the context of speech. But a powerful set of norms deriving from Locke's reflections on spoken communication emerge in the mid-eighteenth century in writings on rhetoric and belles lettres by Adam Smith and others. Smith built on such "effective critics of the old rhetoric as [Robert] Boyle, [Thomas] Sprat, and Locke," yet it was Smith who finally "gave that new rhetoric its earlier and most independent expression."[61] The New Rhetoric, reorienting the focus of rhetoric from persuasion to communication, and with a focus on writing (expository prose), offered nothing less than a modern theory of communication.[62] Through his lectures, Smith attempted to teach a style of writing purified of two main flaws—foreign words (especially Latinate words) and figurative language—and he promulgated the stylistic standards of perspicuity, precision and brevity, and purity.

There is an illustrative moment for the concerns of this book in Smith's *Lectures on Rhetoric and Belles Lettres* (1762; a course first given in 1748). The foundational theory of communication offered in the *Lectures*, and the influential stylistic norms that go with it, project a myth of communication—a dream, as we will see, in more than one sense. So intent is Smith on advancing a form of writing made "plain" as possible—thoroughly characterized by "perspicuity," "purity," and a perfected "order of expression"—that he imagines a form of writing that nearly erases writing itself and nearly eliminates altogether the labor of reading.[63] The scenario ends up verging on thought transfer. (We will see Keats's epistolary and epic versions of a similar scenario in Chapter 4.) During a discussion of "precision," a standard closely tied to "perspicuity," Smith recommends a writing style defined by its brevity ("there are no words that are superfluous") and simple syntax (readers are "not obliged to hunt backwards and forwards" for the sense). Writing that attains to this ideal is what he calls "easy writing": "a natural order of expression . . . which makes the sense of the author flow naturally upon our mind."[64] With "easy writing," it is as though the author's meaning flows by itself, freed from the media of language and writing, directly into readers' minds. But "easy" for whom? The stylistic standards of the *Lectures* are meant to work on writers and their compositions, but readers are also a problem. Like I. A. Richards's later presumption, in *Principles of Literary Criticism* (1924), *Practical Criticism* (1929), and other works, of "total, controllable communication," Smith's pedagogy confronts the problem of ungovernable, unpredictable readers, which in Smith's case would undermine any notion like "easy writing" by forcing that fantasy into contact with the real diversity of readers, the real difficulty of reading, regardless of perspicuity, precision, or plainness.[65]

Smith's workaround in order to maintain the dream of communication is to posit the dreaming reader—or, better to say, half-dreaming, because "half asleep."[66] As intriguing as the other characters who populate Smith's philosophical works (for instance, the "impartial spectator"), the "half asleep" reader is both very real (familiar to us from reading in bed or on airplanes) and purely hypothetical, someone engaged in a kind of not-reading reading—we might call it "dozing reading." In the relevant passage, Smith holds up his recurrent stylistic models of Henry Bolingbroke's and Jonathan Swift's writings, and introduces this lethargic figure:

> We find that . . . [Bolingbroke's and Swift's] writings are so plain that one half asleep may carry the sense along with him. Nay if we happen to lose a word or two, the rest of the sentence is so naturally connected with it as that it comes into our mind of its own accord. On the other hand[,] Writers who do not observe this rule often become so obscure that their meaning is not to be discovered without great attention and being altogether awake.[67]

The Smithian "half asleep" reader, someone not giving "great attention" to the writing before him, has a close relative in the "sauntering" child reader. In *Some Thoughts Concerning Education* (1693), Locke gives this quasi-technical name to the behavior of incurious, languid children who do not have a "busy, inquisitive temper"; Locke's sense of "sauntering"— "to loiter over one's work, to dawdle"—blends two senses of "saunter," to be lost in a reverie (the sauntering child, writes Locke, "lazily and listlessly dreams away his time") and to wander aimlessly. A child who is of "the sauntering temper" is as "negligent and sluggish" in his play as he is in reading books.[68] Following Locke, Maria and Richard Lovell Edgeworth, in their treatise *Practical Education* (1798), distinguish curable young "book-saunterers" from those who suffer from a chronic version of "sluggish attention."[69] It is in this context that in Wordsworth's "The Idiot Boy," Betty Foy describes her son, Johnny, as "a little idle sauntering thing," and Wordsworth is able with that single word ("sauntering") to implicate not only Johnny, but aspects of his own ambivalent stance on literary brevity (see Chapter 2).[70] But in Smith, the emphasis is not on bringing "sauntering" children around to the pleasures of reading, but to envision writing as a nearly immediate, unmediated transmission of sense: the sense "comes into our mind of its own accord."[71] The fix is not about the pedagogy as much as it is about perfecting the medium for the single goal of communication. The figure of the "half asleep" reader permits Smith at once to presuppose a general type of "reader" (many readers made theoretically homogeneous because indifferently inattentive) and to heighten the communicative effectiveness of this "plain" style (even a "half asleep" reader can get and follow the "sense"). If Smith's situation sounds more like a description of someone listening to speech while nodding off ("it comes into our mind of its own accord")—that is, if it seems unlikely that a reader who is not "altogether awake" and yet looking at words receives much "sense" at all, the preciseness of the writing notwithstanding—that is because the desire for perfectible contact exceeds the stylistic standard. At this telling moment in Smith's *Lectures*, the standard of easy writing takes on a hyperbolic cast because of the fantasy on which it depends, which in turn gets reinforced by it: the dream of communication chases after the very possibility that something like easy writing, flowing into a sleepy reader's mind, can be realized.

Smith's easy writing provides a helpful way to preview some of the instantiations of the dream of communication examined later in this book. The term "easy writing" sounds like an advertisement for something "user friendly." But it also sounds like a method for writers: Learn Easy Writing in just a few days! Easy writing sounds especially like shorthand, because shorthand systems also promoted a version of the dream of communication. One can look at shorthand as taking a different approach to the fantasy of perfectible communication. For shorthand systems, the fix is an alternative script system that can be so quickly written, so easily mastered that it can transcribe speech in real time, thus making it possible to record spoken performances (sermons, speeches, legal proceedings) for the ages. At the same time, one can look at shorthand as continuous with New Rhetorical stylistic norms, with similar strategies (such as concision) pursued to the extreme—words and phrases are so short that they are condensed into single symbols. Easy writing could also be a name for the logic of the standardized blank forms that Wordsworth processed. With predetermined blank fields, and asking only for certain "particulars," forms were imagined to be easy for citizens to fill out, easy for the state to amass and process information—an ease as fantastical as that of an easy style.

From Smith's New Rhetorical norms to Wordsworth's "simple and unelaborated expressions" in his "Preface" to Strunk and White's *Elements of Style* to Rudolf Flesch's mid-twentieth-century notion of "plain talk" to the Plain Writing Act of 2010 passed by the U.S. Congress, the dream of communication is alive and well.[72] But it is still a dream, as much of a dream as what might be unfolding in the "mind" of Smith's "half asleep" reader.

From the Normal Method to Normal Romanticism

The method of *The Connected Condition*—its more or less consistent orientation to literary writings, other archival documents (such as tax forms and stenography manuals), and historical context, and how it tends to interpret their interrelations—may be called the *normal method*. And the picture of Romanticism that emerges from this book may accurately be called a *normal Romanticism*, which might at first sound like a contradiction. The normal method by no means entails the extolling of normativity. Rather, the perspective that this method brings to its objects of study is an emphasis, or re-emphasis, on norms and standards, with the aim of studying the interaction of what is normal and what is abnormal, standard and non-standard.

It is worth remembering that the Romantic period, though strongly associated with change and revolution, is also a period definable by what Michel Foucault called "the Norm" and its emergence:

> The power of the Norm appears through the disciplines. Is this the new law of the modern society? Let us say rather that, since the eighteenth century, it has joined other powers—the Law, the Word . . . and the Text, Tradition—imposing new delimitations upon them.[73]

"The power of the Norm" applies to norms pertaining to communication. These norms exert considerable pressure on literary works, and are therefore partly (though not fully) responsible for the form verbal artworks take. Norms like brevity, clarity, and precision in writing impose "new delimitations" on communicative practices as a whole, including literature. Moreover, as Andrew Elfenbein points out in connection with Romantic authors' mixed relation—of obedience and resistance—to standard English, "if you were going to prove your genius by breaking the rules, you needed rules to break"; the authority of "linguistic determination" (of eighteenth-century prescriptivism) "chipped away at the imagination's autonomy."[74] In short, it seems important to appreciate how literary works—and especially, works from a period synonymous with "the power of the Norm"—subscribed to linguistic-communicative norms as much as they may have also deviated from them.[75]

Here is an illustration. Keats's densely figurative and allusive poetic style can be said to transgress his period's norm of good style for written communication as defined by the New Rhetoric. The norm was—and still is—writing that is clear, brief, precise, and not overly reliant on figurative language. Keats's style could be a building block for a hypothetical argument that would stress his linguistic-stylistic subversiveness, perhaps eventually making a claim about a political subversiveness. But the normal method stresses too the ways that the writer adheres to stylistic tenets. And only then can we examine the relation between his uniqueness and his conformity. There are moments in Keats's poetry and other writings where he seems to stick to, even channel, the norm and the fantasy behind the norm, espousing the imaginary condition of transparency in language that motivates the period's standards of style. Consider this statement:

> We hate poetry that has a palpable design upon us. . . . Poetry should be great & unobtrusive, a thing which enters into one's soul, and does not startle it or amaze it with itself but with its subject.—How beautiful are the retired flowers! how would they lose their beauty were they to throng into the highway crying out, "admire me I am a violet! dote upon me I am a primrose!"[76]

There are many ways to read this letter, but I would emphasize that Keats seems to be imagining poetic language in a manner entirely consistent with the prevailing norms of composition of his time, as we have seen above. Language should be brought as closely as possible to the condition of transparency so that the "subject" can be easily accessed by the recipient; poetic language should not draw attention to itself as a medium, should not "startle . . . or amaze . . . with itself." As with Adam Smith's fantasy that "easy writing" would "come into [a half asleep reader's] mind of its own accord," Keats imagines poetry as "a thing which enters into one's soul" effortlessly and immediately—the unobtrusive poetic medium conveys "its subject" without drawing attention to itself. By contrast, having a "palpable design" on readers can be read not only as a poem's intent to moralize, to be didactic—to teach "precepts . . . clowdily enwrapped in Allegoricall devises" (to borrow from Spenser)[77]—but also the very kinds of figures, allegorical devices, ornaments, and other forms of palpable design that the New Rhetoric sought to purge from writing. Understanding Keats means, in other words, accounting for both his florid literary style and the broader social norm of a communicative style whose verbal flowers (if there are any flowers at all) are as "retired" and inconspicuous as can be. Most importantly, the norm impacts the form: as I go on to suggest about Keats, the tensions around the norm—the standard versus his style—are one way to consider the fragmentary form in which he leaves his attempts at *Hyperion*.

Here is another illustration, this one from a later period. One of the best, and most bracing, declarations against the normal and the commonplace is Vladimir Nabokov's essay "The Art of Literature and Commonsense."[78] Like Keats's poetics, Nabokov's aesthetic philosophy—both despite and because of Nabokov's aristocratic background and his classical liberalism—seems ripe for an interpretation that would like to celebrate nonconformity:

> It is instructive to think that there is not a single person in this room, or for that matter in any room in the world, who, at some nicely chosen point in historical space-time would not be put to death there and then, here and now, by a commonsensical majority in righteous rage. The color of one's creed, neckties, eyes, thoughts, manners, speech, is sure to meet somewhere in time or space with a fatal objection from a mob that hates that particular tone. And the more brilliant, the more unusual the man, the nearer he is to the stake. *Stranger* always rhymes with *danger*. . . . And this being so, let us bless them, let us bless the freak.

The normal method endorses Nabokov's decree: "let us bless the freak." But it would also consider how Nabokov, despite his many screeds against standardization, held up standard English as the only suitable language for literary composition (in this same essay, and elsewhere, he dismisses "apostrophic dialect" and other written renderings of folk speech).[79] Above all, given the kinds of standards this approach looks for, the normal method would consider the generic-medial-technological object with which he composed his novels, namely the card (more specifically, the index card), which is among the most significant objects in the history of information management precisely due to its standardized size and formatting, and the norms and ideals that can be said to be attached to it.[80] And the next question would address the friction between his philosophy and standards, the latter including the standardized media of communication and recordkeeping with which he wrote his works, and how they might have shaped his novels.

The normal method is one possible example of the "postcritical reading" that Rita Felski has proposed—or, perhaps not quite *post*critical but a more even-handed version of reading. As Felski explains in her indispensable *The Limits of Critique* (2015), the "mood" and "thought style" of literary study for the last several decades can be described as "critique."[81] By "critique," Felski means many things. One of them is the critic's now familiar oppositional stance—a kind of "antinormative normativity"— relative to texts: "a spirit of skeptical questioning or outright condemnation" of a literary work or scholarship for its perceived politics.[82] But the feature of critique relevant here is an appositional stance, where work and critic align. Wishing criticism to be "engaged in some kind of radical intellectual and/or political work," critics look for how literary works are themselves engaging in critique:

> All too often, we see critics tying themselves into knots in order to prove that a text harbors signs of dissonance and dissent—as if there were no other conceivable way of justifying its merits. . . . Both aesthetic and social worth, it seems, can only be cashed out in terms of a rhetoric of *againstness*. . . . Critics [scour] works of literature for every last crumb of real or imagined resistance. We shortchange the significance of art by focusing on the "de" prefix ([art's] power to demystify, destabilize, denaturalize).[83]

One could imagine a list of cognitive biases in literary study, and overestimating in interpretation a text's emancipatory "message," and fantasizing of a similar potency for the scholarly analysis itself, may be one of the more frequently occurring, familiar habits of our discipline. Like Felski, this discussion rejects the notion that "any questioning of critique can only be a reactionary gesture or a conservative conspiracy," and wonders what we can learn from seeing how authors submit to norms as much as they might "critique," "resist," or "interrogate" them.[84] Unlike Felski's proposals, however, the normal method is less against critique per se than it is intent on noticing the relation between the norm and the strategies around and against it; in my case the normal method is concerned to show the degree to which a poet follows, and strays from, the rules of communication in modernity.

The chapters of this book add up to a sketch of a normal Romanticism. It is a Romanticism defined not by way of the critique paradigm (whether the Romantics' or our own) but by those norms that exerted pressure on the Romantics, who, in turn, exerted pressure on the norms. As I have begun to suggest already, it is a Romanticism routed through the control revolution—that is, nothing less than the emergence of an information society—as much as other political revolutions of the time. From this perspective, the normal, typically taken-for-granted information infrastructures of modernity—for example, information storage systems, telecommunications, informational genres like forms—command, rather than recede from, our attention.[85] It is a Romanticism of "boring things," whether bureaucratic routines, paperwork, standards, or administrators: I look at Wordsworth's administrative work, but there is also Charles Lamb, Robert Burns, Thomas Love Peacock, and other Romantic paper pushers who were charged with collecting and processing information in their administrative capacities.[86] As Foucault reminds us, Romanticism occurs in the wake of the emergence of "the power of the Norm"—joining and inflecting other forms of power ("the Law, the Word . . . and the Text, Tradition"), and shaping the disciplines—and the study of Romanticism needs must always be, to some degree, the study of the normal.[87]

Some Versions of Difficulty and Medial Difficulty

Readers may notice that *The Connected Condition* has much to say about literary difficulty, poetic difficulty in particular—the ways that poetry can be said to be "difficult." Though this recurring motif might seem incompatible with the book's insistence on what Foucault calls "the power of the Norm," in fact, difficulty can be recognized as the product of the tensions between the norms of communication and artistic expression. Discussions of poetic difficulty tend to focus on modernism more than Romanticism, often invoking T. S. Eliot's famous statement, in his essay "The Metaphysical Poets," that "it appears likely that poets in our civilization, as it exists at present, must be difficult."[88] I. A. Richards's comments on Eliot's "The Waste Land" also come to mind. Richards describes the poem's disconnectedness and its allusiveness as a "technical device for compression," and although it is a device used at the cost of alienating readers, Richards defends the technique of condensation: "'The Waste Land' is the equivalent in content to an epic."[89] Richards's own taxonomy of misreading in *Practical Criticism* (1929) and William Empson's master-piece, *Seven Types of Ambiguity* (1930), also belong to this moment.

Of course, many different kinds of "difficulty" arise before the idea is theorized, and to a great extent made normative, in the twentieth century. For example, in textual criticism, there is the principle of *difficilior lectio potior* (the more difficult reading is preferable): because scribes tended to alter texts in the direction of simplification (trivialization) by, for example, modernizing archaisms or simplifying a "complex process of thought," the critic facing alternative readings chooses the more difficult one.[90] And there are also useful treatments of Romantic poetic difficulty: Leonard Epp, considering the Burkean sublime, the 1790s revolution debate, and Coleridge's work demonstrates how the two opposing qualities of "obscurity" and "clarity" could tactically take on either positive or negative values depending on the context; William Christie discusses Romantic poets in terms of his typology of difficulty (obfuscation, obscurity, and difficulty); and Paul H. Fry pinpoints Wordsworth's peculiar brand of difficult simplicity, noting that "if Coleridge's expression is sometimes obscure, Wordsworth's premises are nearly always obscure."[91]

Among the most helpful accounts is George Steiner's essay "On Difficulty," which also offers a typology of poetic difficulty. He names four kinds. "Contingent" difficulties, the most common kind, are also the most easily overcome, and include "a word, a phrase, or a reference" needing to be looked up.[92] "Modal" difficulties occur when we do not quite get the "rationale" of a poem: "the poem . . . articulates a stance towards human conditions which we find essentially inaccessible or alien"; much of this has to do with readers' remoteness from a poem's historically and philosophically specific texture, for example.[93] Steiner also offers "tactical" difficulties: "the poet may choose to be obscure to achieve certain specific and stylistic effects," oftentimes to renovate the possibilities of inherently conventional linguistic expression.[94] And finally, there are "ontological" difficulties, the most radical form. Difficulties of this kind "confront us with blank questions about the nature of human speech, about the status of significance, about the necessity and purpose of the construct which we have, with more or less rough and ready consensus, come to perceive as a poem."[95] Yet the type of poetic difficulty that is a secondary motif in this book is not quite covered by Steiner, although he comes closest to it in his brief discussion of some of the historical developments that lead up to modern "ontological" difficulty:

> The transformation of the visionary elements in the Enlightenment and French Revolution into the philistine positivism of the industrial and mercantile structure of the nineteenth century, brought on a drastic mutual disenchantment of artist and society. . . . At the same time, the rapid proliferation of journalistic and popular media of communication—the press, the *feuilleton*, the cheap book—while beneficial to prose fiction, accentuated the minority status of the poem.[96]

Reading like a paraphrase of Wordsworth's "Preface" to *Lyrical Ballads* and Shelley's *A Defence of Poetry*, Steiner's account alludes to the developments I have noted earlier in this introduction—the developments that suggest that the time of Romanticism saw, in many ways, the emergence of an information society and the first efficiency movement. If we add to Steiner's account New Rhetorical norms such as clarity and concision— and the poetic impulse both to yield to and to frustrate these norms—we approach the kind of difficulty this book has in mind.

The poems in this book, although they are not the most difficult in the language, all feature a certain kind of difficulty. Whether any individual reader finds them to be difficult or not, they are very much "difficulty" poems in the sense that they seem quite self-consciously to be about poetic difficulty, to advertise their own *potential* for difficulty—how the poetic medium can be manipulated in different ways—at the same time that they make certain concessions to the dream of communication (such as writing speed and reading ease). Coleridge's "Rime of the Ancient Mariner" contains, but is also about, inscrutable poetic symbols; Wordsworth's contributions to *Lyrical Ballads* and his long poem *The Excursion* reflect on, and themselves test, the limits of literary lengthiness and tedium. Shelley's *Epipsychidion* is nominally an amatory poem, but it is framed by his thoughts on poetic intelligibility and unintelligibility; and Keats's letters and poems are always pointing to their own figurative "darkness" or obscurity. As the chapters will show, these kinds of difficulty can be understood as—among other things—a response to the modern communications order defined by the desideratum of efficient communication. In other words, some versions of the questions addressed by Alan Liu in *The Laws of Cool: Knowledge Work and the Culture of Information* in the context of post-industrial knowledge work—the status of literature in a "culture of information," and the nature of a "future literary" aesthetic suited for informationalism—start to be asked during Romantic-era industrialism.[97] Some of the artistic strategies of the future literary, including "delay, displacement, oblique representation, and stylization"—and perhaps even what Liu calls the "ethos of the unknown," where "those who live and work nowhere but inside the system of contemporary knowledge can paradoxically, and with more than the normal (and normalizing) irony of cool, seem to stand outside it"—were tried out by the poets of this earlier epoch.[98] Some defining features of certain Romantic poems—for example, ornateness, obscurity, or tediousness—are recognizable as functions of literary writing finding itself in a culture of information. We may call this kind of difficulty, *medial* difficulty: a poetry for—influenced by as well as positioned against—communicative efficiency, informationalism, and their premises, norms, and practices. This kind of difficulty plays with poetic communication mainly from the understanding that one can be half in love with easeful contact, but only half.

The Chapters

Because this book is about communication, perhaps it is not too self-indulgent to reflect briefly on scholarly communication in the form of the monograph. The predominant way of thinking about the chapters in a monograph might be called the "single file" view. In this view, the chapters line up like school children. Sometimes casually described as "case studies," chapters back up the book's argument: each chapter builds intellectually or historically on the previous chapter(s), repeatedly confirming the thesis with different materials. The single file view is probably why—life being short and many books being long—scholars usually need only to skim or read a monograph's introduction, taking in the entire linear trajectory from there, unless they are interested in specialist matters, in which case they might dip into or study individual chapters. The chapters of this book too are accordingly designed to illustrate the variety of ways that Romantic poets engaged the dream of communication, and the chapters line up more or less in single file. At the same time, I would ask readers not to lose sight of them as separate essays, a view that can be described as a "subway system" view: the essays all begin from a center (the dream of communication), but like multiple city subway lines, they run out in different directions, toward different neighborhoods. The subway system view appreciates the degree to which chapters are essays written and revised at different times—resulting in an elusive, shifting sense of how they fit together—as much as (or far more than) they are a group of probative pieces. Nevertheless, as with subway systems, connections or transfers are possible between the separate chapters at points well beyond the main theme.

Coleridge, the subject of Chapter I, is mostly known for being an unpredictable, digressive, and copious talker who was impossible to transcribe. But in this chapter, I recover another side of him: Coleridge the transcriber, theorist of transcription practices, and inventor of his own idiosyncratic shorthand. Considering Coleridge's time as a parliamentary reporter, his self-reflexive notebook entries featuring the character of the rushed note-taker as well as meditations on note-taking, inscription, and transcription, and above all, the shorthand practices of the Romantic era, this chapter posits that Coleridge pursued a "shorthand for thoughts." On the one hand, Coleridge's shorthand for thoughts participates in the fantasy behind all stenographic systems: a notation system rapid enough to keep pace in real time with speech, and capable of recording for posterity the events of the present as they are in the process of unfolding. Moreover, the ciphers Coleridge uses in his notebooks to encrypt certain entries use the same time-saving strategies as contemporaneous shorthand systems— they consider, for example, which words appear frequently enough in English that they can be abbreviated and represented by a single character rather than a string of letters. On the other hand, Coleridge departs from the phonocentrism of contemporaneous shorthand practices, and focuses on developing note-taking techniques for his own silent thoughts. He also looks at obsessive shorthand system inventors (whom he ironically calls "scribble-scrabble-geniuses") with significant skepticism. Furthermore, against the stenographic fantasy of an alternative, non-English script that could "be read . . . at first Sight," Coleridge takes particular interest in what I call, drawing parallels between shorthand and today's optical character recognition software, the *shorthand effect*: when letters, word parts, or whole words uncannily become illegible shapes, and non-linguistic shapes come to look like linguistic signs. The chapter culminates in a reading of the "signs" in "The Rime of the Ancient Mariner," which appear to experiment with the shorthand effect in the medium of poetry, and which have posed the problem for readers—from Wordsworth to Robert Penn Warren and William Empson—of how to read or not read "picture language."

Chapter 2 sets out to answer the following question: How might Wordsworth's *other* job, as a civil servant processing tax documents, have affected his poetry? This chapter expands on Wordsworth's thirty-year career as Distributor of Stamps—an ode to duty of a different kind—to consider more broadly how Romantic literature was shaped by several intertwined developments: the formation of a fiscal bureaucracy in Britain during the long eighteenth century, the attendant proliferation of bureaucratic genres and media, and utilitarian theories of administrative efficiency. Although Wordsworth never mentions his administrative work in his literary writing, some of his major writings are responsive to the priorities espoused by administrative paperwork, particularly by the documentary subgenre crucial to his distributorship: the standardized blank form, what Wordsworth calls "certain papers called Forms." I introduce the concept of *bureaucratic form* to describe the various forms taken by writing when the efficient capturing and communicating of data, or "particulars," are the principal considerations, the standardized form being a prime example. Bureaucratic form—operating in concert with the contemporaneous ideal of brevity in writing (widely taught to students in Wordsworth's time) and long-standing concerns about *brevitas* (the idea that literary works should be the appropriate length so as not to be tedious)—made the economical collection and delivery of information an ideal for all kinds of writing. I show that *Lyrical Ballads* (1798), *Essays upon Epitaphs* (comp. 1810), and above all, *The Excursion* (1814) accommodate, as much as they ignore, the rule of streamlined writing. Even *The Excursion*, criticized for being long and boring, makes concessions to bureaucratic form while also flouting it. In these ways, Wordsworth's writing can be appreciated for its prescient sensitivity and idiosyncratic response to the early, formative phases of the information-centric society we live in today.

Chapter 3 considers the feelings of connectedness and disconnectedness that come with networked life. There are several works from contemporary media studies that shed light on the contradictory feeling of "alone-togetherness," but they tend to have a brief historical perspective. Meanwhile, many works focused on the eighteenth century and Romanticism emphasize infrastructural connectedness during this epoch, perhaps not emphasizing enough the pervasive sense of social disintegration (as exemplified by Adam Ferguson's 1767 epithet for his time, the "age of separations") and the problem of social relations in differentiated societies, the inaugural problem of sociology during this period. This chapter approaches this period as an instructive earlier moment for today's digitally networked life, and views Shelley's poetics as offering a compelling way of being a networked being, then and perhaps now. Shelley sat at the nexus of two contemporaneous discourses: proto-sociological discourse found in Scottish conjectural histories and Romantic-era reflections on poetic communication. From this position, Shelley can engage in nuanced sociological thought while remaining attentive to the formal and medial specificities of artistic works. I demonstrate that Shelley provisionally offers the "cloud[y]" medium of abstract poetry as a model for a specific form of social interaction suited to modernity: an interaction that would forge a middle way between a purely commercial kind of social bond and the total intersubjective identification that he calls "love." In other words, during the age of separations—when individuals in a society frequently transacted business yet lacked a sense of solidarity—Shelley views poetic communication as capable of facilitating immersive, interpersonal connections in a manner that surpasses merely economic interdependence. At the same time, Shelley understands unclear media—like his poetry—as a paradigm of sociality that could protect individuals from intersubjective encroachments or agglutination, an undesirable tendency of "love" that worries Shelley in his later works. Reading *Epipsychidion* (1821) in light of these concerns, and positing a poetry of ambiversion that allows for both connection and disconnection, I suggest that he arrives at a modern communication ethos that is neither purely economic interestedness (what Émile Durkheim will name "organic solidarity") nor entirely amatory, but rightly called poetic.

Chapter 4 proposes a new way to read Keats's most famous letters and his two fragmentary attempts at epic, *Hyperion* (1819–1820). There is a major, although overlooked, dissonance throughout Keats's letters and poetry. On the one hand, they dramatize his wish for rapid, intuitive communication between individuals at a distance, a fantasy fueled by the period's advancements in telegraphy. On the other, Keats's writing reveals a commitment to laborious, meandering reading—a mode of reading encouraged by the densely figurative poetic language of the literary tradition that he idolizes, and which abjures his period's ideal of reading ease and perspicacious composition. I trace this mode of reading to its origins in the allegorical language of scripture, and the rhetorical concept of *ductus*, which describes a reader's path or "way" through dark conceits. Ranging over Keats's letters on the death of his brother Tom, a "Mansion of Many Apartments," and a "life of Allegory," as well as various moments from his verse, this chapter culminates in a reading of *Hyperion*. The discordance between Keats's two tendencies or "ways"—rapid transmission and slow reading—precipitates the impasses that prevent him from continuing *Hyperion*.

Readers may find helpful the following notices of connections between chapters. Chapters 1 and 2 try out alternative kinds of "formalist" reading than are usually conducted under that name. In the first instance, I "look" at "forms" in the sense of letterforms, letter-like shapes, and shape-like letters, as they begin to blend into one another due to the shorthand effect and as they recur in Coleridge's "Rime of the Ancient Mariner." The second chapter studies "forms" in the sense of printed standardized blank forms soliciting handwritten answers: their verbal *form*ula, their *form*atting, and the documentary subgenre itself, the *form*. As these chapters show, not only is there a far wider range of forms beyond the familiar units typically examined under the banner of poetic form, but the now more interesting questions concern the relation between these other, underexamined forms and poetry.[99] Furthermore, both of these chapters join Michelle Levy and Betty A. Schellenberg, for example, in emphasizing the persistence of manuscript culture in the Romantic period, along with the intricate interactions of chirography, print, printed handwriting, and features of forms (blanks to be filled in, tables).[100] Both of these first two chapters also portray the dream of perfecting written communication through speed and ease. Speaking of speed: Chapters 1 and 4 suggest a link between the very similar technologies of stenography and telegraphy; as I observe in Chapter 1, "tachygraphy" (that is, swift writing) was a name given both to the earliest optical telegraph and to shorthand systems. Chapters 3 and 4 are of a piece in their interest in different forms of poetic obscurity, although as I have noted above, the other chapters also have something to say about poetic difficulty. The process of reading figures largely in all of the chapters: the problem of reading "picture images" in the context of Coleridge, the proper limits of a literary work without boring readers (discussed in terms of the rhetorical concepts *brevitas, taedium,* and *fastidium*), slow reading in Keats (the idea of *ductus* and making one's way through a dark textual channel), and Shelley's radical sense that poetry can both connect or disconnect, be an "open" or a "closed" book. All of the chapters would like to suggest—though one hopes this is not merely a different kind of dream—that the Romantic poets have much to teach us about living in a world of modern communications, as well as the fortunes of the literary in it.

Systems of notation become, in practice, more than that; become indeed, though always in variable degrees, means of composition, apparently in their own right . . . means of direct intellectual composition.

Raymond Williams, Contact

The question is bound to arise of whether many of these symbols do not occur with a permanently fixed meaning, like the "grammalogues" in shorthand.

Sigmund Freud, The Interpretation of Dreams

1 SCRIBBLE-SCRABBLE GENIUS

Coleridge, Transcription, and the Shorthand Effect

Coleridge and Rapid Writing

Let us consider two stories that together get at the concern of this chapter: a communication fantasy that enthralled Samuel Taylor Coleridge, though not as much as it did the professional scribes of his time. Both stories, as it happens, feature Coleridge, sleeping, and jotting things down. The first story, the more familiar of the two, is none other than Coleridge's legendary account of the composition of "Kubla Khan." His sleeping mind somehow generated hundreds of lines of a poem, and they somehow remained with him upon his waking up. As he started quickly writing down the poem, a visit from a person from Porlock interrupted him. After the visitor departed, Coleridge realized that the poem was gone from his mind. It is a well-known story, but it is worth looking again at his description:

> The author continued for about three hours in a profound sleep, at least of the external senses, during which time he has the most vivid

confidence, that he could not have composed less than from two to three hundred lines; if that indeed can be called composition in which all the images rose up before him as *things*, with a parallel production of the correspondent expressions, without any sensation or consciousness of effort. On awaking he appeared to himself to have a distinct recollection of the whole, and taking his pen, ink, and paper, instantly and eagerly wrote down the lines that are here preserved. At this moment he was unfortunately called out by a person on business from Porlock, and detained by him above an hour, and on his return to his room, found to his no small surprise and mortification, that though he still retained some vague and dim recollection of the general purpose of the vision, yet, with the exception of some eight or ten scattered lines and images, all the rest had passed away. . . . ("Of the Fragment of Kubla Khan," 180–81)[1]

Suppose we took Coleridge at his word for the moment, rather than treating this account as an allegory of artistic inspiration and/or failure. He composed in his sleep "two to three hundred lines," but managed to save on "paper" fifty-four lines (which is the length of the "preserved" poem) as well as "some eight or ten scattered lines and images" after he returns to his room. All told, he lost somewhere from around one hundred and thirty-seven to around two hundred and thirty-seven lines.

But what is the nature of this loss? Some of Coleridge's wording (especially the several mentions of "recollection") emphasizes that losing the poem was due to forgetting: the disruption caused by the person from Porlock abetted the natural decay of memory, perhaps also the forgetting of dreams overseen by the censoring consciousness posited by Freud, leaving Coleridge with only a "vague and dim recollection of . . . the vision."[2] But other aspects of his wording would have us think about the lost lines in an additional way: Coleridge had written a "composition" that needed to be quickly copied out by himself, now acting as his own "amanuensis," as Kenneth Burke has aptly described the situation.[3] After all, Coleridge describes the "Kubla Khan" that came to him in his sleep as already a piece of writing; it is paradoxically a "composition" that has not yet been outered or written down, yet a "composition" that has been mentally written out.

And the parts that make up this composition are not only the units of a dream—the component persons, "things," images, or words that appear as the dream's manifest content—but also the recognizable units of a written literary work: "lines," "expressions," and therefore "images" in the technical literary sense too.[4] In other words, the story implicates not only forgetting but also the problem of *transcription*. There is a longer composition in one set of media (the language of the dream, poetry, immaterial writing) and a shorter material record of that composition in other media (language written out with "pen, ink" on "paper," poetry). The "deep Romantic chasm" ("Kubla Khan," 12) into which the missing lines fell is theoretically the same chasm opened up by every act of note-taking and transcription because of the possibility of loss and error these acts introduce.[5] In which case, the usually overlooked earlier interval of time—the interval of furious scribbling—comes to matter as much as the "above an hour" he was detained and distracted. How much time did Coleridge have to write out the fifty-four lines that he did manage to get on paper before he was "called out"? Or to ask it another way: at what rate could Coleridge transcribe a thought composition into a handwritten one? Would there be much more of "Kubla Khan" for us to study—maybe closer to the "whole" of it—had Coleridge access, if not to more time before the visitor, then to an inscription method other than one using chirographic English alphabetical letters? But, then, what kind of method would that be, which could turn a mental poem into a manuscript one with the most speed and fidelity?

Story number two provides a clue. Coleridge circulated an anecdote, also quite possibly apocryphal, about his short-lived assignment in February 1800 as an amateur parliamentary reporter during his affiliation with the London newspaper the *Morning Post*. On one occasion, he fell asleep in the middle of a speech by the Prime Minister, William Pitt. Having only "scanty" notes due to sleeping, Coleridge invented much of the eloquent digest that went to press. If the parliamentary report published in the opposition newspaper made Pitt (whom Coleridge considered "a stupid insipid Charlatan") sound half decent, it was because—Coleridge wanted people to know—he had "volunteered" the text.[6] So the story goes. David V. Erdman and, more recently, Nikki Hessell have closely examined the accuracy of his parliamentary reporting (Coleridge was a quite passable reporter) and their studies remind us of something important. Erdman and Hessell can evaluate the accuracy of newspaper summaries like Coleridge's—identifying which parts were probably the reporter's faithful invention, so to speak, and which parts were actually said—by collating them with lengthier, more comprehensive records: shorthand-based transcripts, produced by professional parliamentary reporters for publication in pamphlets as well as collections of parliamentary proceedings.[7] Shorthand, or *stenography* (a combination of the Greek words for "narrow" and "writing"), is "the employment of short signs or characters instead of the ordinary letters of the alphabet" for the rapid, real-time transcription of spoken performances (sermons, speeches, lectures, legal and other proceedings) and, less typically, for the recording of one's own thoughts (notes-to-self or memoranda, diaries, journals).[8] Due to the crowded, noisy conditions in which late eighteenth-century parliamentary reporters attempted to take notes of speeches—even after a ban on note-taking in Parliament was lifted in 1783—their shorthand transcripts were never verbatim records of speeches. Still, shorthand was the period's closest thing to modern electronic audio recording technology.[9] The parliamentary speeches expanded from professional reporters' shorthand notes can be identified by their length, being at least six thousand words long and going up to twenty-five thousand words. In contrast, a typical précis, the kind Coleridge and other newspaper reporters wrote, tended to be around five thousand words or shorter.[10] One of the top stenographers of the time, William Isaac Blanchard, who took down "speeches at length" for Debrett's *Parliamentary Register*, boasted that in "one hour and forty minutes" of a speech, he wrote on "208 law sheets, each sheet containing 72 words, in all 14,976 words"—an unimaginable, hyperbolic 150 words per minute.[11]

Taking its inspiration from these two stories, this chapter makes a sequence of claims. The first is that, if Coleridge's account of "Kubla Khan" prompts the wish for a quicker method of transcription that might have allowed him to write out and save more of "Kubla Khan," Coleridge in his notebooks theorizes this very possibility. Several of his notebook entries are about note-taking itself, and they reveal a persistent fantasy about rapid writing methods. While the notebooks have been considered as being many things and serving many purposes—they are commonplace books, diaries (including dream diaries), writings about travel and nature, wastebooks, and more—they are also home to a particularly Coleridgean brand of what this book calls the dream of communication.[12] Moreover, his notes describe experiments with speedy writing—for example, writing "two or three Sheets rapidly" and then examining the missing words—suggesting that what Noel Jackson has called Coleridge's "literature of self-experiment" extends beyond problems in "philosophy, natural philosophy, and medicine" to those pertaining to inscription and transcription.[13] The notebook entries scrutinizing his own handwriting and note-taking tendencies are perhaps among the most acutely reflexive form of Coleridgean auto-analysis: writing experiments undertaken in notebook writing whose subject matter is writing.

Second, and more specifically, Coleridge pursued a "shorthand for thoughts." His shorthand for thoughts is a kind of quick, in-the-moment transcription, one informed by the shorthand practices in his immediate environment, as when he served as a parliamentary reporter. The introduction to this book invoked Carolyn Marvin's notion of "media fantasies," those speculations that "help us determine . . . what thoughts were possible, and what thoughts could not be entertained yet or anymore" in connection with media technologies and communication practices.[14] In the context of this chapter, Coleridge's media fantasies about rapid transcription chart the imaginative horizons of inscription in the Romantic period. Thoughts that could not be entertained yet include the non-inscriptive audio recording technologies we take for granted. But thoughts that were possible about writing rapidly were shaped by the idealistic assumptions and norms of stenography systems. Like others working with those systems, Coleridge gave much thought to techniques of shortening and simplifying, and thus accelerating, the act of taking things down in writing. What if there were an alternative script, more efficient to write in and read than the English alphabet, because made up of fewer letters? Which English words appear frequently enough that they can be abbreviated and represented with a single character rather than a string of letters?

At the same time—now placing emphasis on the *thoughts* in a shorthand for thoughts—Coleridge's inquiries diverge from those of other users of shorthand systems because he was more interested in the recording of the note-taker's own (that is, his own) thoughts rather than another's speech.[15] Celeste Langan has shown in a superb essay that Coleridge, unlike Wordsworth, believed that poetry represents the language of thought rather than of speech.[16] Much before the modernist novel, and contrary to the commonplace that Romantic poems (chiefly ballads) remediate orality—and contrary too to creative writing pedagogy's phonocentrism, its identification of "voice" with composition itself—Coleridge believed that poetry remediated the language of the silent, thinking mind.[17] Poetry is not limited to what is or can be spoken, and therefore does not reproduce voice but rather the "voices" in one's head; the latter is a symptom of psychosis, but it is also, in Coleridge's understanding, the source and substance of poetry. The same is true of his attempts to theorize, and invent his own idiosyncratic kind of, shorthand, a technology not for recording someone else's talk but the flow of his own thoughts. For this reason, although several valuable studies of Romantic literature have looked into the recording, representation, or remediation in print of the human voice during this period, the case of Coleridge adds an interesting twist or two.[18] As the composition of "Kubla Khan" demonstrates, the thought-manuscript interface—the zone of notebook and diary keepers, and in Coleridge's case, poets—was of greater concern to him than the speech-print interface that has been the focus of much scholarship. What is more, shorthand has a special temporal focus that other written remediations of living language do not: the question is, how can language, being uttered in real time—or for Coleridge, *being thought in real time*—be symbolized, shortened, and registered by hand, if at all, for storage and transmission?

The latter sections of this chapter pursue some implications of Coleridge's shorthand for thoughts. In another notebook entry, Coleridge considers a strange visual phenomenon, whereby the letters of written English come to look like hairy shapes or things; in turn, meaningless, illegible shapes come to resemble writing. Understanding this effect in light of shorthand—because of the way shorthand systems uncannily equate

English letters and the squiggles of alternative notation systems—I call this the *shorthand effect*. It is from this perspective that I revisit "The Rime of the Ancient Mariner" (1798; 1817). Approaching the "Rime" by way of a set of "forms" different from the routine concerns of literary form (for example, the formal elements of the ballad), I focus on overlooked forms like the very alphabetical letters (letterforms) in which the poem is composed and which the shorthand effect defamiliarizes, as well as the "certain shape[s]" rendered verbally in the poem. Raymond Williams observed that notational systems can be used to compose and create as much as to copy—can become "means of composition, apparently in their own right"—and I am suggesting that although Coleridge did not write out the "Rime" in shorthand, it might be read as a work composed in linear, letter-like forms that oscillate between mere shape and letter.[19] The poem's "signs" and "images" can be read differently, now in terms of those other kinds of letter-like signs Coleridge invented, scribbled, and theorized. Above all, where shorthand systems imagined a perfect written medium for communication—one that could easily encode information in real time and be easily decoded later—Coleridge's stenographic fantasias and the "Rime" trouble as much as they pursue the idea of "instantaneous intelligibility" in communication.[20] Although Coleridge's embroilment with shorthand may at first seem to belong to the realm of trivia then, it allows us a different way of approaching the role of writing, media, and communication in his thinking.

From Transcribed to Transcriber: Notes on Coleridgean Note-Taking

Why might have Coleridge's speculations on note-taking, transcription, and shorthand gone unnoticed? These practices concern the crucial process of conversion when ideal might become inked composition, and implicate nothing less than the possibility or impossibility of a historical record. Shorthand, for its part, was the single most important speech- and thought-recording technology prior to the phonograph and in Coleridge's time, not to mention for centuries before.[21] Last but not least, Coleridge is, of course, one of English literary history's most prominent notebook keepers—Seamus Perry justly hails his notebooks as a "prose masterpiece of the age"—and from this recognition it is only a small leap to the hypothesis that Coleridge's notes might reflect on the practice of note-taking itself.[22] My guess is that such matters have been overlooked because it is far more customary to frame Coleridge as someone who needed to be transcribed (but could not be), rather than someone thinking about transcription. With a mythic reputation as a digressive yet scintillating speaker whose discourse was impossible to capture in writing, Coleridge—probably more than any other Romantic-era writer—induces the counterfactual wish for an audio recording of him speaking. In a far-reaching account, Jon Klancher has tracked the series of "transmission failures" that ensued from Coleridge's 1811 lectures on Shakespeare. The professional stenographers in the audience were unable to take down Coleridge's lectures with any kind of accuracy, and distortions and embellishments followed from there—culminating in John Payne Collier's egregious, purple rewriting of the lectures based on the spotty shorthand notes, and extending even to scholarly collected editions of Coleridge's writings.[23]

A well-known anecdote about William Brodie Gurney—a stenographer who came from a family of shorthand systematizers, and who served as an official parliamentary reporter—explains why Coleridge's lectures could not be captured by shorthand.

> With regard to every other speaker whom he [Gurney] had ever heard, however rapid or involved, he could almost always, by long experience in his art, guess the form of the latter part, or apodosis, of the sentence by the form of the beginning; but . . . the conclusion of every one of Coleridge's sentences was a surprise upon him. He was obliged to listen to the last word.[24]

In identifying the unpredictability of the conclusions ("the latter part, or apodosis") to Coleridge's spoken sentences, Gurney discloses a principal strategy in taking shorthand. Inasmuch as the technology depended on handwriting, and because language takes longer to inscribe (even with simplified scripts and word abbreviations) than to utter, shorthand relied on the scribe's anticipation of the speaker's words and phrases to come.

This technology, which aimed for certainty and storage, depended much on uncertain predictions about words not yet spoken; saving the present for the future hinged on guessing the nearer future of the utterance. Commonplaces, rhetorical formulas, and clichés won the scrambling stenographer little bits of time, closing a little the gap between talk and the transcription lagging behind.[25] This legerdemain or trick of shorthand was known from shorthand's earliest uses.[26] An ancient Roman poem on shorthand by Ausonius gives a hyperbolic portrayal of this facet of the art, turning the note-taker's forecasting into an illicit, invasive form of mind reading: "Tell me, then, since you precede my imagination—tell me who has betrayed me? Who has revealed to you what I was meditating? How many thefts does your hand make in my soul[?]"[27] According to Coleridge's reputation as a speaker, it was impossible to guess what he was meditating, to steal from his soul, and a stenographer "obliged to listen to the last word" of Coleridge's formulations was no longer really listening, anticipating, or writing stenographically. On the question of Coleridge and shorthand, then, it is easy to assume that the case is closed, because he was—if not by intention, then by result—a skeptic of shorthand: a speaker who could, simply by holding forth, defeat this obsessive art and expose how shorthand fell short.

Yet when Coleridge in his notebooks is, in his words, "writing on my writing" (*Notebooks*, 3:3325), he reflects on precisely such scenarios of transcription and transmission failure. For example, there is an 1803 entry, which is a transcription of his thoughts about transcription:

> Careful to be accurate, I wrote down what was before my eyes while it was before my eyes, and took down the words from the man's mouth/ but in a hurry I wrote rather scramblingly, &c, & 3 years after made unwittingly a great error in the whole account by transcribing it wrong, & . . . mistaking or misreading a word.—This I mean for my Book of Calumny, Credulity, Causes of mistake. (*Notebooks*, 1:1572)

The occasion described in the entry is unclear. He might be recalling the recording of a speech, as in his parliamentary reporting three years prior; a dream composition, as in his account of "Kubla Khan"'s conception ("I wrote down what was before my eyes"); or *ekphrasis*, in the broadest sense of a literary visual description, not limited to a description of an artwork. But the main point of interest is clear enough: the phenomenon of rushed and sloppy note-taking in the moment of the event, compounded by "mistaking or misreading" later as the writer tries to decipher, expand, and copy out his initial notes—all this amounting to "great error." Since "transcribing it wrong" on both occasions (in the moment and when revisiting the notes) is an ordinary, maybe even expected, occurrence, the fact that an instance of this leads him to project a "Book of Calumny, Credulity, Causes of mistake" may mean that the speech acts and sights he was trying to record were of some legal consequence. In any case, Coleridge's note-to-self, which records a present thought for a future book, self-reflexively recognizes that the humble, haphazard act of note-taking "in a hurry" and "scramblingly" held grave implications for truth, witnessing, evidence, knowledge, and history—and especially, as his entry stresses, their vulnerability to a cascading series of errors set off by the initial act of note-taking.[28] In other words, on the one hand, the existence of the entry—that Coleridge wrote this note or any notes at all—buys into the promise held out by note-taking, the possibility of a written record of the present for safekeeping, for posterity. On the other hand, the content of his entry—the subject Coleridge treats—describes the disappointment of this same promise of transcription, when the medium entrusted with storage (writing) is also the site of "mistaking or misreading." The duality of his entry is in this way reminiscent of Linda Orr's observation about French Revolution–era *logographes* in the Legislative Assembly, the on-the-scene journalistic scribes who jotted down the revolution for posterity: Romantic-era transcription practices projected a historiographical ideal—that "nothing would be lost . . . [and] at last history would be both significant and faithful, loyal to its objects"— and in doing so, proved the impossibility of this wished-for "legitimating correspondence" between historical subject and object, between the writing witness and the unfolding present.[29]

A later notebook entry returns to the same problem of note-taking with celerity, this one planning not a future book on "Calumny, Credulity,

Causes of mistake," but an experiment. "After having written on for two or three Sheets rapidly and as a first Copy, without correcting," Coleridge explains, he wants to "examine every word omitted" (*Notebooks*, 2:3217). This is a recurring scenario featuring a familiar self-portrait in his notebooks: Coleridge himself deep in thought and writing automatically—in a state where he is "unconscious that [he is] writing"—and the occasion for this unconscious writing is to probe the act of writing itself (*Notebooks*, 3:3325). Behind this particular inquiry is a concern with the strategies of omission that his writing automatically adopts in such a state. He observes that when "writing earnestly while we are thinking, we omit words necessary to the sense" or otherwise miswrite such words. For example, in a preceding entry, he had meant to write, "there is no medium between . . . ," but in fact wrote, "there is medium between . . . ," leaving out the "no" (*Notebooks*, 2:3217).[30] This leads Coleridge to a hypothesis: when one is deep or lost in thought, and unselfconsciously writing out those thoughts, the notes are sure to include things found in the world (that is, "the material word," "verbum materiale," or "stuff"), but tend to leave out or mistake words associated with active operations of the mind upon those things ("the word by which the mind expresses its modification of the verbum materiale"), including negations (for example, the "no" in "no medium"). There is, according to Coleridge's hypothesis, a kind of distribution of mnemonic responsibility, of storage. With respect to the former class of words, "the mind borrows the materia from without, & is passive with regard to it . . . [and] a simple event of memory takes place," and by "simple event of memory," he means note-taking-as-memory.[31] But the latter class of words represents the actions of one's own mind, and so a sense of "inward Having with its sense of security passes for the outward Having" (*Notebooks*, 2:3217). Therefore, when writing "rapidly" and "earnestly," the mind's sense of possessing its own acts of "modification" carries over onto the page, unconsciously compelling the omission of those words that it feels to be safe in its own mnemonic storehouse. As with the earlier notebook entry on "transcribing it wrong," we find Coleridge fascinated by what happens when writing down one's own thoughts quickly, and the errors one is liable to make: writing notes "scramblingly" in the moment and then "transcribing [them] wrong, & mistaking or misreading a word," or, in this case, failing to write important words, "necessary to the sense."

But there is a key difference in this entry, a difference that is consequential for this discussion moving forward: the transcription error of omission points to the possibility of a transcription *strategy*, a shorthand. With a delegation of mnemonic burden between inscribed notes and one's memory, and the attendant ability to skip certain words in the note—trusting memory and context will help him recall them—it might be possible to transcribe the flow of thought or speech with greater speed. Looking into both the limitations of transcription—that writing is (to repurpose Coleridge's words) "no medium," or rather an imperfect one for record-keeping—and the possibilities of streamlining transcription via mnemonic and inscriptive shortcuts, Coleridge invested a great deal of thought into the pitfalls and potential of rapid writing. Reworking Wordsworth's phrase for the connected condition, "the rapid communication of intelligence," we might say that there is in Coleridge an abiding concern with the rapid chirography of intelligence, a problem he took as seriously as the professional stenographers who tried desperately to save his speech. As the following section shows, he also took very seriously the *script systems* of shorthand, as seriously as the legions of inventors who thought up alternative notations for the purpose of rapid transcription.

Coleridge among the Scribble-Scrabble-Geniuses

Not only was Coleridge in the midst of stenographers—when he was serving as a parliamentary reporter or when he was giving his Shakespeare lectures—he also directly engaged shorthand premises and practices in a notebook entry from sometime in January 1805. In this entry he simultaneously shares in the exercise motivating shorthand systems—that is, to dream up a simplified script for use in note-taking and transcription—and parodies shorthand. It is worth reproducing the full entry, including the asemic writing comprised of hypothetical letters that he came up with to illustrate his conjecture:

> We have traced picture into hieroglyphic and hieroglyphic into arbitrary character—but go further! see the handwriting of men who

write much yet not for others, as Scribes, but for themselves & for their own reading—see! how few diversities of character there are, so as often to make it impossible except by the sense to know whether a certain mark be an "e" or an "i" (or an "a," or an "o" or an "u") or an "n" or an "r" or an "l," or even an "m" or "u" or "w" . . . eleven letters have certainly been expressed by one mark—and see that "ly" at the end of "certainly" in the line above, who could distinguish it, by itself, from an ill-written GG?—So by increase & habit of increased Intellect may not any one thing come to mean all things?

The foregoing observation seems a mere sophism[.] [A] certain number of distinct marks preceding and awaking the idea[,] it will no doubt turn any pothooks and hangers into the exponents of those ideas that necessarily connect the last distinct mark with the following [but] What if they all were [a series of illegible and invented alphabetical marks; see Figure 1.1]—which characters perhaps may have been made by the scribble-scrabble-geniuses to mean every & each Letter—what if they were all to come together, much more if . . . any *one* were to be uniformly repeated, what would the sublimest Intellect make of it?—No! all we can deduce is this, that the assimilating Intellect may reduce all forms into any one, and make any one in its place representative of all; but still Intellect demands Distinction, as its Essence, & Distinction implies diversity in the co-existent vision. That form which is now an "n" may elsewhere be an "a" or "w" or "i" or "r" or even a "d"—but no six similar characters could without foregoing & following diversity of distinct letters convey the word "inward." N.B. half a page wasted in Nonsense, and a whole page in the confutation of it. But such is the nature of exercise—I walk a mile for health—& then another to return home again. (*Notebooks*, 2:2406)

This entry is easy to dismiss because the thoughts verge on *reductio ad absurdum*, and he twice rejects the proposition he twice floats. Yet one can—in the spirit of Coleridge's own final salutary conceit—consider this mental perambulation, though it will end up where it started, as explorative of the boundaries of the Romantic stenographic—and more broadly, inscriptive—imagination.

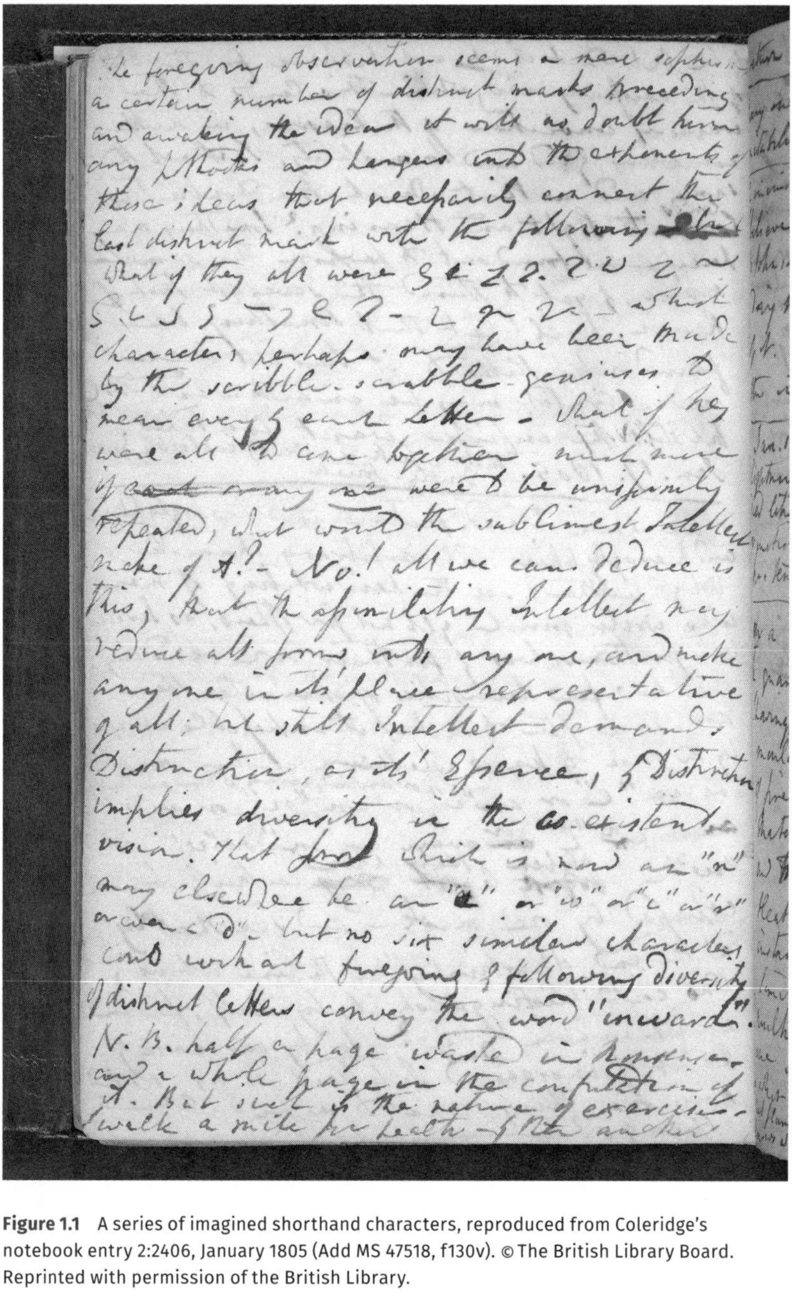

Figure 1.1 A series of imagined shorthand characters, reproduced from Coleridge's notebook entry 2:2406, January 1805 (Add MS 47518, f130v). © The British Library Board. Reprinted with permission of the British Library.

On the topic of Coleridge's views on communication, scholars before me have emphasized his attraction to natural language doctrine and Berkeleyan "divine language," especially during the Somerset years. An ancient and yet perseverant idea that can be found in Plato's *Cratylus* and subsequent theories of an "Adamic language," natural language doctrine involves the fantasy of a more perfect relation between language and its referents, and thus opposes or complicates the idea of linguistic arbitrariness or conventionalism often associated with Locke's *An Essay Concerning Human Understanding* (1690).[32] Yet the semiotic sequence with which Coleridge begins this entry—"picture" to "hieroglyphic" to "arbitrary character"—portrays Coleridge thinking about communication in a different way, one clearly accepting of arbitrariness, beginning at the level of the letter. Here he is interested not in the possibility of Nature's "one mighty alphabet," but in arbitrary alphabets, including that of English itself.[33] The sequence, in highly compressed form, partakes in a genre that Paula McDowell has labelled, following the work of Clifford Siskin and William B. Warner, a "history of mediation."[34] Or in other words, this is a Eurocentric stadial history of signs, one in which advancement is defined by the emergence of writing after pictorial representation, followed by the increasing arbitrariness—or decreasing iconicity or motivatedness—of written signifiers relative to their signifieds. Coleridge begins with "pictures," and then moves on to hieroglyphic writing (written signs that visually resemble their referents, and have some degree of iconicity, like ideograms and logograms), and finally to "arbitrary characters," in this case, graphemes linked only conventionally or arbitrarily to the phonemes they represent.[35] Indeed, Coleridge's thought experiment tries to push the idea of arbitrariness to its extreme: "Go further!" Given "how few diversities of character" there appear to be in the nearly illegible handwriting of that recurring portrait of the copious note-taker—that is, given that such writers seem to rely on so few distinct letters, and it is difficult to know whether any mark of theirs is an "e," i," "a, "o" "u," "n," "r," "l," "m," "u," or "w"—would it not be imaginable that a single arbitrary letter "uniformly repeated" could serve as the basis for writing? That is, in the next evolutionary leap to be taken by writing in tandem with the advancement of "increased Intellect" (reminiscent of what Keats will go on to call the "grand March of Intellect"), might it come to be that "characters" are even further dissociated from their signifieds, such that a set of different letters no longer corresponds even conventionally to a set of speech sounds, and instead there is a single arbitrary mark standing for all sounds? As Coleridge puts it, "May not any one thing come to mean all things?"

The entry ponders this thought a couple of times, only to dismiss it each time: the first time, Coleridge rejects his own premise that any single uncertain mark could mean any and all other letters, because the "distinct marks" before and after the illegible mark(s) usually allow the reader to infer the word and conjure the "idea"; the second time, he rejects the idea of a hypothetical alphabet comprised of a single arbitrary letter by concluding that "Intellect demands Distinction," and goes on to elaborate on that thought. Although Coleridge rejects his own speculations, one may classify this entry, as I have begun to suggest, as media fantasy: a record of what thoughts were possible about alphabets and writing. But then, what is the ground from which these speculations launch? What was making possible these thoughts about what was possible? And why would it have been worthwhile to imagine an alternative alphabet—with a sublime perceiver or reader to match—reduced to only a single arbitrary sign? His hypothetical alphabet, along with his references to "scribble-scrabble-geniuses" and "pothooks and hangers," indicates shorthand. Though he may have been, as a talker, famously inimical to this transcription technology, as a note-taker he pursued the same questions that had exercised shorthand script devisers since antiquity. The following excursus offers some background on shorthand, as well as its status in the Romantic period, so we can further parse Coleridge's cryptic entry.

Shorthand and Romanticism

Shorthand has been called many things, and listing the zany aliases thought up by shorthand system inventors throughout history is a topos in the literature. Isaac Pitman's *A History of Shorthand* (1847) adds to the terms "shorthand" and "stenography," the following: "polygraphy," "cryptography," "phoögraphy," "radiography" and "facilography." More recently, Lisa Gitelman has named "tachygraphy," "brachygraphy," and "phonography," and Leah Price has added "Zeitography, Zeiglography, Semigraphy, or Semography."[36] Whatever the name, every system promises the ability to write at the speed of speech, a simple, easy-to-learn set of signs, and a variety of other benefits. On the long historical timeline of shorthand, some conventional highlights are the following: the invention in antiquity of Tironean shorthand, or *notae Tironianae* (the system devised by Cicero's freedman and amanuensis, Tiro [94 BC to 4 AD); the invention around the turn of the seventeenth century of the earliest shorthand systems for English—Timothy Bright's *Charactertie; An Art of Short, Swift, and Secret Writing, by Character* (1588) and John Willis's *The Art of Stenographie, or Short Writing, by Spelling Characterie* (1602)—and the subsequent "short-hand driven information revolution of the seventeenth century," which saw the rise of reported sermons, trials, and speeches; and finally, coinciding with the beginning of the Victorian era, the publication of the first modern and very successful shorthand system, Pitman's *Phonography; or Writing by Sound* (1837).[37]

Although shorthand is not frequently associated with the historical stretch of British Romanticism, at least not as frequently as it is with other times (for example, the seventeenth century or the Victorian era), it was very much a Romantic-era transcription technology too.[38] The first significant historical survey of shorthand, James Henry Lewis's *An Historical Account of the Rise and Progress of Short Hand* (1816), dedicated to Lord Byron, was a product of the period.[39] Lewis's characterization in 1816 of shorthand as "a science, now so generally prevalent and necessary," might be discounted due to blatant self-interest—Lewis was a tireless promoter of his own system, "The Lewisian System of Penmanship," which Byron and Walter Scott apparently endorsed—but other reasons lend credence to his claim of shorthand's prevalence.[40] Shorthand practice took on renewed prominence when Parliament lifted the ban on parliamentary note-taking in 1783, a prominence perhaps comparable to its seventeenth-century heyday. Newspapers that covered Parliament, such as the *Morning Post* (for which Coleridge wrote three parliamentary reports, one of which was discussed earlier), the *Morning Chronicle*, and the evening *Courier* (for which

Coleridge also wrote, in 1811), rationalized the work of transcription into a relay system in which teams of reporters divvied up the scribal work into two-hour shifts, with "the best [teams] led by shorthand men."[41] And by my count, the frequency with which new shorthand systems were published throughout the later eighteenth century and up through Lewis's *Historical Account*—with a new title appearing every year or so—equals or surpasses the rate at which systems appeared during the "short-hand driven information revolution of the seventeenth century."[42]

What may be of greatest interest to literary historians is that Romantic-era shorthand practices shared with Romantic literary culture certain defining concerns. A brief guessing game illustrates this point. Which of the following quotations—(1) or (2)—is from the stenographer, and which from the Romantic poet? (1) This art necessitates that his or her "pen is prompt in turning to shape" what it seeks to record. (2) This art gives "permanence to the effusions" and ensures that what would have otherwise "perished on the vacant air" is "preserved from destruction, to the probable benefit of ourselves and our posterity."[43] The first thought is from William Wordsworth's "Preface" to his *Poems* of 1815, but with the figure of a prompt pen, Wordsworth plucks a commonplace from shorthand manuals—that each manual's system can teach a student how to write fast enough to keep pace with compositions in speech or in thought—and from the titles of certain systems, such as William Mason's *A Pen Pluck't from an Eagles Wing* (1672). The second instance composites phrases from Lewis's *Historical Account*. Lewis's case for the importance of shorthand—that it records speech for transmission down the ages— stems from the same anxiety about impermanent communications that shapes, for example, Wordsworth's worries in *The Prelude* ("these must perish") or Keats's in *The Fall of Hyperion* ("Pity these have not/Trac'd upon vellum or wild Indian leaf/The shadows of melodious utterance").[44] The poets and stenographers, though they have different motives—literary immortality versus perfectible note-taking, canonical versus clerical concerns—can be difficult to distinguish from one another because both dream about the saving of linguistic expression through a "graphic art" made as swift as possible.[45]

Most systems offer three classes of signs: an alphabet; signs for prefixes, suffixes, participles, prepositions, terminations, and very short words; and finally, "arbitrary characters."[46] Shorthand systems sell their alphabetical signs as a simpler alternative to the English alphabet (see Figure 1.2). They usually offer fewer than the twenty-six marks of the Roman alphabet by assigning similar speech sounds to a single mark. In Byrom's *Universal English Short-hand*, a backslash-like symbol (\) stands for both "f" and "v," and a dash (-) for both "s" and "z"; in other systems "c," "k," and "q" might share a single symbol.[47] Shorthand alphabets also try to assign the simplest shapes for the most frequently occurring letters, marks that can be written with one quick stroke of the pen. An allied consideration is to make these important, frequently occurring marks easy to connect with adjacent marks—to ensure, as Gurney explains, that "those most used [shorthand letters] are of the sort which will easily join" to other letters.[48] Vowels in the middle of words are typically treated differently and give rise to all kinds of proposals.[49] Much like Coleridge's notebook entry concerning the skipping over of words about which the mind has a "sense of security," Blanchard's and others' strategy of leaving out vowels (or representing only some of them with simple signs) presupposes that the mind can fill in the omissions later.

As for the second type of sign: many systems reuse their alphabetical letters to represent these signs, including commonly occurring prefixes, suffixes, participles, conjunctions, prepositions, and other short, very common words. For example, the mark for "d" (or the "d" sound) might also serve as the prefixes "de-" and "dis-," and the termination "-ed"; similarly, the shorthand equivalent of "b" might serve as "be," "but," "be-," or "-ble" and "-able." Sometimes, however, systems offer supplementary signs for other short words and affixes.[50]

The third and final class of sign and the most controversial is arbitrary characters. Actually, all shorthand signs are arbitrary—as arbitrary as the standard Roman letters they purport to be re-forming and reforming—but in the stenographic context *arbitrary character* is a technical term denoting a single sign that stands for the largest units captured by shorthand: frequently occurring words (usually longer than those represented by the second class of symbols) and commonplace phrases in sermonic rhetoric and political-legal discourse—such as "magistrate," "governing," "heart," "covetous," and "wilderness."[51] The arbitrary characters for words are essentially logograms and grammalogues; or in ancient Roman stenographic practice, *notae non literae*; in the Coleridgean context—given his insistence that written signs represent not words but thoughts—ideograms.[52] But there are arbitrary characters for entire phrases too: Gurney's system has arbitrary characters for phrases like "of Heaven" and "false doctrine," and for longer formulas like "the greatest part of the world."[53] Systematizers criticized earlier and rival systems for the impractically long word lists and corresponding number of arbitrary signs that these systems asked students to commit to memory, even as the later systems offered lengthy lists of

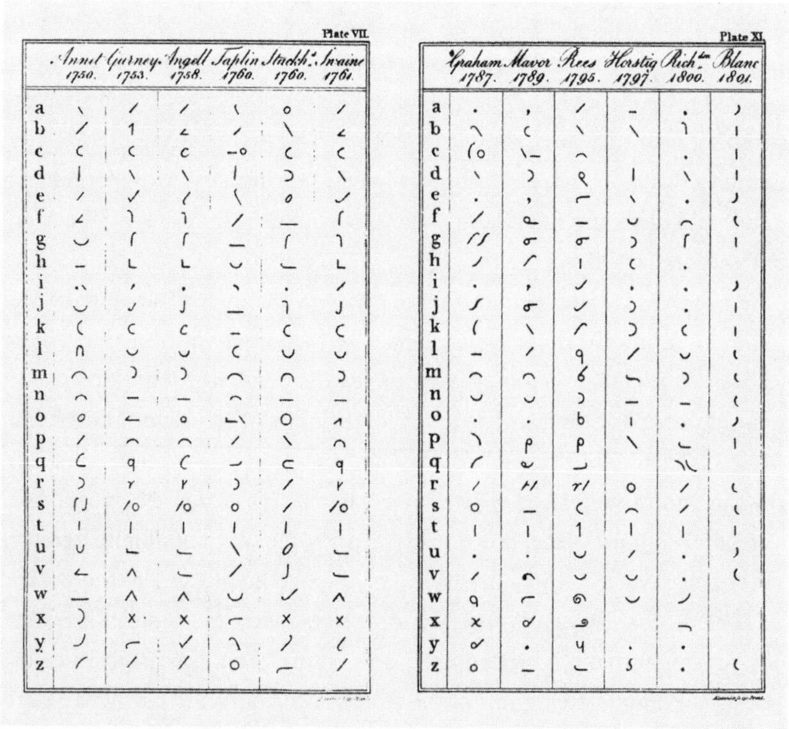

Figure 1.2 A comparison of different shorthand alphabets, reproduced from James Henry Lewis's *An Historical Account of the Rise and Progress of Short Hand*[. . .] (London: Sherwood, Neeley, and Jones, 1816).

their own. What is confusing—or another amusing contradiction—is that the arbitrary characters are usually the least arbitrary or artificial of all the shorthand signs. The shorthand alphabets are more or less arbitrary in relation to the speech sounds or English letters they replace, but the arbitrary characters tend to be the most "iconic" signs, each visually resembling to some degree its signified. For example, Gurney's character for the formula "the greatest part of the world" and all his other symbols for sermonic phrases including "the world" ("this world," "the other world," "world without end") are variations on a small circle representing the world.[54]

Coleridge's Shorthand for Thoughts

Returning now to Coleridge's meditations, the parameters of his media fantasy are set by shorthand, but he also diverges from the priorities of shorthand inventors. Like the scribble-scrabble-geniuses, Coleridge aims at the ideal of a more efficient notation. Consistent with his earlier notebook entry about the omission of words when writing "rapidly," the entry from January 1805 quoted earlier picks up on the time- and effort-saving techniques used by experienced note-takers, who streamline handwriting and work with fewer, simpler marks, even at the expense of illegibility to others: it seems that in such handwriting, "eleven letters have certainly been expressed by one mark." It is meaningful too, then, that Coleridge's imaginary alphabet has fewer than twenty-six letters. More important than any surface resemblance to the meaningless squiggles of shorthand alphabets is that it parallels the logic of stenographic systems: to reduce the total number of letters in an alphabet is somehow to simplify and improve it. And when Coleridge observes that the legible marks surrounding illegible pothooks and hangers make it possible to perceive recognizable words ("exponents of . . . ideas"), the phrase "pothooks and hangers" broadly means inscrutable handwritten marks, like "chicken scratches," but he has stenography on his mind too.[55] As Leah Price has shown in treating Charles Dickens's connection with Gurney's shorthand system, and as the *Oxford English Dictionary* also notes, "pothooks and hangers" was a slang term for shorthand in the nineteenth century.[56] Coleridge recognizes the apparent absurdity of his ideas, and raises logical objections to them, but it is still significant, I think, that he tries twice, against his better judgment, to imagine a script featuring "*one* [sign] uniformly repeated." This media fantasy is one and the same as that harbored by the scribble-scrabble-geniuses: coming up with a simple code, made up of a small number of signs that can be written in a few strokes and easily connected to one another. In Coleridge's nonsensical yet radical fantasy, he imagines the shortest conceivable form of shorthand—other than having a limitless memory or engaging in thought "theft" of the kind Ausonius described—namely, *a shorthand of one sign.*

There are similar stenographic impulses in the ciphers Coleridge used to encrypt some of his notebook entries. These cipher systems have never been categorized as such, but they ought to be tagged as a form of shorthand too.[57] Such a recognition most immediately serves to recall the long relation in the history of communication between quick and coded writing; shorthand systems promoted their scripts for the secondary application of secrecy, and devisers of secret writing also promised transmission quickness by virtue of codedness.[58] For example, some of Coleridge's ciphers engage in the same substitution of words by single characters as is seen in the use of stenographic symbols for affixes and the arbitrary characters (the second and third types of shorthand sign). Both Coleridge and the scribble-scrabble-geniuses generate a list of high frequency words to which symbols are assigned: Coleridge, for example, has his own shorthand symbols to stand for "to," "they," "of," "with," "from," and so forth (see Figure 1.3).

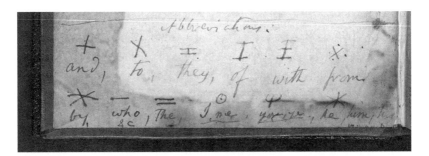

Figure 1.3 Coleridge's shorthand and cipher for frequently occurring words, found on the inside cover of Notebook 21½ (notebook entry 2:2383) (Add MS 47519, f1v). ©The British Library Board. Reprinted with permission of the British Library.

Such common words—typically left out of literary concordances and called *stop words* in natural language processing, and yet quite important for author attribution and certain other statistical investigations into literary works—are the kinds of words that mattered most to devisers of shorthand, whether for widely adopted systems or idiosyncratic ones like Coleridge's. For some purposes, like concordance making, these words are too numerous and insignificant, noise to be minimized from the top of any word frequency list in order to discern patterns involving words of greater interest. But if one's purpose is, in Coleridge's words, to write "for two or three Sheets rapidly"—or, at the longer extreme, as the parliamentary reporter William Isaac Blanchard put it, to produce "208 law sheets, each sheet containing 72 words, in all 14,976 words"—these stop words are the top words of interest. No other words are a bigger priority for symbolizing and shortening. Finally, like shorthand systems, Coleridge's signs had multiple significations, from phoneme to word. Most remarkable is his use of the Hebrew letter *shin*—"ש" and "שׁ" (with a dot over the right side)—which he used as short for the "sh-" sound, the pronoun "she," and the object of his extramarital infatuation, Sarah Hutchinson (via the initials "S.H."). In shorthand terms, this sign, borrowed from Hebrew, is an "alphabetical character," but also serves as a character of the second type (pronouns, affixes, and the like), and as an arbitrary character (a name). In sum, Coleridge invented his own shorthand along the lines of other shorthand systems.

At the same time, and in line with the tone of ironic admiration with which he refers to those other scribble-scrabble-geniuses, he also departs from standard shorthand practice. His nonsensical string of twenty or so scrawls, the kind of alphabet that would stand for "every & each Letter" of the Roman alphabet, satirizes shorthand alphabets. For students struggling to learn shorthand scripts, or for rival systematizers intent on criticizing all but their own alphabets, or even for the uninitiated non-stenographer, the individual signs of shorthand are difficult to discriminate from one another, and Coleridge's scribbles seem designed to point up this fact. In Gurney's *Brachygraphy*, for example, the slash-based signs for "a," "e," "j," and "z" can easily be confused for one another (see Figure 1.2, left plate). And one is struck by all manner of other impracticalities. Chief among them is the time it would take to commit these signs to memory and then attain a proficiency in transcription that is significantly faster than note-taking with the Roman alphabet and one's own unsystematic, idiosyncratic set of abbreviations.

Most of all, Coleridge diverges from the scribble-scrabble-geniuses in order to imagine the possibility of his own shorthand for thoughts rather than for speech. His main preoccupation is the handwriting of note-takers who "write much" but only "for themselves & for their own reading"—that is, note-takers like himself. The apparent comparison Coleridge is making is between the handwriting of "those who write much . . . for others"— "scribes," amanuenses, clerks—where individual letters need to be distinctly recognizable to those "others" and the personal shorthand of those whose audience is their own future selves revisiting their earlier notes. But a less obvious and more important difference is Coleridge's interest in shorthand as a private medium for one's own thoughts and notes—this against the dominant orientation of shorthand systems, from the seventeenth through the nineteenth centuries, toward the transcription and storage of speech. It is true that since antiquity, non-speech applications for shorthand scripts were recognized: enciphering correspondence one wanted to keep private between sender and addressee, or adding a layer of security to personal memoranda, as Coleridge did too. Yet with regard to seventeenth-century stenography, Michael Mendle has remarked that "all systems . . . showed their primary market was sermon note-takers," over more "esoteric uses" like cryptography, although systems would mention these alternative uses too.[59] Similarly, with regard to Victorian-era stenography, Ivan Kreilkamp argues that systems like Pitman's popular *Phonography* idealized shorthand as writing suffused with the living human voice—a form of writing that was an antidote to the standardized, dead letter of printed matter, an answer for "print-culture guilt."[60] The phonocentric situation was similar in Coleridge's own time. Lewis's *Historical Account* differentiates shorthand's "direct utility" from its "indirect utility." The former is the rapid transcription of speech events: its main use is "the application of Short-hand to its most obvious and important purpose—that of embodying the oral eloquence of the Orator and the Divine."[61] In contrast, the "indirect" uses have mostly to do with private note-taking functions; auxiliary uses include "commit[ting] memorandums to paper almost as instantaneously as they are conceived," and writing in code for the purpose of secrecy. The paradoxical but dominant ideology of stenography for several centuries can be characterized as a fetishization of the human voice and, at the same time, a demotion of voice for its ephemerality relative to the celebrated durability of inscription.

Coleridge's shorthand ruminations are thus also at odds with mainstream stenographic discourse. Not only is his focus the idiosyncratic shorthand of individual note-takers, like himself: unlike the devisers of any of the many competing systems on the market, he is most intent to explore the use of shorthand for the comparatively minor function of the transcription of thoughts rather than speech. We have seen Coleridge interested in transcription as a general problem, inclusive of speech transcription ("I . . . took down the words from the man's mouth"), but he devotes as much thought to notes-to-self, to a shorthand for thoughts. He was after a way to write out his thoughts "in short," a way that appears both to learn and differ from the ways of the scribble-scrabble-geniuses. As the other chapters of this book also suggest—whether considering Wordsworth and the ideal of registering bits of information as efficiently as possible, or Keats and the possibility of instantaneous communication at a distance—Romantic poets were drawn to such schemes, systems, genres, media, technologies, and above all, fantasies of perfectible communication, as much as they may have doubted them. This is also the case with Coleridge and the fantasy of rapid writing.

The Shorthand Effect

One of the main effects of shorthand scripts as a technology is the profound defamiliarization of written English, whose shapes are not typically the object of much attention—a blurring of legible writing into shape form and vice versa. As mentioned earlier, I call this the shorthand effect. Within Romantic literature, William Blake's "composite art," with its "visual-verbal dialectics," is the most prominent, much studied version of writing-shape interactions.[62] But Coleridge's media fantasies, too, deal with such interactions, which take on a different cast in the framework of Coleridgean theories of writing, and lead to different implications about legibility and illegibility, effectiveness through efficiency (speed, abbreviations), and notation system to notation system transfers, than they do when considered with regard to Blake's illuminated poetry. Needless to say, any bi- or multi-lingual reader and writer, including Coleridge himself—or more precisely, any multi-notational reader or writer, when, for example, Greek, Hebrew, or Chinese writing is involved—is familiar with switching between English writing and non-English written forms, along with any attendant uncanny, perceptual effects; it makes a great deal of sense that shorthand and Chinese characters alike were called "pothooks and hangers" by Britons. Nevertheless, the abiding interest we have seen across several of Coleridge's notebook entries suggests a distinct strain of thinking, not so much about translation as about note-taking and transcription. These entries intimate that shorthand—in the limited sense of particular published systems and also in the general sense of transcription under the pressure of time, the volume needing to be written, and/or habit—held the strange power to establish an ambiguous equivalence between written English and shapes. Letters, word parts (morphemes), words, and entire phrases can appear as pothooks and hangers, and vice versa. There is something about shorthand and its logic that can, in Leah Price's words, reduce "letters to pure visuality," making them things to be "looked at, not read," while making non-linguistic markings "look like alphabetical characters."[63] For Coleridge, we recall, the act of mistranscription—taking bad initial notes due to rushing and then "mistaking or misreading" them later— means the degeneration of notes into illegible, or incompletely legible, marks. Even good notes can look like a sequence of indistinguishable scrawls to another reader: experienced and copious note-takers write in such a way—that is, in their own kind of idiosyncratic shorthand—that to any reader other than themselves it may look as though "eleven letters have certainly been expressed by one mark."

At the same time, and in the other direction, shorthand systems enthusiastically equated their squiggles with phonemes, letters, affixes and terminations, words, and formulas. Lewis's tables compiled for his historical survey of shorthand (Figure 1.2), and visually configured in such a way that the alphabets of different systems are compared against English letters, are entirely in keeping with the logic and the tables found within individual systems, where English letters and shorthand signs are placed side by side as exchangeable marks. In *Brachygraphy*, Gurney assured his readers that his shorthand signs would, after being learned, come to read just like legible English writing: "there is no Room to doubt but they will be read again at first Sight."[64] Coleridge too, in his own cipher-cum-shorthand, assumed a certain equivalence between non-English marks for words. In one notebook entry addressing Sara Hutchinson (imaginatively "addressing," as it is really addressed only to himself), he refers to his "habit of half unconsciously writing your name ["Sara Hutchinson"] or its Symbol invented by me to express it," describing the unthinking ease ("or its Symbol") with which he can replace her initials or full name with his repurposed symbol for it, the Hebrew letter *shin*.

The semiotic sequence with which Coleridge began his scribble-scrabble-geniuses entry—"picture into hieroglyphic and hieroglyphic into arbitrary character"—is thus complicated by the shorthand effect implied by the rest of the same entry. Stenography prompts revisions to, and reversals of, this trajectory of linguistic advancement. By turning the perceptible marks of written English into non-signifying scrawls, and by virtue of shorthand's status as a secondary, parasitic notation system operating on English, the shorthand effect projects a second degree of arbitrary character: picture → hieroglyphic → the arbitrary characters of written English → *the pothooks and hangers that shorthand and defamiliarized English can both sometimes appear to be*. Or, to look at it another way, the shorthand effect reverts both English writing and shorthand signs to the status of "picture" or "hieroglyphic" representations, but they are representations that, signifying or indexing nothing beyond themselves (that is, representing no speech sounds), are images of themselves as shapes or things.

Around the time Coleridge was developing his cipher-cum-shorthand, he added a late night entry in his notebook describing this very phenomenon, writing taking on the appearance of a thing. Catching a glimpse of his own writing not as a language but as unfamiliar, hairy forms, he observes:

> The words appear *fasericht* [fibrous]—hairy, ragged—with a rough ir-regular *nap* upon them/this last is the real feeling—& yet something resembling words written on blotting paper—not the mere sinking or running of the Letters, but that *fasericht* nappy essence of each Let-ter. (*Notebooks*, 2:2394)

The "words" and "Letters" have taken on a strange quality as "hairy, ragged" shapes. At the same time, he maintains some perception of them as meaningful words and signifying letters in the act of more or less co-herently describing this phenomenon in his entry; but then again, in writ-ing the very letters that make up the words—w, o, r, d, s—and in writing the words themselves, "the real feeling" is that these are things more than they are alphabetical or semantic units. Such is the shorthand effect.

An analogy with something contemporary comes to mind. Something akin to the shorthand effect occurs with *optical character recognition* (OCR), the artificial-intelligence software used in mass book digitization projects; alternatively, the shorthand effect anticipates the shape-letter entangle-ments characteristic of OCR. Lisa Gitelman and Ryan Cordell, in their respective, brilliant accounts, explain that OCR software, in scanning and "reading" pages from printed books, breaks down words into letters and then treats printed letters not as letters but as shapes: each letter is com-pared against a database of letterforms, and then the software makes a best guess as to the printed letter, giving a confidence rating reflecting the pro-gram's degree of certainty.[65] Words become letters become shapes become letters. Meanwhile, on the user end, we researchers often confuse the let-ter- and word-images on our interface—those presented on the facsimile page image on computer screens—as actual letters and words, even though they are not. Cordell points out that we tend to think that our search que-ries are scanning the letter- and word-images shown in the page images that we see on our screens; the highlighting of matching search terms on the page image reinforces this effect. But in fact, searches are being done on underlying, machine-readable text files that are hidden from users.[66] The "words" we see on our screens are not really—not functionally— words or letters so much as images. Not unlike these intricate transactions between writing and shapes/images associated with OCR software and the scholarly databases that depend on them, the shorthand effect—albeit originating much earlier and for different reasons—leads to similar kinds of transactions. And as with OCR, the writing-shape relation in shorthand changes with medial and interfacial combinations and crossings—among and between manuscript, print, and printed versions of manuscript short- hand signs. For example, printed shorthand manuals reproduce pages and pages of handwritten shorthand shapes in print—scrawls printed to retain a handwritten look, but at the same time codified by printing so that each individual scrawl is uniform. All the while, the shorthand signs are pitched by inventors in a way that suggests their exchangeability with legible English handwriting or print. And yet, due to their proximity to printed English writing (that is, the explanatory prose of the system), the shapes tend to appear more hopelessly illegible, different from the familiar, standardized letters surrounding them.

In turn, set against the mechanically reproducible letter types of print—and more broadly, the powerful and pervasive force of linguistic standardization in the eighteenth century—shorthand systems doggedly un- and re-standardized English. System after system offered non-standard non-English scripts, centered on handwriting with all its individual vari- ability, advanced alternative orthography (with phonetic-minded ab- breviation techniques), and proposed a semiotic system that worked in a fundamentally different way from written English (for example, by allow- ing words or entire phrases to be replaced by a single sign). The standard- ization of English that determines so much Romantic literary culture, as Andrew Elfenbein has shown, is thus coextensive with stenographic proj- ects that took apart codified English in order to propose shadow codes that could (the manuals claimed) be written more quickly and function better as a recording technology.[67] Shorthand was a paradoxical, perhaps inevitable response to linguistic standardization, then. On the one hand, shorthand joined the standardization effort insofar as it tried to standardize English even further, to outdo standardization by coming up with an even more rationalized language. On the other hand, these systems were insistent upon revealing how unstandardized or irrational standardized written English remained when it came to the practical applications of note-taking, transcription, or any other occasion for rapid writing. The plethora of such systems—each one vying to become *the* standard—appears as a chaotic marketplace of semiotic options. All of these systems, however, shared and sold one dream: better written signs than those of English, signs that could also be "read . . . at first Sight."

The Picture Language of "The Rime of the Ancient Mariner"

Shapes as written language and written language as shapes: the phenomenon of the shorthand effect seems entirely conventional at first when transplanted to the context of literary writing. We are, of course, accustomed to shapes, objects, scenes, landscapes, other artworks, and other visually perceived things being represented or remediated in writing. Nothing could be more routine than the poetic image, the literary description. Yet there is something else occurring in Coleridge's writing, something that can be seen in "The Rime of the Ancient Mariner" too.[68] In this final section, I revisit certain scenes and problems from the "Rime," aiming not only to read but to *look*—in a more literal sense than usual, or somewhat like the way OCR software looks at pages—at the "Rime" in a different way. I propose to read the poem in light of Coleridgean speculations about notational signs discussed above, and in doing so, make the case that the poem's images may be understood not in terms of symbol or allegory but rather as the shorthand effect attempted in the poetic medium. This means analyzing "forms" that are not the customary units of poetic form (such as rhyme, alliteration, and meter) but are instead the linear forms or shapes that the poem makes so conspicuous: the letterforms of the English alphabet, as well as the bars, grates, and other skeletonized forms that recur in the poem and that feature so prominently in responses to the poem (such as Alexander Calder's line drawings, and the Warren-Empson dispute on the poem's words as "shapes on the page"). This also means reading the poem not in light of other symbologies than have already been brought to bear on it—for example, the approach to biblical hermeneutics of the eighteenth-century "higher criticism"—but rather in light of the signs and symbols most closely associated with the scribble-scrabble-geniuses.[69] Indeed, the "signs" presented in the poem (and noted also in a marginal gloss: "The ancient Mariner beholdeth a sign in the element afar off" [69]) and the words of the poem themselves blur in a manner described by the shorthand effect—at one moment coming into focus and legibility in the way stenographers fantasized, at the next moment becoming mere pothooks and hangers.

The passage of interest is the beginning of Part III, when the Ancient Mariner sees the approaching skeleton ship in the distance:

> I saw a something in the Sky
>   No bigger than my fist;
> At first it seem'd a little speck
>   And then it seem'd a mist:
> It mov'd and mov'd, and took at last
>   A certain shape, I wist.
>
> A speck, a mist, a shape, I wist!
>   And still it ner'd and ner'd;
>
> . . .
>
> The western wave was all a flame,
>   The day was well nigh done!
> Almost upon the western wave
>   Rested the broad bright Sun;
> When that strange shape drove suddenly
>   Betwixt us and the Sun.
>
> And strait the Sun was fleck'd with bars
>
> . . .
>
> As if thro' a dungeon grate he peer'd
>   With broad and burning face.

. . .

Are those *her* Sails that glance in the Sun
  Like restless gossameres?

Are those *her* naked ribs, which fleck'd
  The sun that did behind them peer? (1798.167–178)

Readers of Coleridge have noticed the pictorial, imagistic tendency of his writing, as exemplified here. For example, Raimondo Modiano, focusing on Coleridge's landscape-inspired notebook entries between 1798 and 1806, describes these entries as "word pictures." In these entries, Coleridge converted natural landscapes into picturesque paintings (he looked at landscapes "with a painter's eye"), and then represented those paintings in writing, going for "paintings in the domain of language."[70] As Modiano puts it, these entries reproduce "visual phenomena in verbal discourse"— that is, in the form of a "verbal sign."[71] Perhaps having in mind passages like the description of the approaching specter ship, Wordsworth pointed out something similar about the "Rime," the poem's enthusiasm for such "word pictures." His 1800 "Note to the Ancient Mariner" observes, in a negative way, that "the imagery is somewhat too laboriously accumulated," and in a less negative way, that "a great number of the stanzas present beautiful images."[72] Alexander Calder's mid-twentieth-century line drawings for an illustrated edition of the poem seem entirely consistent with these other reactions to Coleridge and the "Rime" in particular.[73] Calder's primitivistic images—the denuded, Adamic human figures, the basic sketches of the sun, moon, bird, ship, water-snakes, and church— complement well Warren's "archetypal" reading of the poem that is reprinted in this illustrated edition, but they are also reminders of the poem's conspicuous visuality. The illustrations reinforce the poem's own preoccupation with illustration, but illustration using words.

Yet Coleridge's writings do something slightly more than and different from what can be characterized as presenting images or description in the medium of writing. They draw attention to themselves as attempts to render visual matter in written notation in a way that also draws attention—

in the peculiar manner of shorthand writing—to the visual dimension of the notation itself. For Coleridge, the presentation of "visual phenomena in verbal discourse" has a flip side, which is the quality of "verbal discourse" and its signs as "visual phenomena"; letters and words are, apart from and alongside any signifying function, also fibrous things with a "*fasericht* nappy essence." And the "Rime" invites the shorthand effect and the kinds of looking that goes with it. One can read differently Wordsworth's appreciation of the "stanzas" of "beautiful images" in the "Rime," given that stanzas are visual as much as aural units, images in themselves (groups of lines of writing on a page). The marginal gloss mentioned earlier, which first appears in the version of the poem included in *Sibylline Leaves* (1817), activates the same effect, drawing attention to formatting, document design, and other features of visual layout.[74] In the illustrated edition of the "Rime," the line drawings that the poem inspired in Calder sit alongside the printed poem in a way that reminds one that the printed poem (its alphabet, its letterforms) can be looked at as a set of linear shapes too.

William Empson thus pinpoints an intriguing quality of the "Rime" in his response to Robert Penn Warren's "symbolist" interpretation of the poem. "To read the passage in the Symbolist way, in fact, you must pretend that *the words are just shapes on the page*, not capable of telling a story, not representing any natural use of the spoken language," Empson complains, before grumbling, "I am surprised that anyone has the patience."[75] But it does not require subscribing to Warren's reading to observe that Coleridge himself and the "Rime" especially allow the reader to look at "words [as] . . . just shapes on the page," and to look at the poem as presenting shapes as words on the page. A significant part of Warren's reading requires demonstrating that "good events take place under the aegis of the moon, the bad events under that of the sun," so it is important to his reading that after the Mariner recounts shooting the albatross, the very next line (the start of a new section, Part II) is "The Sun came up upon the right" (1798.81).[76] In Warren's words, "the crime, as it were, brings the sun."[77] Empson responds that the sun has been rising in the east ever since the albatross had started visiting the ship (and that, besides, there are other less sinister moments that occur in sunlight): therefore the first line of Part II captures the Mariner recalling the northward trajectory of the ship as he resumes his narration at the start of Part II. That is to say, Warren's interpretation, according to Empson, ignores the flow of the Mariner's tale and the section breaks; the exercise of tracking the symbolism of the sun and moon (and associated other things in each of their symbol clusters) entails treating these images in isolation and making claims about them by virtue of their proximity to "bad events."[78] In writing that the symbolist method treats words as "just shapes on the pages," I take Empson to be referring to the shapes or forms of the "symbols" themselves (the sun, the moon, the cross) to which Warren assigns predetermined meanings or associations irrespective of the context in which they appear (so Empson argues). But Empson's wording—"the words are just shapes on the page"—also points to the non-symbolic words in the poem that Warren ignores through the same archetypal reading: these words too are reduced to mere "shapes on the page," in the sense of careless reading.

But from early on, Coleridge's poem treats its own writing as "shapes on the page." Coleridge offers the reader the simile "as idle as a painted Ship/Upon a painted Ocean" (1798.113-114). The poem acknowledges its intention to operate in terms of images: the simile likens the unmoving ship to a painted ship, but also implies the poem's likeness to a painting.[79] The phrase has the quality of *hypermediacy*—a sense of media profusion— where a ship is represented in the medium of painting (one might even read two layers of painting, a ship painted "upon" an existing painting of an ocean), which is represented in written-poetic media. But what is most compelling about the phrase's hypermediacy is the ensuing interplay of written language and shape: the poem is describing an image (in a painting), but that image defamiliarizes the very words we are reading, making them painted or inked forms on the page. That is to say, "painted Ship" and "painted Ocean" also describe the individual letters that make up the words "Ship" and "Ocean," characterizing the letters themselves as perceptible shapes painted on the page we are reading.

Such images in the poem cannot adequately be characterized as either symbol or allegory: they function—that is to say, they oscillate— more along the lines of the shorthand effect. In Coleridge's well-known,

though inconsistently maintained, distinction between symbol and allegory, he devalues the latter as "but a translation of abstract notions into a
picture-language," whereas the former "partakes of the Reality which it renders intelligible" ("Lay Sermons," 360). By most explanations, Coleridgean
allegory is a figure involving an arbitrary substitution, and his definition of
symbol is close to the figure of synecdoche. At first, the ghostly ship seems
to be a good example of symbol: the marginal gloss announces the ship's
significance ("The ancient Mariner beholdeth a sign in the element afar
off" [69]), and when the Mariner cries out, "A sail, a sail!" (1798.153), he is,
as readers have noted, rehearsing Coleridge's very definition of symbol as
synecdoche.[80] But the gloss's identification of the ship as a "sign" simplifies,
and makes sense of, "a certain shape" that the Mariner can perceive only
vaguely and negatively as indeterminacy and insignificance, and that he
struggles to describe in positive, meaningful terms: "a something," "a little
speck," "it seem'd a mist," "a shape." As Frances Ferguson puts it, the gloss
and the fictive scholar writing it consistently impose a sense of "significance and interpretability, but only by reading ahead of—or beyond—the
main text."[81] Moreover, even if the Mariner makes a symbolic utterance
when he cries out, "a sail!" to stand for a ship, it is the wrong symbolic
question, mistaking the ship as the tenor (with sail as vehicle and part), as it
were, when it is the vehicle: the entire scene is concerned with what the approaching, mysterious skeleton ship might mean, if anything—and not only
or especially the significance of the sail.[82] The strongest case for reading
this scene symbolically is, of course, Empson's historical reading. His essay
impugns at every available opportunity Warren's reading, but pointedly
remarks that one of the most important symbols in "Rime"—the specter
ship—had completely eluded Warren's symbolist interpretation: "Coleridge
really was writing in a Symbolist manner here, for once."[83] According to
Empson, the abolitionist Coleridge is responsible for the series of linear
images—the "bars" like a "dungeon grate," and the exposed "naked ribs" of
the ship (an image repeated in Death's bony frame)—that refer to the sight
of docked slave ships under repair, their planks needing to be removed and
replaced after several voyages because they would have been "rotted off by
the insanitary exudations of the dying slaves."[84] In brief, the skeleton ship

symbolizes the "maritime expansion of the Western Europeans," most of all the slave trade.[85] But then again, this same "certain shape" appears in different variations throughout the poem: the skeletonized sails that are like "restless gossameres," the Mariner's hand that is like the "ribb'd Sea-sand" (1798.219), and the skeletonized "leaves" (1798.566) that the Hermit sees.[86] And these other shapes from other scenes in the poem are not as easily classified as symbols, eluding both Empson's and Warren's symbolist readings. What all of these images can be said to have in common is that they are "a certain shape," a "strange shape."[87]

But neither are these images allegorical: they are indeed a picture-language, but not in the context of Coleridgean allegory. Rather, they are a form of picture-language in the self-conscious way I have been noting: words as shapes on the page, and shapes rendered as words on the page. Recall that in the framework of Coleridge's shorthand-inspired theories of writing, arbitrary signs are not an inferior version of symbol, and the term "picture" itself is highly ambiguous. For Coleridge, in the context of communication, arbitrary signs are more progressive than signs possessing any degree of iconicity (that is, "partak[ing]" in or resembling in any degree their referents); indeed, they are the very marker of linguistic modernity and the advancement of "intellect." And picture is not necessarily a pejorative quality: even though pictures and hieroglyphics are less advanced as semiotic systems than arbitrary characters are, Coleridge's engagement with shorthand also leads to the strange sense that legible English writing and alternative notation systems alike are both to some degree pictures.

Therefore Coleridge's descriptions of the approaching, and then arrived, specter ship operate much more like shorthand than either symbol or allegory. In a manner and to a degree not captured by either of those concepts, the images of the "Rime" hover between writing and shape, between legible letters and words (on one side) and linear forms that resemble them and yet do not signify in the same way (on the other). This begins to suggest why the poem is so deliberate about lighting effects: linear shapes—shapes resembling grates, gossamers, ribs—overlaid on the sun, and darkened to blackness by intense backlighting. As Empson observes, "the sun has to shine between the ribs of the Ghost Ship."[88] But the same images suggest in turn, even as they may be suggested by, the defamiliarized view of writing as, in Coleridge's words, "black marks printed on white paper" (*Notebooks*, 3:4066). If the "Rime" offers a "sign" with and through this series of memorable images, as the gloss insists, it is closest to the signs and symbols of the kind Coleridge speculated about in the context of shorthand. And yet, the "Rime" understands that the wish underlying shorthand—a set of symbols that can "be read again at first Sight"—is undermined by unpredictable effects, like the blurring of shapes into writing and vice versa, rendering writing and shapes merely "a something," even for capable readers like Warren. The idea that "images [rise] up . . . as *things*, with a parallel production of the correspondent expressions" (as Coleridge described the composition of "Kubla Khan"), and the desire for a script quick enough to transcribe dream writing, thoughts, or speech are one part of the dream of communication. The other part of the dream is a stranger vision, where the dreamer sees "images" and cannot make out whether they are "expressions" or "things." *[shorthand symbols]* Using another image from the poem, one might say that Coleridge, not unlike the Mariner, saw something like "water-snakes," curved and "coil'd" (1798.272), and in them saw signs and shapes, meaningfulness and meaninglessness. And no tongue their significance might declare.[89]

The duty of a Distributor of Stamps is, upon application made by him to receive Stamps from the Head Office to supply the demands of his District. These Stamps are forwarded by him to his Subdistributors in the quantity required by them. . . . The Collection of Legacy Duty which is naturally attached to this Office is performed by supplying to Executors and Administrators certain papers called Forms to be by them filled up according to the directions contained in them and returned to the Distributor.

William Wordsworth to William Lowther
(Viscount Lowther), March 28, 1821

To humbler functions, awful Power!
I call thee . . .

William Wordsworth, "Ode to Duty"

2   WORDSWORTH AND BUREAUCRATIC FORM

Our Poet Distributor

In 1813, William Wordsworth began his job as Distributor of Stamps, and he worked in that capacity for three decades until his retirement from the office. He initially served as distributor for the Westmorland, Whitehaven, and Penrith districts, but came to be responsible for additional areas as he continually sought to increase his official purview and profit. During these years, in order to support his family, Wordsworth divided his time between his artistic and administrative occupations. "Our Poet Distributor" is the dual title by which his wife, Mary, refers to him in a letter to relatives, where she also muses that "his skill in *numbers* as a Poet" prepared him well "to do justice to the accounts of the Stamp Off[ice]," alluding to his metrical and financial know-how.[1] During this segment of his poetic career, his contemporaries too were unable to think about Wordsworth's poetry without thinking about his other job. Byron begins *Don Juan* (1819) by censuring *The Excursion* (1814) and

observing that "Wordsworth has his place in the Excise" (actually Wordsworth worked for the Stamp Office, but Byron's mistake either retains
or sharpens the comment's edge).[2] Similarly, Francis Jeffrey's review of
Wordsworth's *Memorials of a Tour on the Continent* (1822) observes that
"since [Wordsworth] has openly taken to the office of a publican, and exchanged the company of leech-gatherers for that of tax-gatherers, he has
fallen into a way of writing which is equally distasteful to his old friends
and his old monitors."[3] From Wordsworth's own closest family members
to other Romantic poets and unsympathetic reviewers in the periodical
press, many of his contemporaries regarded him—whether positively or
negatively—in terms of his dual work as "Poet Distributor."

Yet what is most curious is that despite his identity as "Poet Distributor," Wordsworth's literary writings seem never to have been influenced by
his tax-collecting job at all. If Wordsworth scholarship has, with few exceptions, avoided using the distributorship as an interpretive frame for the poetry, it is probably not only because the context of taxation can be a boring
topic or that greater scholarly attention is still accorded to Wordsworth's
poetry before that career, focusing on works from the "Great Decade," but
also because Wordsworth's literary writings never explicitly bring up his
other vocation or taxation in general (although other policy and political
issues to which he was much less directly connected appear in them). Moreover, it is not immediately apparent that his poetry was affected at all upon
"exchang[ing] the company of leech-gatherers for that of tax-gatherers."[4]
How best to approach this puzzle? His poetic silence about his civil service
work might be referred to the concepts of displacement, effacement, and
the like, all of which were activated and rigorously theorized in connection
with New Historicist methodologies in Romantic studies. Or, better yet,
because the problem at hand concerns the relation between literary genres
and genres that belong in part to the fiscal domain (for example, tax forms),
the problem can be referred to Mary Poovey's argument in *Genres of the
Credit Economy*, especially her account of Wordsworth's role in "generic
differentiation."[5] According to Poovey, Wordsworth played an exemplary
role in the Romantic contraction of imaginative writing to "Literary writing," and then the consequential differentiation of "Literary writing" from

monetary genres and financial commentary.[6] The partition Wordsworth
kept up between literary genres (his poetry, essays, and prefaces) and financial genres (money and writing about money)—notwithstanding the
proximity of these two sets of genres in his actual life as "Poet Distributor,"
his interest in book sales, his worries about supporting his family—could
be said to confirm Wordsworth's commitment to the ideological exaltation
of literary writing at the exclusion and suppression of non-literary genres
from non-literary discourses.

I would nevertheless like to show how I reach different conclusions
based on the biographical datum of Wordsworth's career in the British
civil service and on the question of how his job distributing stamps and
processing tax forms might have shaped his poetry. This chapter approaches Wordsworth by way of the dramatic development of the British
fiscal-bureaucratic system during the eighteenth century and the Romantic era, including the media, genres, and practices of impression and inscription generated by, and comprising, this bureaucratic infrastructure.[7]
Occurring at the same time as the Romantic differentiation of literary
writing from other genres was *another* process (a reverse process, more
or less) by which imaginative writing absorbed communicative norms
from bureaucratic genres; what was happening, to borrow one of Kenneth Burke's formulas, was the "bureaucratization of the imaginative."[8]
Wordsworth's *Lyrical Ballads* (1798), *Essays upon Epitaphs* (comp. 1810), and
The Excursion negotiate the communicative norms of administrative, informational media—norms aimed at the efficient communication, collection,
and processing of information. This chapter calls the instantiation of such
norms in writing *bureaucratic form*, and attempts a "formal" reading of
Wordsworth where *form* indicates the implementation of a utilitarian logic
of efficiency in written genres—a logic exemplified by the standardized
blank forms Wordsworth processed as part of his second job.[9] Although
Wordsworth's contemporaries, chiefly Jeffrey, posited a direct mimetic
relation between Wordsworth's later poetry and a generalized notion of the
"prosy," "feeble" language of bureaucratic administration, my argument
supposes that Wordsworth's writings respond *not to bureaucratese but to
bureaucratic form.*[10] As we will see, Wordsworth's writings acknowledge,

but also ignore, the social imperative to be short and swift in the so-called delivery of information. That Wordsworth's literary writings from both before and after his distributor career show the impact of bureaucratic form suggests that the start of his government job was not the only factor involved: bureaucratic form gained social force from being in mutually reinforcing relations with the later eighteenth-century New Rhetorical curriculum, which drilled British students in the norm of brevity in writing and the older, traditional rhetorical-literary principle of *brevitas*.[11] All three of these factors made efficiency in writing, and attempts to reduce writing to information, the order of the day—a dream of perfectly streamlined communication.

The account I am proposing leads to a twofold recognition, one relating to the sociology of modern officialdom, and the other relating to what Foucault calls "the power of the Norm" (see my discussion of this concept in the introduction).[12] The first recognition lets us view Wordsworth's strict compartmentalization of his administrative work in terms of the specialized, professional, modern bureaucrat.[13] The gradual formation of this figure, for our purposes, stretches from the quasi-rationalization of the British state's administrative infrastructure during the reforms of the later eighteenth and early nineteenth centuries, up through the mid-twentieth-century compartmentalization of white-collar work from every other part of the white-collar worker's life—what C. Wright Mills calls "the Big Split."[14] In other words, if Wordsworth appears never to let his publican work bleed into his poetic work, this suggests the not insignificant degree of rationalization and modernization characterizing the still incompletely rationalized and modernized fiscal bureaucracy of which he was a part.[15] At the same time, and this is the second recognition, "the power of the Norm" of efficient inscription emanates from the fiscal-bureaucratic realm and exerts pressure on other genres of writing, including literature, thus overriding to some extent the professional compartmentalization and generic differentiation by which Wordsworth kept his poetic and bureaucratic work separate. *Lyrical Ballads*, *Essays upon Epitaphs*, and *The Excursion* are therefore not about fiscal bureaucracy, but they are in a variety of ways about the exigencies of bureaucratic form.

Ode to Duties

The broadest context for Wordsworth's distributorship is the remarkable growth and organization attained by Great Britain's fiscal-bureaucratic infrastructure in the period.[16] With the state needing to finance one military commitment after the next and trying to avoid bankruptcy, the fiscal-bureaucratic infrastructure—although by all accounts still far from a modern bureaucracy as Max Weber would define it—transformed during this period, growing significantly in number of employees, coordination, and efficiency. There were also staggering increases in the rates and kinds of taxes levied by the government, and a proliferation of the media and genres associated with this expanding bureaucracy. For this reason, according to John Brewer, Britain's transformation into a global economic and military power during the long eighteenth century can be attributed not to military might alone but also to changes in the structure, protocols, and personnel of the centralized government administration: to "bookkeeping not battles," or rather bookkeeping in order to underwrite battles, to borrow Brewer's formulation about the period's rapidly evolving "fiscal-military state."[17]

The ballooning size of the British fiscal bureaucracy's ranks was impressive, as William Blackstone's observation about them conveys:

> Witness the commissioners, and the multitude of dependents on the customs, in every port of the kingdom; the commissioners of excise, and their numerous subalterns, in every inland district; the postmasters, and their servants, planted in every town, and upon every public road; the commissioners of the stamps, and their distributors, which are full as scattered and full as numerous; the officers of the salt duty, which, though a species of excise and conducted in the same manner, are yet made a distinct corps from the ordinary managers of that revenue; the surveyors of houses and windows; the receivers of the land tax; the managers of lotteries; and the commissioners of hackney coaches.[18]

Wordsworth was just one of these multitudes of administrative personnel and, even within the Stamp Office, just one of the "distributors . . . full as scattered and full as numerous" as Blackstone put it. Yet we know the specific tasks that Wordsworth performed because of a job description he was compelled to write about his own position. In 1821, the utilitarian reformer Joseph Hume invoked Wordsworth as an example of the venal political practices that eighteenth-century and Romantic-era radicals called "Old Corruption," and characterized the poet's appointment as a sinecure. This left Wordsworth having to answer the same question that the speaker in "Resolution and Independence" puts to the Leech-Gatherer: "How is it that you live, and what is it you do?" (126). Defending himself, he substantiated his responsibilities in a description that he drafted, which eventually made its way up to, and passed muster with, England's Solicitor General.[19] Here is his description, a different kind of ode to duty:

> The duty of a Distributor of Stamps is, upon application made by him to receive Stamps from the Head Office to supply the demands of his District. These Stamps are forwarded by him to his Subdistributors in the quantity required by them. . . . The Collection of Legacy Duty which is naturally attached to this Office is performed by supplying to Executors and Administrators certain papers called Forms to be by them filled up according to the directions contained in them and returned to the Distributor.[20]

His responsibilities can be broken down into three areas: (1) the distribution of "Stamps," that is, stamped paper, in order "to supply the demands of his District"; (2) the collection of other kinds of "stamp" duties on consumer goods and certain kinds of licenses, which he does not mention above, but which we know about from his bond of office; and (3) "the Collection of Legacy Duty" and the processing of the paperwork associated with it.[21] The three main responsibilities of Wordsworth's position— stamped paper, duties on goods and licenses, and the legacy duty—each seem to deal with disparate species of taxation, but they reflect the motley assortment of taxes that over the course of the eighteenth century came under the control of the Stamp Office. These taxes were locally collected by distributors like Wordsworth, "a single cog in an ever-moving mechanism" (as Max Weber would characterize the official) or, in Wordsworth's own terms, "a tool/Or implement, a passive Thing employed/As a brute mean" (*The Excursion*, 9.116–18).[22] The part of Wordsworth's job involving the collection of the legacy duty is the most relevant for bureaucratic form as it relates to Wordsworth's poetry. Still, it is worth briefly describing his other responsibilities, because they provide us with a sense of the ubiquity of fiscal-bureaucratic genres and media.

Stamped Paper

By "Stamps," Wordsworth is referring not to postage stamps (which were not introduced in Britain until 1840), but stamped paper. After the General Stamp Act of 1694, and a steady series of related laws after it, the paper, parchment, or vellum on which legal and business documents were written needed to be embossed, or "stamped," with an official mark in order to be valid, like today's embossed notary seals required on certain legal documents. At first there were six denominations of stamps, but newer stamps of different values continually appeared as the duties on documents kept rising during the eighteenth century. The range of legal and business documents that came to be taxed was nearly comprehensive: most documents in legal proceedings and also deeds, bonds, contracts, leases, marriage certificates, wills, passports, insurance policies, certificates of admission to the college of physicians or the Inns of Court, academic degrees, and more.[23] Looking back over the period from the introduction of stamp duties up to 1815, the Victorian lawyer and legal historian Stephen Dowell concludes that "every species of written or printed document necessary for carrying on the business of mankind . . . had now been drawn within the grasp of the stamp laws."[24] These documents could be taken to the Stamp Office after they were written in large hand (that is, engrossed), at which point the duty could be paid and the document stamped: if the document was paper, it could be directly embossed; if the document was vellum or parchment, it would have a small embossed piece of paper (an escutcheon) affixed to it, since skins did not hold impressions as well as paper. But individuals could also purchase blank pre-stamped paper on which to inscribe a variety of transactions and instruments, and these are the government-issued stamps that Wordsworth distributed.[25] (This kind of blank, pre-stamped paper was the very sort that caused American colonists to protest violently the Stamp Act of 1765 in the lead-up to the American Revolution.)[26] Wordsworth hired and supervised a crew of "Subdistributors," or "subs" as they were called, who sold the stamped paper to individuals and from whom he collected earnings.[27] In turn, he reported and sent revenue back up to his superordinates: "at the close of every quarter, an account is sent to the Head Office in London of the Stamps on Hand, and at the same time Money is remitted to the amount of those sold."[28]

Other Stamp Duties

In Wordsworth's time, "stamps" referred to other kinds of duties too.[29] The state introduced these other sorts of stamp duties during the eighteenth century as it sought to increase revenue beyond that earned from the taxing of documents, and in some cases, in order to control social activities (for example, gambling) and the circulation of information (for example, via almanacs and newspapers). Although some of these duties were quite unlike those charged on the paperwork "necessary for carrying on the business of mankind," they too involved stamps in the sense of official impressions or markings and during this period were also under the management of the Stamp Office. For example, there were stamp duties on certain consumer items that were required to feature an official mark: these items included playing cards, dice, lottery tickets, gloves, hats, hair powder, horses, and medicines. Then there were the so-called taxes on knowledge, which notoriously levied taxes on, and attempted to regulate, newspapers and almanacs. The Stamp Office also administered duties on licenses for certain kinds of work, such as the work done by hawkers and pedlars, tavern keepers, bankers, and lawyers.[30] Although Wordsworth celebrates, and strives to identify himself with, "Pedlarism" ("Fenwick Note," 1216) in The Excursion, he was much less an instance of Pedlarism than he was a functionary in the state regulation of it. The fact that his position entailed licensing individuals in that line of work suggests that Wordsworth's administrative work and the British fiscal-bureaucratic system at large need to be central considerations in thinking through the different forms of labor treated in *The Excursion* and instanced by the literary work itself.[31] In short, it was simply impossible in the eighteenth century and the Romantic period not only to carry on the "business of mankind" but also to indulge in quotidian consumer activities without coming into contact with stamps—along with the documentary media and genres connected with them, as well as the practices of impression, inscription, seeing, using, reading, and paying associated with them.

The Legacy Duty and "Certain Papers Called Forms"

Often categorized under the genus of death duties, the legacy duty was a tax on personal property passed on by death to another individual—that is, a tax on "legacies" or "successions." In general, the remoter an inheritor's relation was to the deceased, the steeper the tax as a percentage of the value of the bequest.[32] Legacies figure largely in Wordsworth's own life, or perhaps one should say livelihood. As is well known, he was himself a legatee in 1795, when he received a £900 legacy upon the death of Raisley Calvert, the brother of a grammar school friend, which allowed him to write poetry rather than to find other employment at a critical juncture early in his career.[33]

Recall that Wordsworth's job entailed "supplying to Executors and Administrators certain papers called Forms to be by them filled up according to the directions contained in them and returned to the Distributor." The Legacy Act of 1796 had introduced the provision that the Stamp Office board of commissioners would "appoint proper persons to collect and receive the duties hereby imposed, and to keep proper accounts thereof, to be transmitted to the head office of the said commissioners."[34] Wordsworth was one of these persons. If the Calvert Legacy is a familiar landmark in Wordsworth's biography, less well known is that Wordsworth later on, as distributor, had to carry out the grim task of vigilantly discovering deaths in his region—especially those associated with wealthy estates—so that he could collect the legacy duty, these occasions yielding rare windfalls much greater than the office's other forms of revenue through stamped paper and the other kinds of stamp duty.[35]

Furthermore, the 1796 Act mandates the printing of a standardized form, but also provides that an entirely handwritten document ("entirely handwritten" because even printed standardized forms call for handwritten answers) containing the same information will be valid:

> It shall be lawful for the said commissioners of stamp duties, from time to time, to provide sufficient quantities of paper adapted for such receipts or discharges as aforesaid, and to cause to be printed thereon the form of words in the schedule hereunto annexed; and it shall also be lawful for any of His Majesty's subjects, requiring such receipts or discharges, to cause the same to be duly filled up with sums, names, and date, according to the provisions before-mentioned, and also upon any vellum or parchment, or upon any other paper not provided by the said commissioners, to use the like form whenever there shall be occasion.[36]

Appended to the Act is the exemplary "schedule" of the government-issued printed form that was to serve as the basis for the vellum or parchment version of the same form (see Figure 2.1).

This is the form to which Wordsworth alludes when he writes of "certain papers called Forms." While the Act frames the form primarily as a receipt or discharge, Wordsworth's description of his job responsibilities reveals that the form served additional important functions as it circulated. Blank forms tend to evoke a sense of fixity, even deadened stasis, yet Lisa Gitelman has observed that blank forms are equally definable by their mobility.[37] The Romantic-era legacy duty form is no exception in this regard. After the Stamp Office provided sheets of the printed blank form to distributors like Wordsworth, these distributors provided the form to executors and administrators. At this point, the form functioned as a means for the British government to collect data in a manner consistent with its increasing function as an "information state."[38] Meanwhile, the form acted also like a bill in that it compelled payment of the tax from the legatee or the executor or administrator. Next, Wordsworth checked with "minute attention" each completed form for the correctness of its information and payment amount, and then sent off batches of the forms to the central Stamp Office.[39] Presumably Wordsworth dealt as well with entirely manuscript versions of the forms on vellum or parchment, but in his job description he focuses on the printed paper forms that are "filled up" with handwriting. Next, "these papers are forwarded by him once a month to the Head Office where (if found correct) they are stamped, then returned to the Distributor."[40] At these stages, the form served as an "original,"

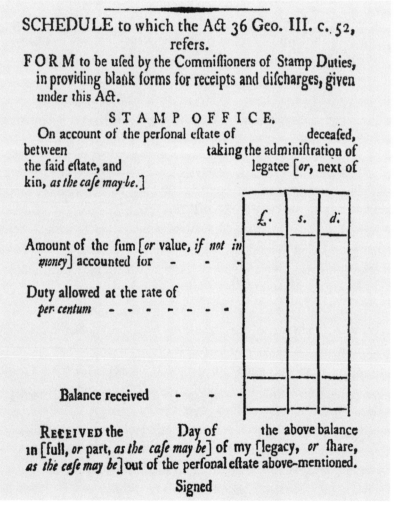

SCHEDULE to which the Act 36 Geo. III. c. 52, refers.

FORM to be used by the Commissioners of Stamp Duties, in providing blank forms for receipts and discharges, given under this Act.

STAMP OFFICE.

On account of the personal estate of   deceased, between   taking the administration of the said estate, and   legatee [or, next of kin, *as the case may be.*]

£.	s.	d.

Amount of the sum [*or* value, *if not in money*] accounted for   -   -   -

Duty allowed at the rate of *per centum*   -   -   -   -   -   -

Balance received   -   -   -

RECEIVED the   Day of   the above balance in [full, *or* part, *as the case may be*] of my [legacy, *or* share, *as the case may be*] out of the personal estate above-mentioned.

Signed

Figure 2.1   The 1796 Legacy Duty form. Reproduced from Peter Lovelass, *An Abstract of, and Observations on, the Statutes Imposing Stamp Duty. . .* (London: 1796).

whose information was transcribed and duplicated for recordkeeping in both Wordsworth's and the central Stamp Office's account books.[41] Finally, in Wordsworth's words, the form was "from him forwarded through his Subdistributors to the Executors, who in these papers receive a Discharge for the Duty due under the Will."[42] When the form made its way back to executors or administrators by way of Wordsworth and his "subs," it became a receipt or discharge. As Section 27 of the 1796 Act states, "no legacy [is] liable to the duty, to be paid without a receipt, containing certain particulars."[43] These "particulars" are those pieces of information that populate the blank fields of the form shown in Figure 2.1:

1. Name of the deceased individual leaving the legacy (the testator or testatrix)
2. Name of the executor or administrator
3. Name of the legatee
4. Value of the legacy
5. Rate ("at the rate of _____ per centum") and amount of the duty on that legacy
6. Balance received by the legatee after paying the legacy duty
7. Month and date when the legatee received the balance
8. Signature of the legatee

The same particulars recorded by the government served, then, as key details of the form in its function as proof of payment by the legatee or executor or administrator. By now, it will come as no surprise that, in order to be a valid receipt, the form—whether printed with handwritten answers or entirely handwritten—needed to bear a stamp, like all the other "document[s] necessary for carrying on the business of mankind."

Bureaucratic Form

The legacy duty form as a document may or may not be interesting in itself, but for this argument it is of interest as an especially vivid example of bureaucratic form. *Bureaucratic form* names a set of features of writing, features that can traverse media (paper or vellum or parchment) and genres (those belonging to fiscal-bureaucratic or to literary discourse). Bureaucratic form manifests itself in writing in which the efficient communicating and recording of information are the principal considerations. Defining characteristics of bureaucratic form thus include rationalization by way of simplification, abstraction, quantification, and standardization; as James R. Beniger puts it, "rationalization might be defined as the destruction or ignoring of information in order to facilitate its processing," and "one example from within bureaucracy is the development of standardized paper forms."[44] Bureaucratic form is related to but different from long-winded and obscurantist bureaucratese—another style associated with administrative writing—because it is motivated by the reductions that typify "seeing like a state," and what Foucault has analyzed as "biopolitics." Viewing human beings as a population, states see only what they need or want to see, and perform "the administrative ordering of nature and society" through "transformative . . . simplifications."[45] By these simplifications, human and social matters are reduced to certain particulars that are then aggregable and subject to "forecasts, statistical estimates, and overall measures."[46] The legacy duty form, for example, reduces a gift left by a deceased relative, along with everything else that gift may have meant to the benefactor and may mean to the recipient and other living individuals, into a relatively simple series of discrete pieces of information that matter to the government for the purposes of enforcing the payment of a duty in order to wage war elsewhere. The all-important Calvert Legacy, without which Wordsworth probably would not have had a poetic career at all, could be reduced in the same way—if one were "seeing like a state"—to "sums, names, and date," as the 1796 Act states. A donation can be converted into data, but that conversion comes with not only gains (the ability to aggregate data) but also losses (simplification).

For literary scholars, including those of Romantic literature, *form* usually signifies, among other things, the features involved in literary genres or literariness itself. But we may also note that in the later eighteenth century, the word *form* did not possess wide currency in any sense relating to literature; it was not associated with any of the later literary-critical concerns of "formalism."[47] My intention is not to insist that there is one right way to understand *form*, whether it denotes the familiar features of "literary form" or some other kind of form. Rather, I hope to reconstruct as richly as possible what "certain papers called Forms" were for Wordsworth—given his location at the intersection of bureaucracy and poetry—while also advancing a concept of form that may be used to examine the writings of other historical periods. For example, Samuel Johnson's *Dictionary of the English Language* (1755) offers thirteen denotations of *form* as noun, seven of *form* as verb, seven of the adjective *formal*, four of the adverb *formally*, one for the noun *formalist*, and so on, yet not a single one of these definitions and their related quotations refers to literature or its genres.[48] Some of the broader senses may have been used to describe literature in a loosely metaphorical way, but what is striking is that Johnson does not apply even these senses to literature, even though many of Johnson's quotations are, of course, drawn from a literary archive. A perusal of the archive Eighteenth Century Collections Online (ECCO) similarly shows that *form* was seldom used in connection with literary writing, aside from a few scattered instances: "poetic form" appears only fifteen times across the entire archive, "literary form" yields a single result, "sonnet form" none.[49] According to Johnson's *Dictionary*, *form* typically denotes shapes, methods, rituals, and the arrangements of things (including words) in the world, particularly in the domains of the law, the church, the school, and the military.

This semantic due diligence of a historically specific sort allows one to appreciate that the word *form* in the eighteenth century was seldom uttered, written, or imagined in connection with literary writing. Neither did it point primarily to the fiscal-bureaucratic domain. *But senses of form widely operative in the later eighteenth century—originating in religious and legal discourse, among other areas—along with the emergent sense captured by Wordsworth's "certain papers called Forms" (that is, the standardized form) are carrying into, and constituting, bureaucratic form.* In other words, the concept of bureaucratic form is a key site for *form*, in the various senses used in the Romantic era and before. What follows is a disquisition on three overlapping senses of the word—senses that meet in, and help to make, bureaucratic form what it was in Wordsworth's time.

First, there is *form* as we have seen it used in the 1796 Act: "it shall be lawful for the said commissioners of stamp duties . . . to cause to be printed thereon the *form of words*" (emphasis mine). Bureaucratic form depends on such "form[s] of words," that is, prescribed, standardized sequences of words and numerical information as well as blank spaces on the document, whether in a combination of print and manuscript or entirely handwritten: for example, "On account of the personal estate of _____ deceased, between _____ taking the administration of the said estate, and _____ legatee." In Johnson's *Dictionary*, "form of words" appears under the word *form* defined as "Particular model of modification," and the citation, from Addison, refers to prayer ("form of words that are uttered in the ordinary method of religions worship"), but it is also close to the denotation "Stated method; established practice."[50] *Form* in this sense overlaps a great deal with *formulary*. *Formulary* can be either a noun referring to a book or manual containing religious, legal, or letter-writing procedures and templates, or, of more relevance here, an adjective describing a prescribed arrangement of words—that is, a formula. In anticipation of this chapter's later engagement of Wordsworth's *Essays upon Epitaphs*, I note that elsewhere Johnson observes that in an epitaph, the "part of it . . . which tells the birth and marriage is *formulary, and can be expressed only one way*" (emphasis mine).[51] Tombstone inscriptions and documents manifesting bureaucratic form (like tax forms) both involve formula or "form of words."

Second, in addition to *form*-as-formulariness, bureaucratic form relies on a closely related sense of *form* as *formatting*, the arranging of information on documents.[52] For instance, Sir John Sinclair, in compiling his *Statistical Account of Scotland* (1791-1799)—with which Wordsworth was familiar and which may even have partly inspired "We Are Seven"—provided clergy throughout Scotland with "a particular *form* . . . for drawing up the Statistical Account of their respective Parishes."[53] That form took the shape of a list of prompts (basically a questionnaire), compelling those completing the prompts to provide certain kinds of information: "The name [of the parish], and its origin"; "Situation and extent of the parish"; "Number of acres"; and so on.[54] Although the words *format* and *formatting* do not appear until later, in the nineteenth and twentieth centuries, the word *form* is used in a manner that suggests an increasing coordination of information with visual-spatial strategies of ordering that information in various administrative genres, like Sinclair's "particular form." True, there is much earlier evidence, in medieval accounting documents, of formatting, or what the field of technical writing has since the 1970s called, and analyzed under the subject of, "document design."[55] But there is also sufficient evidence of a marked rise in printed forms (that is, printed but soliciting handwriting) in the later eighteenth and early nineteenth centuries, and on these printed forms, it was becoming more and more common to find formatting, especially tabular configurations.[56] Studying British census forms and income tax forms, Mike Esbester has concluded that tables were increasingly common on early nineteenth-century printed forms. He explains, "although information recorded in tables could have been gathered by sentence-completion tasks, tables offered the advantage that they could incorporate unanticipated details from respondents, while retaining a standardized layout that made data-processing more efficient."[57] The Romantic-era legacy duty form perhaps captures the transitional moment when tabular layout on forms becomes more and more commonplace: transitional because, on the one hand, the law still allowed for handwritten versions of the form, presumably without tabular configuration, and on the other hand, the printed legacy duty form issued by the state, much like the British census form of 1801, relies on this kind of form (that is, formatting) within the printed form for what is imagined to be the easy filling-in and efficient processing of particulars.[58] There is good reason to believe that Romantic-era forms increasingly relied on form-as-formatting.

Third, and intertwined with form-as-formulariness and form-as-formatting, bureaucratic form is instantiated materially in the subgenre of the informational document, "the form" itself. Wordsworth's phrasing about forms—"certain papers called Forms"—implies that he is invoking a largely obscure class of object. This is curious, because historical research on blank forms, which has been undertaken by scholars in diverse fields—book and media history, technical and business writing, and information design— suggests that they long predate the Romantic era. Peter Stallybrass, Pamela Neville-Sington, Lisa Gitelman, and others have demonstrated that the earliest printed standardized forms were the later fifteenth-century forms for Catholic indulgences, which featured blanks soliciting manuscript bits of information such as the purchaser's name, the date, and the place. As these scholars remind us, the first things printed by Gutenberg and by Caxton were not Bibles—were not books at all—but indulgences, and these unbound sheets were printed in the millions.[59] These papal indulgence forms were the model for the earliest printed *fiscal-bureaucratic* forms, devised around 1512 by Henry VIII's Lord Chancellor, Cardinal Wolsey, for the collection of the subsidy (essentially a kind of income tax) to raise money for war with France.[60] The legacy duty form that Wordsworth distributed and processed beginning in 1813 is thus one of many distant descendants of the tax form used by Wolsey to tax citizens for the same purpose of war. And yet Wordsworth is also watching the form—specifically by that name, "form"—either just approaching, or in the process of crossing, or just having passed, a threshold of cultural salience in the Romantic period.[61] It is quite late in the history of formulary documents that the specific medial-generic object, the document itself, rather than the formulaic language found on it, comes to be known as a "form." The *OED* cites Charles Dickens's *Little Dorrit* (1856) as the earliest example of the word *form* in the sense of "a formulary document with blanks for the insertion of particulars."[62] Yet the government forms that were so central to Wordsworth's distributorship come earlier than the *OED* suggests, intimating that the form-as-blank-form is coming into being, in Wordsworth's moment, as a medial-generic object by that name.[63] The Designing Information for Everyday Life, 1815–1914, project suggests that "by the late eighteenth century it became more economical to print forms using movable type," and adduces, for example, catalogues and advertisements by printers from 1780 and the 1820s offering to print various kinds of "blank forms."[64] Similarly, Jeremy Bentham and his brother, Samuel, in their writings on accounting methods, recommended that organizations—whether Jeremy's planned prisons and poorhouses (ca. 1798), or the Admiralty's dockyards for which Samuel came up with a bookkeeping system—use standardized or uniform "blank books or forms" for more effective management.[65] Wordsworth witnessed the blank form approaching or achieving a kind of social recognizability.

To summarize this disquisition on form, then: "bureaucratic form" is a highly charged locus that attracts, intermingles and relies upon various kinds of form in the senses that were active or emergent in the eighteenth and early nineteenth centuries: formulariness, formatting, and the standardized blank form. Bureaucratic form is perhaps the single most important site for form in Wordsworth's time, and it lives on as modernity's ideal of efficiency in writing, an ideal with which literature has had to reckon ever since.

The Long and Short of It: *Brevitas*, Brevity, and Bureaucratic Form in *Lyrical Ballads*

In Wordsworth's time, bureaucratic form operated in concert with at least a few other norms pertaining to economical writing; bureaucratic form exerts pressure on Romantic literature, but it does not act alone. For example, the strain of Romantic literary writing that embraces an aesthetic of minimalism can be seen also to be modeling the ethical and ecological imperative of making the most of finite resources, as Anahid Nersessian has argued recently.[66] Yet Romantic minimalism is also to a great extent determined by the tangle of priorities involved in bureaucratic form, along with the norm of brevity deriving from the New Rhetorical curriculum, and a related norm internal to the literary tradition, namely *brevitas*. Beginning with the older literary norm of *brevitas*: I surmise that starting in the later eighteenth century, the New Rhetorical curriculum and bureaucratic form amplified the residual, long-standing concern with *brevitas*, but it can be appreciated too that *brevitas*, the imperative that authors observe decorous length, is a relatively consistent concern persevering throughout the long history of rhetoric and literature itself, before the New Rhetoric or bureaucratic form. On the roots of *brevitas*, E. R. Curtius's account remains an illuminating resource. Curtius tracks *brevitas* from its treatment in classical rhetoric as one of the fundamental *virtute narrationis* through its considerable, unruly expansion in medieval poetry and rhetoric into a much theorized and generalized form of poetic artifice. *Brevitas* and *brevitas* topoi in poetry are in many ways inseparable from their opposites, *taedium* and *fastidium*, both of which point to the reader's side and the phenomenology of reading, and indicate the worry of eliciting the reader's distaste through tiresome, excessive length—these worries too are articulated through recognizable topoi.[67]

In *Lyrical Ballads* (1798; 1800), Wordsworth works through his fascination with *brevitas* and *taedium/fastidium* by assuming that stories have an appropriate length, and that the greater violation is lengthiness rather than concision. These would be tacit, nearly imperceptible features of the poems, were it not for two closely related markers. The first is Wordsworth's recurring signature for these concerns: the premise that readers' time or words can be "wasted." His narrators share (quite casually or in asides) their worries about the time or space extraneous words might take up. His storytellers fret about verbal redundancies and superfluities, about imposing on and detaining readerly attention beyond the bounds of propriety. One gets the sense that Wordsworth's narrators are always counting words. Alternatively, they imagine themselves, and their addressees, to be on the clock—perhaps the "clock" that is the time discipline of industrial capitalism, best exemplified, in Wordsworth's moment and in his mind, by the Wedgwood pottery manufactories.[68] But the poems' acknowledgments of *brevitas* also often take the second form of ignoring the imperative to be brief: the poems thematize various kinds of wastefulness or inefficiency, or the poems themselves perform their own contrarian acts of long-windedness, delay, deferral, and digression. These latter responses do not amount to a critique of brevity—because the poems in *Lyrical Ballads* tend to be on be brief side—so much as to subtle answers to the norm of efficient communication guiding not only referential, informational genres but literary writing too.

Conventional *brevitas* and *taedium/fastidium* formulas are especially noticeable in narrative gestures toward omissions. As for what is left out, the gestures come close to the rhetorical device of paralepsis, but the things readers are spared, or rather alerted to being spared, are characterized in Wordsworth's poems not so much as events as extraneous *words*. In "The Idiot Boy," for example, Betty is said to curse Johnny with a series of "*other names, an endless string,/* But now that time is gone and past" (170–171; emphasis mine): the "endless string" of names is gestured

to but never recounted, presumably for the sake of time.[69] The strangeness
of such conspicuous indications of verbal parsimony is only heightened
by the excessive repetitions and refrains of this and other ballads; after all,
recurring strings of words, often the same words, are a defining stylistic
feature of "The Idiot Boy." Still, the reason for this particular omission
("But now that time is gone and past") points to a heightened sense of the
value of time, that there is little use taking up the present time with what
has already taken up "time" in the past. Similarly, Johnny's speech is not
(or not only) meaningless noise ("his lips with joy they burr at you" [19]),
but an abundance of meaningful words: "his words were not a few,/Which
Betty well could understand" (75–76). But these words too are skipped over.
Even when the poem gives a positive portrait of Johnny's particular brand
of volubility ("his words were not a few"), the narrator mentions these
"words" or speech sounds, but does not quote them, perhaps in this case
too because "that time is gone and past."

Nevertheless, the same poem at other moments gleefully suspends the
same *brevitas* principle it seems to have internalized. The poem's narrator,
for his or her part, prepares the reader to expect an account of Johnny's
adventures—"Oh reader! now that I might tell/What Johnny and his horse
are doing" (322–23)—only to begin these anaphoric stanzas:

> Perhaps, and no unlikely thought!
> He with his pony now doth roam
>
> . . .
>
> Perhaps he's turned himself about,
> His face unto his horse's tail
>
> . . .
>
> And now, perhaps, he's hunting sheep,
> A fierce and dreadful hunter he!
>
> . . .
>
> Perhaps, with head and heels on fire . . . (337–342)

As the poem nears its conclusion, the narrator, rather remarkably,
stalls for several stanzas with a series of conjectures about what Johnny
might have been doing, each marked by "perhaps." Like the image of

Johnny himself riding his horse backward ("perhaps he's turned himself about,/His face unto his horse's tail"), the poem fails to move forward in a predictable manner, looping back to utter certain refrains (most memorably those on Johnny's burring), or, in this case, dawdling to entertain a series of hypotheticals. The poem delays when it should be wrapping up. "The Idiot Boy" as a tale revolves around Johnny's "sauntering," an aimless circuitousness; as I noted in the introduction, "sauntering" was also a term used to describe a wandering, inattentive reader, usually a child.[70] But the poem itself, mimicking its central figure's sauntering journey, meanders in its telling. There is thus a tension between the poem's own intention to proceed expeditiously by invoking but omitting strings of words, and the value it places on generating strings of words whose only function appears to be to delay.

The deferral strategies in "The Idiot Boy" complicate the poem's time-saving or (as we might say) time-sensitive gestures, and prompt us to read the poem's ending differently too:

> "The cocks did crow to-whoo, to-whoo,
> And the sun did shine so cold."
> —Thus answered Johnny in his glory,
> And that was all his travel's story. (460–63)

When the poem finally reaches its conclusion, Wordsworth leaves us with a brilliant parody of brevity, a pointed rejoinder about the limits of short reports. Answering his mother's questions—"Tell us Johnny, do,/Where all this *long night* you have been" (448–49; emphasis mine)—Johnny gives a most laconic account of his "long night." But his synopsis aligns brevity not with explanatory, informational, or communicative value: rather, we get a confused inversion of archetypal elements (owls and cocks, moon and sun, night and day) and paradoxical combinations of objects and features (as in the "cold" sun). The poem's final comment on brevity is akin to a vexing epigram or proto-Imagist poem: "The cocks did crow to-whoo, to-whoo/And the sun did shine so cold." And that was all. The final line in the poem (like Robert Frost's use of "and that was all" as the final line in his Wordsworthian poem "The Most of It") captures the poem's reflections on quantity, length, and comprehensiveness: "that was all" in the sense of littleness or shortness, and "that was all" as in "that was everything."[71]

"Simon Lee" likewise negotiates the principle of verbal economy. At times, like "The Idiot Boy," the poem indicates, only to withhold, the words that spill out of that character: "And thanks and praises seemed to run/So fast out of his heart, I thought/They never would have done" (98–100). Here too, it is as though the narrator senses that this "endless string" of words would be too excessive, too voluminous to quote in the poem, and thus glosses over what sounds possibly worth retelling, namely, the "thanks and praises" that prompt the narrator's culminating meditation about "gratitude" (103). The most memorable lines in "Simon Lee" are, of course, the narrator's address to the reader (reminiscent of the similar kinds of address in "The Idiot Boy," described earlier): Wordsworth portrays a solicitous-sounding narrator anxious about *brevitas*, who apologizes, "my gentle reader, I perceive/How patiently you've waited" (69–70), and who also tries to reassure us that "What more I have to say is *short*" (77; emphasis mine). Then again, although the poem is concerned to be "short," readers cannot help but notice the narrator's inefficiencies in storytelling, which do not delight so much as delay, as in "The Idiot Boy." The title promises an "incident," but also deliberately subordinates it to the character portrait ("The Old Huntsman, with an Incident . . . "), making the incident a kind of afterthought. True to form, the narrator does not get to the incident until the poem is nearly over. As a strategy bound to provoke self-awareness (at best) or annoyance (at worst) in readers inhabiting modern life and with their "craving for extraordinary *incident*" ("Preface," 294; emphasis mine), the poem defers incident for three-quarters of its duration by a series of contrasting sketches of young versus old Simon Lee, which give the poem an oscillating, rather than forward-propelling, effect. And, of course, the incident is hardly an incident, and when we do arrive at it, it is quickly glossed over.

In addition to performing its own acts of deferral, "Simon Lee" figures inefficiency in an important description of the labor of Simon Lee and Old Ruth:

> And though you with your utmost skill
> From labor could not wean them,
> Alas! 'tis very little, all
> Which they can do between them. (53–56)

There is a perverse kind of celebration of inefficacy, a gap between a greater input and a lesser output. First, there is the addressed reader expending "utmost skill," but failing to "wean them" from their work, a futile endeavor; and second, we have Simon Lee and Old Ruth themselves expending their energy only to do "very little." The poem self-consciously describes an excess of invested energy and a poverty of yield. If some passages in "Simon Lee," like those in "The Idiot Boy," betray an anxiety about getting to the point—about keeping things "short" and respecting the reader's patience—other passages, like this one, intimate a poetic license to be inefficient. The description of Simon Lee that seems to go nowhere, the deferred telling of the incident, and the testing of readers who are waiting "patiently" for some kind of significance ("the tale") in the story: all of these instantiate Wordsworth's interest in exploring a ratio between "labor" (the poem's, the narrator's, the readers') and the resulting "very little," which is insignificant or significant depending on any given reader's capacity for appreciation ("but should you think,/Perhaps a tale you'll make it" [79–80]).

Where "The Idiot Boy" and "Simon Lee" gesture to their attempts at brevity even as they disregard the principle, "Michael" features a justification about an inclusion, about something left in the poem:

> Not with a *waste of words*, but for the sake
> Of pleasure, which I know that I shall give
> To many living now, I of this Lamp
> Speak thus minutely. (131–134; emphasis mine)

The narrator pauses the poem to interpolate a rationale for the forty or so lines on the cottage's lamp. This description might seem to be, but it is not, the narrator assures us, superfluous. But given that the poem begins by framing itself assuredly as the transmission of a lengthy "Tale" (27) for future generations—for "youthful Poets, who among these Hills/Will be my second self when I am gone" (38–39)—what is causing the defensive justification about "a waste of words" if not the *brevitas* expectation itself? The poem discloses a sensitivity to the possibility of wasting the reader's time, to the assumption that the poem should be economical in its telling: "not with a *waste* of words," meaning at once excessive and barren verbiage. Wordsworth's statements elsewhere that *Lyrical Ballads* is an experiment about "language ... in a state of vivid sensation" ("Preface," 287) or what "impassioned feelings" do to our words ("Note on 'The Thorn,'" 332) would have us expect that the narrators of the poems should feel entirely authorized to narrate precisely such moments involving "impassioned feelings" like "pleasure." But the fact that these moments are deliberately passed over by the poems—or, as in the case of "Michael," told only with great anxiety about a perceived "waste of words"—suggests the potency of the rule of appropriate length. Wordsworth's poetic experiments are highly conscious about the bounds of propriety when it comes to literary length, and he turns to traditional rhetorical and literary formulas for these soundings. And yet, the poems simultaneously skirt or test the *brevitas* principle in both playful and nervous ways. As soon as readers are alerted to the possibility of word "waste," the narrator proceeds anyway to tell us "minutely" of the cottage lamp.

Functioning alongside or on top of this already active concern with *brevitas* was another, closely related norm deriving from the New Rhetorical curriculum: the norm of brevity, not restricted to narrative. As exemplified and disseminated by the tremendously influential lectures of Adam Smith, Hugh Blair, and others, the New Rhetorical curriculum drilled into students the stylistic norm of brevity in written composition in a manner that persists through William Strunk's early twentieth-century lectures at Cornell (which become the basis of *The Elements of Style* [1920]) and crystallized in his version of Smith's and Blair's imperative: "Omit needless words! Omit needless words! Omit needless words!"[72] Bureaucratic form was, I would think, particularly reinforced by this contemporary version of brevity—probably more than it was by *brevitas*—and New

Rhetorical brevity was, in turn, reinforced by bureaucratic form; but both are operating upon long-standing, underlying anxieties about *brevitas* and literary propriety.

The particular cooperative force of the New Rhetorical rule of concision and the utilitarian ideals of bureaucratic form can be glimpsed in Wordsworth's "Note on 'The Thorn.'" There it becomes apparent that he is thinking in terms of "space . . . upon paper" (332). Where several of the poems in *Lyrical Ballads* worry about the problem of the waste of words or readers' time, the "Note" includes a striking revelation that Wordsworth feels himself to be answerable to concerns about economical or uneconomical uses of paper space, a highly material version of the same underlying worry. He writes:

> There is a numerous class of readers who imagine that the same words cannot be repeated without tautology: this is a great error: virtual tautology is more oftener produced by using different words when the meaning is exactly the same. Words, a Poet's words more particularly, ought to be weighed in the balance of feeling, and not measured by the space which they occupy upon paper (332).

Wordsworth's polemic is cogent in large part due to a strategic ambiguity about "space . . . upon paper." On the one hand, he is arguing that it is the poet's prerogative to repeat "the same words" (the good kind of tautology he is arguing for) and occupy as much paper space as he sees fit. He appears to be anticipating that, to an unsympathetic reader, the repetition of the same words may look like an especially egregious form of "waste of words" in the practical, material register of a waste of "space . . . upon paper," given the expensiveness of paper.[73] His response is that the policy of brevity for the sake of the parsimonious use of paper does not apply to the poet. In "Simon Lee," "The Idiot Boy," and "Michael," Wordsworth invokes the ideal of conciseness but reserves the right to ignore it: narrators tease, dawdle, and digress; incidents are invoked but then deferred and then treated in perfunctory fashion; characters like Johnny, the "idiot boy," get lost and wander; and Wordsworth himself indulges in a particularly excessive kind of repetition that critics have noticed since the volume's first appearance.

On the other hand—and indeed his wording allows him to have it both ways—he is claiming that it is the poet's right or responsibility to be brief, and readers are mistaken if they are evaluating poetry on the measure of the space that words occupy upon paper, perhaps against the standard of weightier, lengthier forms like the epic. Rather, fewer words, and the same few words repeated, can be more heavily freighted with feeling than any string of words generated by the unthinking automatic stylistic variation typical of poetic diction. Like Strunk later—"Omit needless words! Omit needless words! Omit needless words!"—Wordsworth recognizes that brevity goes hand in hand with repetition to potent effect.

Thus when Wordsworth later in his "Note" describes words as "efficient" (333) things, the immediate context calls for the idea of efficaciousness or the real materiality of words as "things," but this earlier passage colors that word with a more utilitarian sense: words are ideally efficient in the sense that they communicate maximum feeling with a minimum of words. There is much virtue, argues Wordsworth, in a high feeling/word ratio, in readers getting each word's worth of feeling. In either case, the New Rhetorical compositional ideal of brevity blends with a noticeably administrative- and efficiency-minded way of thinking about the efficient use of "space . . . upon paper"—the very logic we saw in the dimension of bureaucratic form that bears on the streamlined organization of words and on the formatting of information on paper or parchment administrative genres. But for Wordsworth, this ethos of verbal frugality is inextricable from his experiments in excess and inefficiency, which are only recognizable as such because of the norms about shortness. Geoffrey Hartman observed about "The Idiot Boy" that "the release [Wordsworth] feels in telling the story is too wastefully apparent," noticing the strange "delight" Wordsworth derives from the troubling material.[74] But Hartman's invocation of the idea of wastefulness is also revealing and critical to our understanding of Lyrical Ballads: the poems are never able to lose sight of a series of ratios pertaining to efficiency, wastefulness, and productivity in the context of writing itself, in the medium of words.

For us, then, it might remain customary or expedient in pedagogical contexts to emphasize the revolutionary nature of Lyrical Ballads, to rely on a shorthand whereby the volume marks a sudden departure from eighteenth-century poetics and ushers in a particularly modern kind of poetry. But it is equally valuable to recall Wilbur Samuel Howell's observation that "Wordsworth's reforms in poetry were part of a great trend, begun in the Renaissance," a trend consolidated by both the New Rhetoric and bureaucratic form: "the great change in the theory of rhetorical style since [the Renaissance] has been a change from the convention of imperial dress to the convention of the business suit."[75] The gradual, consequential trend toward a business- and bureaucracy-oriented style in communication and writing as *the* standard for all communication and writing impinges on Wordsworth, and his "reforms"—and the parodying of these same reforms— might be most accurately grasped as a piece of that long-term trend. But this also alerts us to the extreme sensitivity of *Lyrical Ballads* to the slower, longer tectonic shift in style that leads to nothing less than rules of communication in modernity. Courses in technical and business writing—oftentimes well-subscribed for obvious reasons—would be wise, then, to look further back historically to figures like Wordsworth, who are reflecting on the implications of informational and communicative efficiency ("waste of words") and perhaps even streamlined document design ("space . . . upon paper") when these desiderata were hardening into our laws of writing.

Seeing Like a Poet; or, How to Do Things with Bureaucratic Form

If *Lyrical Ballads* responds to a bundle of norms of writing, from different domains and belonging to different historical timelines—bureaucratic form around the time of Romanticism, the Enlightenment priority of stylistic brevity, and long-standing *brevitas* from the classical-rhetorical and literary tradition—*Essays upon Epitaphs* (comp. 1810) points to the literary uses to which bureaucratic form, in its starkest manifestations, can be put. The tripartite *Essays* functions as a reminder that the "fill-in-the-blanks" format belongs not only to standardized blank forms but to commemorative practices and literary discourse too, where it is used for very different ends. Above all, the three essays show Wordsworth not only engaging deeply with individual epitaphs but also thinking about epitaphs *en masse* and the large-scale aggregation of information that can be found across "a thousand church-yards" (56).[76] That is, while his turn to sepulchral inscription might seem to correspond to a backward-looking impulse, *Essays* reveals Wordsworth to be comfortable with what today goes by "big data," capably negotiating different scales of information.

Recall Samuel Johnson's comment on the epitaph: "part of it . . . which tells the birth and marriage is *formulary*, and can be expressed only one way." Johnson's note prompts a strange thought: if bureaucratic form is attaining a kind of cultural salience in the later eighteenth century—as this chapter has been arguing—would it not have been drawn into relation with the genre that had since antiquity, and in Johnson's mind, been strongly identified with formulaic writing, namely the epitaphic inscription? It seems at first like a perverse question, yoking together heartfelt memorials and dry documents. But then again, the form of an epitaph is not unlike the form of certain bureaucratic documents, such as the standardized form. Writing in both epitaphic and bureaucratic form must be "brief" (*Essays*, 59), the latter because of the administrative consideration that we have seen Wordsworth call "space . . . upon paper," the former because of the obvious constraint of finite space upon stone.[77] In close relation to brevity is an allied consideration that both epitaphs and administrative forms take into account: the individuals encountering them are, as Wordsworth says about passersby of epitaphs, "busy" (54) or "impatient" (59). Both forms assume the efficient shape that they do not only due to limited space on the medium but also based on certain assumptions about the distracted-ness of people—"men occupied with the cares of the world" in "modern times" (54)—and how best to make the most of their attention for the short time it can be claimed.

Yet these are only adventitious resemblances between epitaphic and bureaucratic form, and it is not until one notices Wordsworth's allusions in *Essays* to other kinds of documents that one begins to recognize that his essays, in their peculiarly insightful way, place epitaphs among other informational genres and practices of Wordsworth's time.[78] One might say that the essays combine and thus contrast those "inscriptions" so influential on Wordsworth's poetry as suggested by Geoffrey Hartman in "Inscriptions and Romantic Nature Poetry," and "inscriptions" in the

documentary, epistemological sense suggested by Bruno Latour in "Drawing Things Together."[79] Wordsworth's reflections on memorials and mortality might have proceeded just as well without reference to the landmark
state administrative project the *Statistical Account of Scotland*—which, as
we have seen, sought to gather certain pieces of information about the
parishes of Scotland—but there it is in the *Essays* (65), making a curious
appearance. Elsewhere Wordsworth compares a village churchyard to the
informational genre of the "report," arguing that the sum of inscriptions
in a churchyard captures more about "a Community . . . than any report
which might be made by a rigorous observer" (64). Finally, Wordsworth
likens the collection of epitaphs in a churchyard to a traditional means
of registering and amassing information, in fact much the same information as epitaphs, but inscribed in books and not on stone: he describes
a graveyard as "a favorable Register" (64) and invokes with this telling
figure the genre of the parish register. By Wordsworth's time, the recording of births, marriages, deaths—sometimes referred to as "hatches,
matches, and dispatches"—in parish registers had been a long-standing
practice.[80] Whatever Wordsworth's other motives may have been for his
extended treatment of epitaphs—his interest in Chiabrera's epitaphs and
in the tradition of Greek epigrammatic inscriptions, the wish to criticize
Pope's epitaphs and Samuel Johnson's writings on the topic, the chance
to continue his polemic against poetic diction and "artifices" (84) begun
in the "Preface" to *Lyrical Ballads*—he sets sepulchral inscriptions against
the backdrop of other inscriptions that attended Great Britain's coming
into being as a modern information state. As the local parish register is
giving way to the establishment of the General Register Office, and amid
systematic endeavors like the *Statistical Account*, the essays juxtapose epitaphs and other administrative writing and point to their similar features,
forms, and functions.

Thus while the essays are on the surface treating the "notion of a
perfect Epitaph" (76) and prosecuting their negative evaluation of bad
inscriptions (literary and lapidary), they are also intimating the underlying similarities between the "massifying" of humans in biopolitics
as described by Foucault—a massifying carried out in part through

documentation—and the "points, of nature and condition, wherein all men resemble each other" (59) as revealed by epitaphs. It would be mistaken to characterize Wordsworth's preoccupation in *Essays, Lyrical Ballads*, and *The Excursion* with what is commonly human as an unappealing form of universalism, naive or presumptuous at best, and effacing socioeconomic differences at worst. On the contrary, there is ample evidence that his interest in what individuals hold in "common with the species" (89), as the *Essays* puts it, is driven by his alertness to the biopolitical logic that grasps its object of administration at the level of "man-as-species"—that is, the management of humans-as-population—and his own corresponding sense that there is a similar version of this logic in the traditional form of the sepulchral inscription.[81] Epitaphic inscriptions too presuppose that "to be born and to die are the two points in which all men feel themselves to be in absolute coincidence" (57), in a manner that is not unlike the biopolitical view of humans as "a global mass that is affected by overall processes characteristic of birth, death, production, illness, and so on."[82] This may help to explain what one notices while reading the essays, that they are rhetorically excessive in insisting on how boring and predictable epitaphs are: "wholly uninteresting" (68) and "even trite" (78) with their "uniform language" (65) and their "monotonous language" (66). Wordsworth insists that epitaphs are homogeneous in terms of the kinds of information they record (for example, hatches, matches, dispatches) and, beyond those particulars, in terms of the utter conventionality of their sentiments: "a husband bewails a wife; a parent breathes a sigh of disappointed hope over a lost child; a son utters a sentiment of filial reverence for a departed father or mother; a friend perhaps inscribes an encomium recording the companionable qualities, or the solid virtues, of the tenant of the grave, whose departure has left a sadness upon his memory" (56). But his hyperbole should tip us off to the secondary agenda operating beneath these meditations, one that brings epitaphs into closer relation with those other "uninteresting," "uniform," and "monotonous" records: standardized paper or parchment records that also presuppose certain regularities of humans when humans are viewed—seeing like a state—as a species.

Wordsworth therefore responds in an unexpected manner to the problem of depersonalization. There is a "want of discrimination in sepulchral memorials" (56), and their clichéd inscriptions are "the language of a thousand church-yards; and it does not often happen that anything, in a greater degree discriminate . . . is to be found in them" (56). One might note the same depersonalizing effects of bureaucratic documents, a frequently lamented fact. Yet his response does not at all entail a lament about depersonalization or dehumanization, either explicitly in connection with epitaphs or implicitly in connection with the administrative data-amassing practices the essays name. Instead these essays undertake a criticism on the subject of epitaphic form, a criticism that foregrounds his appreciation for how good epitaphs have "a due proportion of the common or universal feeling of humanity to sensations excited by a distinct and personal clear conception, conveyed to the reader's mind, of the individual" (57). In other words, administrative records and epitaphs alike reinforce what humans have in common, but they also make perceptible "individualities" (67), details that allow one to discriminate one individual from another. As Frances Ferguson has suggested, large-scale grouping (whether in the context of utilitarianism or in biopolitics) has an oft-overlooked reverse side, and that is the ability to provide social and institutional structures against whose backdrop the crucial ability to "make individuals distinctive" emerges.[83] In short, the massifying of humans—a view that humans form "a global mass that is affected by overall processes"—is at once an eraser and guarantor of individuality, and Wordsworth seems to recognize this in connection with epitaphic and bureaucratic data alike.

At the end of the final essay, Wordsworth leaves readers with a vivid portrayal of the most moving tombstone he ever saw:

> In an obscure corner of a Country Church-yard I once espied . . . a very small Stone laid upon the ground, bearing nothing more than the name of the Deceased with the date of birth and death, importing that it was an Infant which had been born one day and died the following. I know not how far the Reader may be in sympathy with me,

but more awful thoughts of rights conferred, of hopes awakened, of
remembrances stealing away or vanishing were imparted to my mind
by that Inscription there before my eyes than by any other that it has
ever been my lot to meet with upon a Tomb-stone. (93)

Again, Wordsworth's reaction is somewhat unexpected. The cold presentation of three particulars—a name and two dates—does not lead him to
deplore bureaucratic form, but rather to recognize the tombstone as an
aesthetic object that prompts a kind of sympathetic-imaginative "filling-
in": "thoughts of rights conferred, of hopes awakened, of remembrances
stealing away or vanishing." *Essays upon Epitaphs* invites us to ask: if
lapidary and literary epitaphs invite such imaginings, can similar imaginative games be played with the details found on boring standardized
forms, conjectures about the person behind the abstract pieces of data?
Do we not construct similar "thoughts" and narratives about the human
being behind the discrete particulars found in job applications or online
dating profiles? The essays remind us of the other things one can do,
and typically does, with bureaucratic form, particularly when thinking
poetically—beyond thoughtless and hurried filling out, processing, or filing away. Wordsworth's response exemplifies what Robert Mitchell has
astutely identified as "population aesthetics," an aesthetics arising from
biopolitics: "the logic of population establishes the enabling frame for
intense experiences of hope and fear; fundamental judgments concerning what is beautiful and ugly, sublime and mundane; and our intuitive
sense of how individuals ought to relate to collectives."[84] Perhaps more
than we would expect, Wordsworth is surprisingly at ease with a world of
populations and information at large scales, navigating it, and finding in
it the possibility of aesthetic experience. Wordsworth is capable of moving from one "very small Stone" to "the language of a thousand church-
yards." In this context, what may be of greatest interest about *Essays upon
Epitaphs* is that it shares a rare side of Wordsworth, negotiating different
scales of information in modernity—from the individual instance to the
aggregate, from the single epitaph to what Wallace Stevens called "Anecdote of Men by the Thousand."[85]

The Excursion and Efficiency

The Excursion is a poem that in multiple ways demands to be read in connection with Wordsworth's administrative work. While many parts of the poem's composition history are speculative, and complicated due to the poem's entwinement with compositions for the projected long poem *The Recluse* (for example, "The Ruined Cottage," "Home at Grasmere"), we do know that Wordsworth worked on crucial parts of *The Excursion* in the period between early 1813 and May 1814. According to Mark Reed's chronology, Wordsworth composed and reworked substantial portions of Book 2 through Book 9 during these months; it was during this period when the poem truly took on its final form.[86] It was in this same stretch of time that Wordsworth began to seek out a second job, and, succeeding, began his work as Distributor of Stamps. As early as August 1812, Wordsworth and his intermediaries had inquired of Sir William Lowther, Earl of Lonsdale (the longtime patron of the Wordsworth family), about an office. Lowther informed Wordsworth in March 1813 that he had recommended the poet for the office of Distributor of Stamps for Westmorland and Penrith. And a month later, Wordsworth signed his bond of office.[87] The ensuing months are occupied by major work on *The Excursion* alongside a flurry of distributorship business. On top of managing the accounts, Wordsworth hired John Carter for clerical assistance, visited and checked on his subs, identified instances of tax evasion, and more.[88] His job as a tax collector frames the poem in another, more apparent way: *The Excursion* begins with a dedicatory poem to Lowther, a sonnet written by a Wordsworth grateful at the prospect of greater financial security from the appointment. When Wordsworth writes, "I appear / Before thee, LONSDALE, and this Work present" (5–6), the word "Work" indicates *The Excursion*, but as Mark Schoenfield too has noted, one cannot help but think also of the government "work" provided by Lowther.[89] More speculatively, one wonders how it must have felt for Wordsworth to be revising and reviewing passages that might have taken on new significance because of his distributorship. For example, two of the longer stories told during the sequence of embedded narratives, those of the Prodigal (6.285–390) and Oswald the volunteer (7.720–912), are based on the sons of one of Wordsworth's acquaintances, a man who had served as a clerk to one of Wordsworth's predecessors in the distributor position.[90] Wordsworth would have also been collecting the legacy duty at the same time that he was reviewing passages like the "small inheritance [that] had fallen" (7.454) to the Deaf Man's older brother. There is also the Sympson family narrative, which would have been a good potential example of *luctuosa hereditas* under the period's tax law: that is, the situation arising when a parent outlives his or her descendants and is taxed on legacies left by them, rather than the other way around.[91]

Yet these correspondences—some made solid by chronology, others admittedly conjectural—are themselves less interesting than the possibility that, even if Wordsworth in his poem never makes explicit reference to the British fiscal bureaucracy, *The Excursion* works through norms pertaining to efficiency in writing powerfully exemplified in standardized bureaucratic genres. Recall that one of the main contentions of this chapter is that the compartmentalization by which Wordsworth kept his poetic and administrative labors separate indexes the degree to which both kinds of work were in his moment rationalized and professionalized; simultaneously, this specialized seriousness was attended by a countermovement, where certain rules of writing flowed out from the domain of bureaucracy (and business) and into literary writing.

Does *The Excursion* react at all to the social imperative of efficient writing? The most obvious social question toward which the poem tends is not bureaucratization but industrialization—"changes in the Country from the manufacturing spirit" ("Summary of Contents," 46)—the subject of sustained discussion in Books 8 and 9. Yet in Byron's mind, as we have seen, *The Excursion* could not be mentioned without invoking Wordsworth's civil servant job, and the start of his career as a bureaucrat overlapped with his big final push on the poem. It is better to recognize *The Excursion* not only as a poem about industrial work, then, but rather as a poem taking part in a set of interrelations between several different kinds of labor: the factory work that is the pressing, topical problem discussed at the work's culmination; the administrative work that becomes so conspicuous in British society during the long eighteenth century (recall Blackstone:

"Witness the commissioners and the multitude of dependents"), and that occupies Wordsworth himself after 1813; and, of course, the work of poetry as embodied by *The Excursion* itself. Alison Hickey's terrific monograph on *The Excursion* frames the poem as an ambivalent response to various systematizations—the "perceived systemization of the British nation and empire . . . economic systemization, political and military systemization, the manufacturing system"—but one needs to add to Hickey's list the fiscal-bureaucratic system that employed Wordsworth, and more significantly, drove the British fiscal-military state of the long eighteenth century.[92] The poem's vexed response to bureaucratic form can thus be tracked along the coordinates provided by industrial, administrative, and poetic work—or, the Romantic-era complex of blue-collar, white-collar, and poetic worker (Muse-caller?). From this perspective, Wordsworth's poem is remarkably prescient. Standard accounts of the emergence of modern information societies characterize bureaucratic organization as a belated mid- and later nineteenth-century response to the need created by the industrial revolution for rationalized feedback systems; in the view of these narratives, the "control revolution" follows industrialization.[93] Yet we see Wordsworth already thinking through the contemporaneous relation between early bureaucratization (of the administrative state) and manufacturing, and in this context pondering the fate of writing under the dominion of the utilitarian logic of the closely allied bureaucratic and industrial orders. What becomes of literature when writing comes more and more to be viewed as something from which to extract, "mine," or process data? When writing becomes principally about producing "useful" information, about so-called knowledge production?

In this final section of this chapter, I would like to show, focusing mostly on the "oral records" (6.628) narrated in the middle books of *The Excursion* (Books 5 to 7), that Wordsworth internalizes bureaucratic form and its utilitarian spirit, an internalization that helps to account for some of the fascinating contradictions in this frequently unfascinating poem. Most readings of the poem's encounter with utilitarian thought focus on Wordsworth's passing references to the utilitarian instructional approach known as the Madras system, but I would like to focus instead on the poem's response to a utilitarian approach to something much closer to Wordsworth's life and work: *writing*. That an extended exercise in the documenting of human lives and extended ruminations upon the act of documenting sit at the heart of *The Excursion* suggests the poem's engagement with the documentary genres so ubiquitous in its historical moment, not least what Wordsworth called "certain papers called Forms." But the manner in which Wordsworth has his characters carry out these tales, and the ensuing discussions and digressions, portray a contradictory response on Wordsworth's part to the norms of bureaucratic documents. It would overstate matters to characterize *The Excursion* as an intervention into or a critique of bureaucratization or industrialization and more accurate to describe it as an internalization responsible for the poem's paradoxical positions and for the peculiar features and form of the poem. In the spirit of the poem's description of the Prodigal—"within his frame/Two several Souls alternately had lodged" (6.297–98)—one might say that *The Excursion* lodges within its unwieldy frame at least two impulses with regard to writing made utilitarian.

If, as I have suggested, *Essays upon Epitaphs* intimates striking connections between epitaphs and administrative documents insofar as both can be grasped as written records molded by the logic of efficient communication, *The Excursion*'s medial status as a written poem remediating and celebrating speech appears at first to express Wordsworth's notably different, romantic wish to portray a world where humans are documented by means other than writing—other than contemporary paperwork or parchment-work, other even than traditional epitaphic writing. The poet describes a "Church-yard . . . almost wholly free/From interruption of sepulchral stones," and praises the rural dead who "trust/The lingering gleam of their departed Lives/To oral records," that is, to oral tradition or "Depositories faithful and more kind/Than fondest Epitaphs" (6.621–30). The glorification of "oral records" in the poem, then, seems to be an almost apotropaic gesture both acknowledging and warding off records in any medium other than the oral. As we have seen, the inscribed records of Wordsworth's moment are primarily definable by their standardization and radical simplifications—or, recalling James Beniger's words above, by "the destruction or ignoring of information in order to facilitate . . . processing." By design, bureaucratic documents abstract certain particulars about the living, the dead, and the transactions between them (such as legacies) to relatively few data points: for example, the eight particulars recorded in the legacy duty form, the three registered by the British state in "hatches, matches, and dispatches," or the three carved into the most memorable epitaph Wordsworth encountered ("name of the Deceased, with the date of birth and death"). By contrast, *The Excursion* prizes "pathetic Records" by "voice/ . . . delivered" (7.1075–76) precisely because they are meandering as well as unsystematic in the details they include, exclude, or gloss over; unlike administrative documents, these oral records are short on facts, dates, and all manner of otherwise "useful" information.[94] Wordsworth's Fenwick note on this poem, in accounting for his choice to make the Wanderer one of the poem's principals, confesses that "wandering" was his own main passion, and this confession, as much as the work's very title, strongly suggests that the poem quite deliberately suspends for itself the social imperatives related to streamlined writing, perhaps suspending the idea of effective communication more generally ("Fenwick Note," 1215). Another way to view this is that one impulse in *The Excursion* is the one defining the "disorderly abundance" of the responses Sinclair received from parishes in the making of the *Statistical Account of Scotland*: bureaucratic form begat not concise information but unruly, locally tinged, copiousness.[95]

But the poem does *not* fulfill, at least not entirely, the atavistic wish for a world before or without modern bureaucratic recordkeeping systems. Much to Wordsworth's credit, *The Excursion* maintains a saving level of self-ironizing energy. For one thing, the story of the Deaf Man—whose love of books recalls Wordsworth's own, as treated in Book 5 of *The Prelude*— whose very being is defined by reading (7.456–71), or rather the consumption of writing, counters the inscription-aversion elsewhere in the poem. More importantly, the poem identifies an unlikely likeness between its own spoken "depositories" and administrative genres. Wordsworth makes this identification in an involved way: he associates, in a mediated fashion, the poem's own storytelling activity with bureaucratic form by associating the former with the industrial ethos of efficiency ("the manufacturing spirit") that closely parallels the ideals behind bureaucratic form. That is to say, he indirectly discloses the imprint of bureaucratic form on his poem and his historical moment. Wordsworth is thereby able—without engaging in anything like a direct critique of the bureaucratic system of which he is a part, but also without making any overt concessions to bureaucratic form—to observe how the oral records of *The Excursion* paradoxically resemble writing shaped by bureaucratic form by linking those oral records to industrialization, particularly the manufacturing emphasis on input, output, and efficiency.

Nowhere is the poem's drawing of these connections more apparent than when Wordsworth has the Wanderer let slip that the Pastor's oral records should ultimately be about "gain" (6.597). The Wanderer proceeds to puzzle over, and qualify, his own revealing phrasing in a series of questions, the significance of which belies their placement within parentheses: "(Gain shall I call it?—gain of what?—for whom?)" (6.598). Immediately prior, the Solitary had noted that the Pastor's stories about the rural dead all seem to lead to an overwhelming sense of fatality ("Of poor humanity's afflicted will/Struggling in vain with ruthless destiny" [6.571-72]) and are therefore like ready-made tragedies: the deceased "generations are prepared" and their "internal pangs . . . are ready" (6.569-70) to be converted with little effort into literary art by "the tragic Muse" (6.566). The Solitary overstates matters, and with a great deal of cynicism, but we must grant the accuracy of his observation. He is pointing out the utilitarian ethos by which the Pastor's "Authentic epitaphs" (5.653) are "prepared" and "ready"—almost too prepared, too ready—for the function of imparting "genuine knowledge" (6.610), usually aimed at edifying the despondent Solitary himself. That is to say, the Solitary puts his finger on the disconcerting feeling that the group's activity somewhat resembles the industrial processes that become the subject of concern in Books 8 and 9. It is no accident, then, that the Wanderer, in urging the Pastor to steer clear of narrating the most grotesque lives marked by "brutish vice" (6.590), says that such anecdotes would yield only "poor gain" (6.597). "Gain," after all, is *The Excursion*'s byword for the ethos of industrialization and utilitarianism: "Gain—the

Master Idol of the Realm" (8.186).[96] The departed lives are treated like raw materials subject to processing by the Pastor and others, oddly like the industrial materials described throughout *The Excursion*, both sorts of materials being harvested or mined for "gain."

The figural resonances between the spoken narratives and industrial processes aimed at "gain" take different forms. The peasant who bursts into the poem in Book 7 insinuates the uncanny similarity between the activity of producing gain from stories of the dead and his own lumbering. The peasant too makes use of the dead, an arboreal corpse (he hauls a "giant Oak/Stretched on his bier" [7.564-65]), and the Pastor imagines a variety of manufacturing tools as well as products: the wood becomes "strong knee-timbers, and the mast that bears/The loftiest of her pendants" for a ship, a "wheel that turns ten thousand spindles," and "the trunk and body" of "the vast engine laboring in the mine" (6.622-26). As several important readings of the poem have pointed out, the chief figure that bridges the characters' pursuit of learning "truths" from the epitaphic anecdotes and heavy industry is that of *mining*.[97] It appears in the wording of the Wanderer's original request to the Pastor that initiates the sequences of narratives:

> The mine of real life
> Dig for us; and present us, in the shape
> Of virgin ore, that gold which we by pains
> Fruitless as those of aery Alchemists
> Seek from the torturing crucible.
>
> . . .
>
> Epitomize the life; pronounce, You can,
> Authentic epitaphs
>
> . . .
>
> So, by your records, may our doubts be solved. (5.631-56)

The Excursion's main activity of documenting the lives of the dead is a kind of mining—"The mine of real life/Dig for us" enjoins the Wanderer—and it is for a very specific kind of didactic recompense; the storytelling, as Kevis Goodman has aptly put it, "hovers between mining and grave-digging.":[98] Note too the lines that extend the Wanderer's mining conceit: "present us, in the shape/Of virgin ore, that gold . . . " Reminiscent of the Solitary's intuition that the tragic stories of the rural poor seem overly "prepared and "ready" for the purpose of edification, these lines suggest that there is something backward about the group's exercise: so overdetermined is the tendency of the stories toward didactic gold, that it is almost as if the group is not truly mining meaning from the authentic epitaphs so much as being presented didactic gold reverted to look like virgin ore (that is, it is as though the stories have been back-constructed into raw form from a predetermined moral). Notwithstanding the considerable emphasis on the spoken—"pronounce[d]"—status of the epitomes, then, there is always an air of *scriptedness* and fable about them. Or, expanding on the Solitary's comment that the Pastor's narratives resemble "Fictions in form" (6.560), we might say that the pronounced stories have been given the literary treatment—written, formed into fiction—perhaps "literaturized." Wordsworth alloys his didactic poem with a significant degree of self-consciousness—figured in such exchanges about storytelling and mining—that his poem treats narratives, and perhaps poetry at large (including *The Excursion* itself), as something from which didactic gold can be extracted and designed from the outset with this extraction in mind. He resorts to the same imagery when he assures readers that they "will have no difficulty in *extracting*" the poem's philosophical-didactic "system" for themselves ("Preface to *The Excursion*," 39; emphasis mine). In sum, Wordsworth is self-aware that *The Excursion*, though it seems to celebrate unruly orality, oftentimes takes an approach that treats *writing* from the industrial and bureaucratic perspective of efficient processing. The poem acknowledges its management of inputs into outputs with an eye toward gain.

But if, at times, the poem seems too preoccupied with gain, at other moments, it appears to contemplate the advantages and disadvantages of gain and the logic of efficiency. Francis Jeffrey, whose review of *The Excursion* remains as insightful as it is prejudicial, senses that efficiency in writing is the real issue with the poem. In a telling analogy, Jeffrey describes Wordsworth's writing (of *The Excursion* as well as of the projected

Recluse) as a textile manufacturing business: "All this is so much capital already sunk in the concern; which must be sacrificed if it be abandoned: and no man likes to give up for lost the time and talent and labor which he has embodied in any permanent production."[99] It is not only that the poem internally thematizes the problem of gain in its embedded narratives: the poem as a whole, as Jeffrey sensed, can be understood in terms of investments, costs, or expenses ("capital," "labor," and "raw material") to be converted into some sort of "production" (such as "articles of this very fabric") for gain.[100] Furthermore, in Jeffrey's eyes, the poem emblematizes a specific form of failure, defined by excessive input with useless output, something Wordsworth himself portrayed in "Simon Lee." Jeffrey's wording discloses the utilitarian formula for efficiency against which Wordsworth's failed textual production is tacitly being measured. Jeremy Bentham articulated this formula in the form of a motto: aptitude (or, we might say, any desired outcome) maximized, expense minimized.[101] And Bentham insisted that the latter caused the former:

> *Official aptitude maximized; expense minimized* . . . Of these two states of things—these two mutually concomitantly desirable objects—one bears to the other the relation of *cause* to *effect*; for, that from the same arrangement from which the expense so employed will *experience diminution*, the aptitude in question will, in the natural order of things, *receive increase*: in a word, that *caeteris paribus*, the less the expense so bestowed as above, the greater, not the lesser, will be the aptitude.[102]

The utilitarian version of efficiency thus rejects, for example, the idea that more upfront investment might lead to more productivity; nor does it countenance the possibility that expenses and aptitude might interact in more complex ways (for example, that there might be a minimum baseline expense necessary below which aptitude would not increase, or that high aptitude would in the long run make up for earlier expenditure). A simplistic, penurious model, Bentham's efficiency formula posits only that minimized input will lead to maximized output. According to Jeffrey's analysis of *The Excursion*—and as many readers since him have also concluded—the poem flagrantly violates this simple formula, with

Wordsworth having invested so much time, work, words, writing, and pages into something that provides so little of worth. By this logic, he should have poured less effort into his poetic "concern," which would have increased the gain.

But then again, we cannot forget that the Wanderer had *asked* about gain, spoken in the interrogative mood: "Gain shall I call it?—gain of what?—for whom?" In the Fenwick note, Wordsworth explains the background of the Miner anecdote and explains that he had heard stories of little effort followed by great gain leading to madness: "I have heard of sudden influxes of great wealth being followed by derangement & in one instance the shock of good fortune was so great as to produce absolute Idiotcy . . . but *these all happened where there had been little or no previous effort to acquire the riches*" ("Fenwick Note," 1220; emphasis mine). In this case, the utilitarian formula for efficiency—input minimized, output maximized—leads to madness. And there is more: in the actual anecdote of the Miner in *The Excursion*, great expenditure of effort is followed by great wealth, but this too leads to disaster, as the Miner "proved all unable to support the weight/Of prosperous fortune" (6.247–48). It seems to matter little whether the initial effort is small or large: for Wordsworth, the problem lies with the utilitarian formula itself, the way it converts human lives into an administrative or mechanical process. Although the Pastor, in customary fashion, concludes the story with a certain kind of gain—the unconsoling consolation that the Miner has named after him, for posterity, a "Path of Perseverance" (6.264)—the narrative, as much as the scenario narrated in the Fenwick note, casts doubt on the Benthamite efficiency equation. They too seem to ask: Gain shall we call it?

We turn finally to Jeffrey's indictment of *The Excursion*'s notorious lengthiness and perceived tediousness: its "profuse and irrepressible wordiness," its "long words, long sentences," the fact that it is "four hundred and twenty good quarto pages," and so on.[103] In Jeffrey's famous words, "What Mr. Wordsworth's ideas of length are, we have no means of accurately judging." He continues: "the quarto before us contains an account of one of his youthful rambles in the vales of Cumberland, and occupies precisely the period of three days; so that, by the use of a very powerful *calculus,* some estimate may be formed of the probable extent of the entire biography."[104] Yet the sprawling form of *The Excursion* becomes a very different phenomenon once related to bureaucratic form, as in the "certain papers called Forms" that Wordsworth himself processed as he completed the poem. Although we are accustomed to looking for, and discussing, certain things under the headings of literary form or poetic form, perhaps we are missing what is most obvious about the form of *The Excursion*—its sheer length. As we have seen, Wordsworth, without ever explicitly invoking bureaucracy, responds in various ways to the expectations of writing that accompany modernity, the seemingly non-negotiable imperative to present information or particulars in the most streamlined manner. It is no stretch to say that Wordsworth glimpses in bureaucratic form an early version of our world where the rule is TL;DR—internet slang for "too long; didn't read."[105] What might be mined or quickly gained from the present discussion—can it be rendered in bullet points, an instance of bureaucratic form very familiar to us today?

- *Lyrical Ballads* worries about brevity, but also sometimes ignores it.
- *Essays upon Epitaphs* shows Wordsworth surprisingly at ease in a world of big data.
- Written communications should be as short as possible. *The Excursion* knows this, treats this imperative as a theme, and yet it is a very long poem.

One would like to say that such short synopses are not the whole story, and neither are they the gold, but the allure of bureaucratic form—the power of the norm—is strong too. Might we nevertheless ask: Gain shall we call it? Gain of what? For whom?

And it opened its fan-like leaves to the light
And closed them beneath the kisses of night.

Percy Shelley, "The Sensitive Plant"

ambiversion, *n.*: A mental condition characterized by a balance of
extravert and introvert features.

Oxford English Dictionary

3 SHELLEY AMID THE AGE OF SEPARATIONS; OR, A POETRY OF AMBIVERSION FOR NETWORKED LIFE

Connections in the Age of Separations, Separations in the Age of Connections

What are the pros and cons of networked life, of being a connected being? Connectedness mediated by today's digital technologies and platforms involves a messy mix of feelings, and these feelings can be seen in the mix of positions taken on networked life within media studies. For example, Sherry Turkle, in *Alone Together: Why We Expect More from Technology and Less from Each Other*, asks, "Does virtual intimacy degrade our experience of the other kind and, indeed, of all encounters, of any kind?," and answers for the most part in the affirmative. If you spend many hours online or gaming, "there's got to be someplace you're not." "And that someplace you're not," Turkle tells us, "is often with your family and friends—sitting around, playing Scrabble face-to-face, taking a walk, watching a movie together in the old-fashioned way."[1] Where Turkle worries, rather nostalgically, about the deleterious effects of virtual interactions on co-present social life, Nancy K. Baym comes to a different conclusion by asking whom we are spending online time with. It turns out that much mediated socializing is a continuation of "old-fashioned" socializing. Digital interactions are usually with the same friends and family we already know, those we have socialized with offline first. Our collective fascination with digitally facilitated stranger sociality (through such means as dating websites and apps) overshadows the more humdrum existence of "media multiplexity" in our lives: meaning that our existing relationships are "conducted through more than one medium, and that closer relationships use more media."[2] And when new relationships do initially form online, Baym finds, they often lead to offline, face-to-face contact in a highly ritualized, predictable manner: moving, for example, from online communication to texting to meeting in real life.[3] Where Turkle tends to emphasize the "alone" aspect of alone togetherness, Baym emphasizes how digital media reinforce existing "togetherness" and also allow new kinds of togetherness. One last, recent position worth considering is Patrick Jagoda's, which is a blend of, or somewhere between, Baym's and Turkle's views—closer to Baym in embracing online sociality and yet aware of the sorts of concerns raised by Turkle. Jagoda offers "network ambivalence." Being ambivalent about the connected life means fully committing or opting in to social media, but with "a deliberate intensity, patience, and willingness to forgo quick resolution or any finality at all," and also "learning to inhabit a compromised environment with the discomfort, contradiction, and misalignment it entails."[4] "Network ambivalence" sounds perhaps less like a novel "crucial critical position" than a description of the default, inevitable position in which many people living with constant connectedness find themselves, but it is nevertheless a canny assessment.[5] For Turkle, networked life takes away from face-to-face time to a worrying degree. For Baym, it tends to consolidate existing friendships or lead to face-to-face fun. For Jagoda, there is a middle way between polar responses to networks, opting in fully but with what literary historians will recognize as a form of negative capability—a network negative capability.

This chapter derives from a twofold reaction to all these discussions, wishing first to add something to them, and then to add to that initial addition. In the first instance, one cannot help noticing that these discussions of networked life have a very short historical purview. This is by no means a criticism of the works described, which set out to understand the contemporary problem and offer insights of real value. Yet, as this book has been arguing, the connected condition predates digitality, and there is something to gain—even if what is gained is a more unwieldy problem of massive historical and theoretical proportions—from considering a longer version of these problems, including earlier epochs. As I began suggesting in the introduction, the period leading up to Romanticism and then the era itself both show early stirrings of an information society. "Means of bureaucratic organization, the new infrastructures of transportation and telecommunications, and system-wide communication via the new mass media" were more developed than is usually appreciated.[6] A strong version of the view that the eighteenth century is a precursor to today's highly mediated, networked world can be found in Clifford Siskin's and William Warner's introductory "Invitation in the Form of an Argument" in *This Is Enlightenment*, where they describe several developments that "establish[ed] the conditions for the possibility of Enlightenment."[7] They call these developments, all of which can be said to deal with practices and technologies of communication, "cardinal mediations." At certain moments in Siskin's and Warner's argument, "mediations" take on an artifactual, technological cast ("tools," "machines," "mechanical mediations"), but the cardinal mediations quite differently tend to involve wide-ranging processes: the emergence of infrastructures for the transmission and communication of information (for example, postal systems), genres and formats that intensified communication practices (for example, newspapers and other periodicals), associational practices (for example, clubs, societies, the "republic of letters"), and protocols of contact (for example, those associated with mail, credit, and copyright). The overall picture one gets from this valuable account of cardinal mediations is an Enlightenment defined by increased connectedness.[8] Our present-day networked life and the responses that come with it—the sensation of alone togetherness, the feelings attending media multiplexity and our navigation of it, or the attitude of "network ambivalence"—had past lives, though in different forms, in the time of a networked Enlightenment.

But there is something to add now to this account. This earlier age of cardinal mediations was also a cardinal "age of separations," in the words of Adam Ferguson's 1767 *Essay on the History of Civil Society*.[9] Ferguson and his contemporaries were addressing a crisis, a crisis that was the founding problem for Scottish proto-sociological discourse, as typified by Ferguson's *Essay* and related works. The problem was not limited to sociability, and implicated nothing less than the continuation of society, given two developments: the differentiation of the professions or the division of labor (separation), on the one hand, and infrastructural connectedness of the kind formed by cardinal mediations (connection), on the other. To borrow from Turkle, the togetherness allowed by communication and transportation networks was joined by an equally strong sense of alone-ness. Yet this earlier instance of alone-togetherness was less about the perceived decline of "old-fashioned" or meaningful intimacy as a result of mediated interactions, and more about a troublingly diminished sense of collective life amid rampant connectedness primarily for the purposes of conducting business. The "age of separations" was about "the bands of society" loosening perilously or even breaking, because of and despite greater commercial connectedness.[10]

We are not the first to have to bear with networked life, and neither are we the first to think about ways of navigating it. Percy Shelley's writings, including his love poem *Epipsychidion* (1821), reflect on Romantic-era networked life—that is, on the historically specific feeling of social disconnectedness amid heightened communicative and infrastructural connectedness. Participating in contemporaneous sociological discourse addressing this earlier version of alone togetherness and in Romantic poetry's reflections on communication through the medium of poetry, Shelley's works try to figure out how the poetic medium might model a form of relationality that is neither impersonally transactional nor overwhelmingly amatory. For us, living in surprisingly similar and yet surprisingly different networked world, Shelley's writings point to how social beings might take their cue from the ambiversion of literary communication, particularly poetry: poetry can be communicative and yet uncommunicative, some readers might be connected with it while others not, and books may be opened or left closed. This, in turn, suggests a way of being in the connected condition that is "poetic," in the sense of having the capacity—perhaps a saving capacity—to be in a state of connection at some times, disconnection at others.

Poet or Media Theorist or Sociologist

Because of both recent and not so recent work on Romantic poetry, we have proleptic formulations that identify the figure of the Romantic poet as an early theoretician of discourses that will achieve discipline formation only much later—two important examples are media theory and sociology. In the first case, the important work of Celeste Langan and Maureen N. McLane has shown that Romantic poets were deeply engaged in "media theory," with Shelley foremost among his contemporaries in "establish[ing] a horizon for thinking the conditions of mediality." His poems represent, and strive for, a kind of immediacy (as figured, for example, in the "unpremeditated art" of the bird in "To a Sky-Lark" [1820]); there are also important comparative reflections on artistic media in his *A Defence of Poetry* (comp. 1821); he relies on telegraphic imagery in "Ode to Liberty" (1820); and he took great interest in "communication" in the older sense of transportation, an interest discernible in the various modes of conveyance in his poems (chariots, coaches, boats).[11] Here we have Shelley, early media theorist.

Meanwhile, according to Raymond Williams's classic essay "The Romantic Artist," in his book *Culture and Society*, Shelley, like other Romantic poets, was also a sociologist, engaged in the science of society. Williams argues that, "what were seen at the end of the nineteenth century as disparate interests, between which a man must choose and in the act of choice declare himself poet or sociologist, were, normally, at the beginning of the century, seen as interlocking interests: a conclusion about personal feeling became a conclusion about society."[12] In Williams's interviews with the *New Left Review*, his interviewers take him to task because *Culture and Society* appears to ignore the beginnings of sociology, which occurs in the period he covers and took as its inaugural preoccupation the same problems as those taken up by the English writers he studies. "The whole argument of *Culture and Society* was in a sense also the main theme of

European sociology from its founding moment onwards," the interviewers point out, "a system of thought you never mention." They add: "The entire trajectory of the discipline, from Comte and Saint-Simon down to Weber or Durkheim" attempted to address "the disintegrating forces of industrialism and democracy" by proposing "a more organic culture" in the same way that English writers like Southey and Arnold did. Williams answers that "the English tradition" focused more on the "very rapid and brutal experience of industrialization" and the problems engaged by early sociology were only secondary concerns.[13] His interlocutors are right that Williams writes around the continental sociological tradition in *Culture and Society*, and he appears partly to concede this. But from another perspective, as "The Romantic Artist" states, he is treating Romantic poetry as early sociology, from the startling premise that poetry and sociology were more interchangeable or continuous than is easily imaginable after their disciplinary division. A Romantic artist was a sociologist. Williams's understanding of the ties between early sociology and Romanticism tallies with Alvin W. Gouldner's "sociology of sociology," which notes the affinities between the inaugural, positivist strain of sociology in Saint-Simon and Auguste Comte and Romanticism generally.[14]

So we have Shelley as media theorist and as sociologist. From the present perspective, it is commonsensical that communications media and practices are central problems in sociological theory, but it is less obvious how sociological discourse, theories of media and communication, and poetry were joined in the Romantic period—*especially* in the case of Shelley.[15] If Shelley was a poet and simultaneously a media theorist and a sociologist, he is a peculiar case of this triadic appointment because his notoriously difficult poetic style and his theories about poetic communication would seem to divorce Romantic poetry from sociological thought. After all, even though Shelley may not have had to "declare himself poet or sociologist," he is also an exemplary figure in Williams's account of the gradual detachment of the sociological function (particularly its "criticism of industrialism") from poetry, and the subsequent social marginalization of the literary.[16] Williams describes it as follows: "What happened, under the stress of events, was a series of simplifications" whereby "art became a symbolic abstraction for a whole range of general human experience" threatened by the modern industrial order, and thus, "a general social activity was forced into the status of a department or province, and actual works of art were in part converted into a self-pleading ideology." With the conjuncture of developments responsible for the specialization and marginalization of literary culture in full view, he confesses that "the last pages of Shelley's *Defence of Poetry* are painful to read." Williams concludes almost elegiacally that "the bearers of a high imaginative skill become suddenly the 'legislators,' at the very moment when they were being forced into practical exile."[17]

Shelley the poet is thus uneasily joined to Shelley the sociologist, and neither of those two Shelleys is easily reconcilable with media theorist Shelley. This is because Shelley the media theorist poses a problem for, even undermines, any potential poetic-sociological role he might take on. In this *psychomachia* of sorts, the former's assumptions about the linguistic-poetic medium and his typical handling of it—his style—would only exacerbate the broader social shifts under way "to isolate art, to specialize the imaginative faculty to this one kind of activity, and thus to weaken the dynamic function which Shelley proposed for it."[18] At some moments, *A Defence of Poetry* exalts poetry over the other arts because language is the clearest of the "mediums of communication" for thoughts.[19] But at several other moments, Shelley stresses how language, once organized into poetry, is a profoundly unclear medium. He wavers, in William Keach's words, between celebrating "language as the medium of poetry" and displaying a "linguistic skepticism that runs throughout the *Defence* like a counterplot."[20] In another well-known moment in the *Defence*, Shelley describes poetic composition as a "feeble shadow of the original conception."[21] It turns out that poetic language too can function as "a cloud which enfeebles" thought, which is how he described the media used by "sculptors, painters, and musicians," which he demoted below those of poets.[22] And the obscure poetic style he at times adopts further interposes between composition and audience, as though to overlay the linguistic "cloud which enfeebles" the poet's conception with another layer of darkness—a "mist," "veiling," or "figured curtain"—that could enfeeble normative kinds of comprehension and sympathy typically involved in reception.[23]

What good are perceptive sociological theories of modernity when conveyed in a potentially opaque medium made deliberately doubly opaque—or when the poet-media theorist-sociologist becomes a symbol for poetic art's inward-looking tendencies and inefficacy? The embarrassment Williams confesses feeling at the peroration of Shelley's *Defence* appears to be embarrassment at glimpsing Shelley's writing as an emblem of literary discourse in general: Shelley registers and responds to poetry's own declining relevance in a difficult style that serves only "to isolate art, to specialize the imaginative faculty" further, caught in a perturbed, self-defeating pattern.[24]

One way to reconcile Shelley the Romantic poet, the sociologist, and the media theorist is to suppose that his theories of artistic media (of the kind found in the *Defence*), including his thoughts on poetic obscurity, do not disable his poetic sociology and instead play a special role in it. Williams, in another work, *Marxism and Literature*, opens the way to this possibility as he outlines what a Marxist cultural sociology would look like. Overcoming the tendencies of bourgeois sociology, this sociology of culture would avoid neutralizing complex social and class relations into inert abstractions ("mass public," "mass communication") and fully account for imaginative works and the forms they take—all without reducing the imagination to "knowledge," and without reducing the "social forms of language and movement and representation" to categories like "books."[25] This sociology of culture would be "a task distinct from the reduced sociology of institutions, formations, and communicative relationships and yet, as a sociology, radically distinct from the analysis of isolated forms."[26] Briefly, it is "at once a 'sociology' and an 'aesthetics.'"[27] Shelley's writing, in this later view, need not be exclusively "self-pleading ideology" on behalf of literary culture, sociopolitically impotent and uncommunicative. It may be those things too, but it could also be conceived as at once a sociology and an aesthetics, and "aesthetics" can reasonably include "media aesthetics," to the extent that Shelley's writing is a sociology awake to the medial facets and specificities of imaginative works—how they function as "mediums of communication," and the peculiar way poetry goes about "the communication of its influence."[28] Careful to avoid the theoretical reductions and neutralizations that make poetry a transparent index or a deliverer of knowledge or information or which measure poetry on these grounds—as the prompt for Shelley's somewhat humorless response, Thomas Love Peacock's "The Four Ages of Poetry," satirically does—Shelley's *Defence* attempts to account for poetic media, as much as form, within a larger "enquiry into the principles of society itself."[29]

The recognition that Shelley's writings attempt at once a sociology and a media aesthetics may clear up certain problems pertaining to his obscure style. We are not dealing with the fetishization of literary obscurity for its own sake, of course, or even an "analysis of isolated forms" or media. The question of whether or not Shelley's literary difficulty diminishes his political vision also begins to appear less urgent. As the argument goes, the obscurity of works like *Prometheus Unbound* (1820) and the actually miniscule supply and demand for many of Shelley's works—about which William St. Clair's *The Reading Nation in the Romantic Period* provides statistical confirmation—dampen the sociopolitical force of his writing.[30] But a better way to approach Shelley's sometimes unclear style dismisses from the outset the assumptions "that a clear style results in a popular audience and that political engagement requires having the most extensive audience possible," as Michael Warner has put it.[31] In Warner's terms, which happen to characterize Shelley's predicament very well, "those who write [opaquely] might very well feel that they are . . . writing to a public that does not yet exist . . . and finding that their language can circulate only in channels hostile to it, they write in a manner designed to be a placeholder for a future public."[32] Writing for "a future public" is after all, the very point of Shelley's "On Launching Some Bottles Filled with Knowledge into the Bristol Channel," whose contents may at some point "waft . . . to some freeborn soul."[33] But better yet, Shelley's opaque poetry is not only "a placeholder for a future public" but also a set of sociological reflections incorporating, and performed in, the poetic medium. There is therefore more to say beyond the fact that Shelley strategically modulates his style based on his imagined audience, that his poetry can be "exoteric" or "esoteric." This is certainly the case, as Stephen Behrendt's illuminating discussion of Shelley's stylistic decisions shows. Shelley did reflect on the comparative accessibility of individual works: he describes *The Cenci* (1819) as a work "of a more popular kind" (*Letters*, 2:108), the "*sermo pedestris*" of "Julian and Maddalo" (comp. 1819) (*Letters*, 2:196), and the popular orientation of the political songs of 1819, all against the obscurity of *Prometheus Unbound*.[34] But there is also the question of how Shelley imagines the clarity or unclarity of the poetic-linguistic medium beyond its bearing on the circulation of his works. What comes into view when obscurity is removed from the framework of audience or reception and instead recognized as a model of sociality? Can the capacity of obscure literary works to be both communicative and uncommunicative—to satisfy or not satisfy an imperative to make contact, to be connected—intimate a way of being in a networked world?

Connection Problems: The Interval between Us

Recall that, in making the case for the inextricability—perhaps identity—of poetry and sociology during Romanticism, Williams suggested that "a conclusion about personal feeling became a conclusion about society." I then added—following Langan and McLane's account of Shelley's astuteness about the media situation of the Romantic era—that Shelley's "conclusion[s] about society" are remarkable for integrating theories of imaginative media. But Shelley's actual handling of the poetic medium, his style, is in tension with any aspiration he may have had to communicate his ideas about the science of society: one way to approach this conundrum is to comprehend Shelley as engaged in, at once, a sociology and a media aesthetics that offers difficult poetry as a cue for social life.

If the sociological insights of Romantic poet-sociologist-media theorists stem from a "conclusion about a personal feeling," Shelley provides us with a useful starting point with his famous essay fragment "On Love" (comp. 1818). The essay begins from a specific feeling about social dissimilitude in similitude. The superficial, visual resemblances between the speaker and his addressees belie the profound disjunction he feels to be between them:

> I see that in some external attributes they resemble me, but when
> misled by that appearance, I have thought to appeal to something
> in common and unburthen my inmost soul to them I have found my

language misunderstood like one in a distant and savage land. The more opportunities they have afforded me for experience the wider has appeared the interval between us, and to a greater distance have the points of sympathy been withdrawn. . . . I . . . have found only repulse and disappointment. ("On Love," 503)

We might consider these lines not in the context of, for example, sympathy and its difficulties or Shelley's expatriation, but rather from the premise that an additional problem shapes these reflections: the problem of a community whose individuals coalesce by virtue of some similarities yet find themselves growing apart because of some differences. The scenario nominally involves one speaker and a yearning for potential amatory partners, but it senses a larger social transformation wherein those imagined as belonging to the same group or social framework—defined by geographical area, nation, or the like—lack what Shelley refers to as that "something in common."

This essay fragment, in my view, participates in sociological discourse as it addresses the separation of individuals in the specific context of modern societies defined by the division of labor. It joins Ferguson's *Essay on the History of Civil Society* as well as French positivist thought, all of which variously theorized how the division of labor impacted social and class relations. For example, Ferguson observes:

The mighty engine which we suppose to have formed society, only tends to set its members at variance, or to continue their intercourse after the bands of affection are broken.[35] [T]he separation of professions, while it seems to promise improvement of skill, and is actually the cause why the productions of every art become more perfect as commerce advances; yet in its termination, and ultimate effect, serves, in some measure, to break the bands of society.[36]

As John D. Brewer and others point out, Adam Smith, David Hume, and John Millar were more sanguine about the division of labor, believing that commercial interdependence among individuals would ultimately facilitate social cohesion, and thus anticipating Émile Durkheim's notion of "organic solidarity."[37] Ferguson, quite differently, worried that while individuals increasingly had many occasions to conduct business, the more crucial "bands of affection" that guarantee the integrity and overall health of the society were relaxing or tearing. Specialization and repetitive tasks circumscribed the perspective of individuals and therefore slackened, or worse, would totally dissolve the affective-social ties constituting the national body. Likewise, Comte, who studied Ferguson, concludes, in his "Considerations of the Spiritual Power" (1825–1826), that "the necessary result of this constantly developing specialization is that each individual and each people is habitually confined to a more and more limited perspective, and inspired by interests that are more and more particular," thereby diminishing their sense of a collective life.[38] Shelleyan love—the "[thirst] after likeness" ("On Love," 504)—is a feeling specific to a modern social structure viewed from this sociological vantage.

Wordsworth too, in similar sociological reflections, lamented the same problem. The year before Shelley's essay, Wordsworth wrote a letter to Daniel Stuart, the proprietor of the *Morning Post* and *Courier* newspapers. Wordsworth formerly had subscribed to a view shared by Smith, Hume, and Millar, but by the time of this letter, his view is closer to Ferguson's concerns about the weakening of social ties between different orders of society:

> I see clearly that the principal ties which kept the different classes
> of society in a vital and harmonious dependence upon each other
> have, within these 30 years either been greatly impaired or wholly
> dissolved. . . . All that kind of feeling has vanished—in like manner,
> the connexion between the trading and landed interests of country
> towns undergoes no modification whatsoever from personal feeling,
> whereas within my memory it was almost wholly governed by it. A
> country squire, or substantial yeoman, used formerly to resort to the
> same shops which his father had frequented before him, and nothing
> but a serious injury real or supposed would have appeared to him a
> justification for breaking up a connexion which was attended with
> substantial amity and interchanges of hospitality from generation to
> generation. All this moral cement is dissolved, habits and prejudices

are broken and rooted up; nothing being substituted in their place but a quickened self[-]interest, with more extensive views,—and wider dependencies,—but more lax in proportion as they are wider.[39]

Like Ferguson, who describes the commercial "intercourse after the bands of affection are broken," Wordsworth notes that the "connexion" between different classes "undergoes no modification whatsoever from personal feeling." The division of labor, and "self[-]interest," rather than producing a "harmonious dependence" between classes, has only intensified "the cash nexus and class divisions," and has led to the dissolution of "moral cement."[40]

Although it is appealing to dwell on how the Romantic era and the Enlightenment were times of connectedness, and how individuals formed networks (perhaps analogous to today's social media), media in this period did not only bring people together, and the density of communication networks did not necessarily mean a greater overall sense of affective contact or fellow feeling. There is always another side to the connected condition; the dream of communication is inextricable from the reality or anxiety of disconnection. Shelley's fragment hints at this fact insofar as the otherwise similar "external attributes" and an existing, underlying sense of togetherness are what heighten—and go hand in hand with—the pathos of the lamented "interval between us" and the "greater distance" he feels. More to the point, routine contact and more regular communication practices can and did aggravate, rather than alleviate, the feeling of social atomization, or even cause it in the first place. Here is Ferguson's republican version of this thought: "The members of a community may . . . have no common affairs to transact, but those of trade: Connections, indeed, or transactions, in which probity and friendship may still take place; but in which the national spirit, whose ebbs and flows we are now considering, cannot be exerted."[41] Wordsworth's letter too ties the condition of greater connectedness—which allows for "more extensive views . . . and wider dependencies" of business—to the laxity of a different kind of "connexion" founded on, and reinforcing, "personal feeling." From the sociological perspective, communication infrastructures disconnect as much as they connect. Émile Durkheim posits that a more concentrated form of social organization, arising from improvements in communications media and transportation infrastructure, as well as from urbanization, is the very cause of the division of labor: "The number and speed of the means of communication and transmission" (what he calls "material density" and what we would deem good infrastructure) meant that "similar occupations located at different sites over an area enter into fiercer rivalry."[42] This evolutionary mechanism, in turn, drove the creation of newer, narrower specializations.[43] Durkheim emphatically puts it this way: "We state, not that the growth and condensation of societies *permit* a greater division of labor, but that they *necessitate* it. It is not the instrument whereby that division is brought about; but it is its determining cause."[44]

Now, "material density," according to Durkheim, should ordinarily correspond, as it did in France, with "dynamic" or "moral" density, which he defines as the shared feeling of a collective life, where "individuals . . . are effectively engaged not only in commercial but also moral relationships with each other" and "live their life together in common."[45] We can perceive what Durkheim will later call "moral density" in earlier incarnations in Ferguson ("the bands of society," "the national spirit"), in Wordsworth ("personal feeling" at a collective level, "hospitality," "moral cement"), and in Shelley ("love"). When there is a kind of correspondence between material density and moral density, a society is marked by a harmonious organic solidarity. But as Durkheim—along with Ferguson, Wordsworth, and Shelley—suggests, this did not happen in England. Material density did not lead to moral density:

> As for the material density—if this is understood as not only the number of inhabitants per unit of area, but also the development of the means of communication and transmission—this is *normally* in proportion to the dynamic density. . . . However, there are exceptions, and one would expose oneself to serious error if the moral concentration of a community were always judged according to the degree of physical concentration that it represented. Roads, railways, etc. [and one can reasonably include those objects and practices put under the

heading of "communications"] can serve commercial exchanges better than they can serve the fusion of populations, of which they can
give only a very imperfect indication. This is the case in England.[46]

Communicative connectedness in England developed, as did the division of labor and commercial interdependence, without an attendant
sense of large-scale sentimental social coalescence; networks of communication and transportation, far from only connecting people, were at the
same time the very cause of "the interval between us" felt by Shelley.[47]
With respect to analyses of Romantic or other media and communications practices, one might say that ideally they would observe the distinctions between (say) sibling relationality and a connection to a milliner or
a solicitor—even if the latter are "connections, indeed . . . in which probity and friendship may still take place"—rather than reduce the complex dynamics of each interaction by incorporating them all into, or even
positing in the first place, flat networks of affective circulation on the
basis of communicative frequency or density.

Thus it is not only, in Wordsworth's terms from the "Preface" to *Lyrical Ballads* (1800), that "the increasing accumulation of men in cities" and
"the uniformity of their occupations" cause "a craving for extraordinary
incident which the rapid communication of intelligence hourly gratifies."[48] The causality goes in the other direction too; there is a kind of
vicious cycle. As Wordsworth and Shelley sensed too, I think, "the rapid
communication of intelligence" and "the increasing accumulation of
men in cities" were arguably themselves first responsible for the material concentration (that is, Durkheim's "material density") that led to a
greater division of labor and the monotonous "uniformity" of each kind
of work—which, in turn, led to the "craving for extraordinary incident
which the rapid communication of intelligence hourly gratifies." Wordsworth's depiction of his reading audience as those in a state of "savage torpor" is a precise allusion to Smith's figure of "the man whose
whole life is spent in performing a few simple operations . . . and who
has no occasion to exert his understanding": as Smith describes him,
"the torpor of his mind renders him, not only incapable of relishing or

bearing a part in any rational conversation, but of conceiving any generous, noble, or tender sentiment."[49] This kind of "torpor," then, led to yet
more craving for stimulation by the very communication infrastructures
that created the confining "limited perspective" in the first place, and
which Comte linked to specialization. The issue in Romantic-era media
and communications is not exclusively or primarily the fact of connec-
tivity. Instead, the main problems are the historically specific sense of
disconnectedness in concentration or connectedness (recall Ferguson's
identification of "intercourse after the bands of affection are broken"),
and the possibility of connection amid a pervasive, historically specific
sense of disconnectedness (a big issue, among others, to which Romantic
poets and sociologists addressed themselves). Certain familiar lines from
Romantic poetry begin to sound like compressions of significant questions about social structure: lines such as "greetings where no kindness
is" from Wordsworth's "Tintern Abbey," or "some inane and vacant smile"
from The Cenci come first to mind, but there are countless others.[50] Not
mere complaints about personal encounters with coldness and hypocrisy
in social life, they also, taken together, form a poetic-sociological topos,
marking the non-exchange of affects that bind and matter the most, amid
a present characterized by an intensified communications environment.
This too is alone togetherness, or together aloneness.

From the Labor of Love to a Poetry of Ambiversion

In response to the estrangement between individuals, felt to be yawning
to the point that the ties constitutive of society were in danger of dissolution, Shelley in "On Love" proposes or wishes that love is an original psychic human principle that might reconstruct "community" ("On
Love," 503). Colored by necessitarian doctrine, Shelley's essay would
like to believe that what Ferguson diagnosed as the broken "bands of
affection" might be healed, and a social reintegration realized, by the
magnetic, attractive force of "love," a force as natural and universal as
gravitation.[51] Shelleyan love counters Adam Smith's own irreducible
psychic principle, the "trucking disposition": a "certain propensity

in human nature . . . the propensity to truck, barter, and exchange one thing for another."[52] Nevertheless, Shelley eventually intuits the inadequacy of love to resolve the modern problem of sentimental dispersal-in-interconnectedness, the problem of absent moral density within material density.

He does this vividly in *Epipsychidion*. His later disavowal of the poem— "it is a production of a portion of me already dead" (*Letters*, 2:262–63)— may be read as a recognition that his brand of love resembles the ties of interdependence characteristic of modern commercial societies. At first glance, it appears that *Epipsychidion* is articulating a critique of the division of labor. For example, the poem criticizes the practice of monogamy via a conceit that likens it to monotonous, alienated labor:

> Narrow
> The heart that loves, the brain that contemplates,
> The life that wears, the spirit that creates
> One object, and one form, and builds thereby
> A sepulchre for its eternity. (169–73)

We have seen Ferguson, Comte, and Wordsworth attribute this kind of monotony or uniformity to "the separation of professions," by virtue of which a laborer "contemplates" and "creates" only "one object." Yet, if Shelley appears to reject both monogamy and the division of labor, the curious fact that he articulates matters of "the heart" in a vocabulary of the "narrow"-ness of specialization implies that Shelleyan love is not quite the answer to the age of separations: the economic drive toward division defines, and thereby troubles, the poem's central amatory reflections. Even though Shelley seeks to distinguish the dividing or sharing of "love" (that is, free love) from the division of "gold and clay" (where "to divide is . . . to take away" [160–61]) as well as from the division of "suffering and dross" (where to divide is to "Diminish till it is consumed away" [178–79]), one cannot help but find behind Shelley's case for free love the prevailing economic logic of division, the defining sociological concern of his time.

In the same vein, at a different moment in the poem, Shelley figures love using the very terms by which the division of labor was celebrated, that is, as a harmonious system made of distinct parts:

> We—are we not formed, as notes of music are,
> For one another, though dissimilar;
> Such difference without discord, as can make
> Those sweetest sounds, in which all spirits shake
> As trembling leaves in a continuous air? (142–46)

As close to a poetic rendering of Durkheim's organic solidarity as one can find in Romantic poetry, Shelley's "difference without discord" rehearses the unmistakable signature of a social system made up of specialized parts working in concert; the image is analogous to Wordsworth's formerly held sociological assumption of "harmonious dependence." Like later readers of Adam Smith, Shelley in his love poem points to the uncanny similarities between sympathy or love and the specific kind of solidarity which issues from commercial dependencies—in other words, that love itself may be said to love exchange, thirsting after its likeness.[53]

In *Epipsychidion*, such figures depicting love as organic solidarity go beyond a superficial resemblance between the two, because the poem dramatizes quite explicitly how individuals in relationships realize the dynamic of "difference without discord"—giving a new meaning to the phrase, a "labor of love." For example, there is the thinly veiled biographical allegory in which Mary Shelley is the moon and Teresa Viviani is the sun, together the "Twin Spheres of light who rule this passive Earth" (345):

> And all their many-mingled influence blend,
> If equal, yet unlike, to one sweet end;—
> So ye, bright regents, with alternate sway
> Govern my sphere of being, night and day! (358–61)

In a now recognizable motif, the two celestial bodies are portrayed as performing different, yet complementary labor. They are "equal, yet unlike" elements that produce "one sweet end"; their concerted "alternate sway" takes turns to "govern" the earth, in the way the world of work is

also governed in modernity. Perhaps most memorably, in the final movement of the poem, the speaker identifies himself as the property owner
("This isle and house are mine" [513]), and Emily as, dissimilarly yet essentially in this insular division of labor, something like a housewife: the
"lady of the solitude" (514). *Epipsychidion* reflects back at Shelley, when he
is most intent on illustrating how love might work, not the mirror image
of the "ideal prototype of everything excellent or lovely" ("On Love," 504)
but an image of a modern social system of enmeshed, complementary
labor, about which he has been at pains to imagine an alternative. The
poem would like to differentiate the concept of division in the realm of
"pleasure and love and thought" (180) from division as it operates in the
age of separations, but the poem repeatedly falls back on language suggestive of their likeness.

One problem with Shelleyan love, then, is that it is like organic solidarity, the kinds of interactions in a connected world (material density)
devoid of true mutual understanding (moral density)—possibly even, in
Shelley's darker portrait of this kind of world, occasions for "repulse and
disappointment." Another problem with love—this one too thematized
by *Epipsychidion*—comes from the other direction. The amatory poem
intimates that love, when it is not reduced to the model of differentiated
modern labor, is equally in peril of lapsing into a morbid fusion of identi-
ties. As the poem hastens to an end, Shelley writes:

> We shall become the same, we shall be one
> Spirit within two frames, oh! wherefore two?
> . . .
> One hope within two wills, one will beneath
> Two overshadowing minds, one life, one death,
> One Heaven, one Hell, one immortality,
> And one annihilation. (573–74; 584–87)

The poem began with more confident professions of union, of one individual melting into another: "I am not thine: I am a part of *thee*" (52).
The ending to the poem similarly attempts to imagine love as coalescence rather than combination: "oh! wherefore two?" and goes on to

imagine "two meteors" that join and become "the same" (577). But by the end of this passage, the speaker is more skeptical and anxious; thinking through the implications of his words, he equates "love" with "one Hell" and "one annihilation."

The recognition of this other problem with love—as a union that could annihilate both individuals—is no less of a poetic-sociological thought, bringing Shelley close to what Durkheim will refer to as "agglutination."[54] In arguing that an "organic solidarity" based on complementarity ensues from the division of labor, Durkheim warns against this kind of sameness, which would bring to a halt the dynamic system of differences he is outlining. Explaining how individuals imagine and internalize others in society (as "images"), Durkheim explains that "when union derives from the similarity between two images, it consists in an agglutination." Unlike the division of labor, wherein "they remain outside each other and are linked only because they are distinct," in this form of psychic and social lumping, "they fuse completely, becoming one."[55] The implication for *Epipsychidion*—which is thoroughly inflected by sociological thought, or rather thinks through a sociological crisis in terms of relationships between individuals—is that the "scheme of life" proposed by the poem and this Edenic couple would reproduce a social structure that, in swerving away from networks of interest, and in order to maintain true "bands of affection," would veer into the other problems of homogeneity and social stasis.[56] It is likely too that Shelley sees his revamped society for the strikingly regressive vision that it is: a pre-commercial, pre-industrial, pastoral societal phase recognizable from Enlightenment stadial and conjectural histories. The poem concludes with figures of discrete but united individuals, but such figures gradually give way to the repetition of singularity ("One . . . one . . . one . . . "). Evocative of the tyranny of "one will" on another, these final images are disquietingly consistent with the masculine impositions exemplified by mesmeric control and Coleridgean voluntarism, both of which continually troubled Shelley.[57] It is not clear which would be worse for Shelley: love reduced to organic solidarity or to the agglutination of subjectivities, the destruction of two for the sake of unity.

Reframed as poetic-sociological reflections— conversant with contemporaneous sociological discourse, and anticipating later works, like
Durkheim's—*Epipsychidion* shows Shelley in the process of pondering,
through the vehicle of a love poem, the urgent sociological question of
his historical moment: How does one live in an age of separations? At
first, love seems to be the answer, but the poem shows Shelley writing
himself into the recognition about the limits of love: that it might be
only another version of the "separation of professions" or that it might
resemble a deadly agglutination at both personal and societal levels. Yet
still other moments in the poem intimate that if love is not a solution
to the Romantic-era connected condition, poetry might be. In addition
to the poem's sociological dimension, there is the media-theoretical
aspect: it matters a great deal that the entire poem is framed by inquiries into poetic communication. As Andrew Franta rightly points out,
Epipsychidion reflects on its own "reception, dissemination, and transmission." Where Franta demonstrates Shelley's prospective focus on a
future, "proper audience," I wish to comprehend Shelley's poetics not in
terms of audience but as media-theoretical and sociological intimations
about social life.[58]

In particular, the poem occasions in Shelley a serious consideration
of how poetic difficulty allows a poem to be a communicative medium
and, at the same time, not one. Following Thomas Gray's precedent of
envisioning his difficult Pindaric odes as intelligible to some while not
to others—"Vocal to the intelligent alone; but for the crowd they need
interpreters"[59]—Shelley's "Advertisement" for *Epipsychidion* begins by
viewing the poem as a species of communication that may be "suffi-
ciently intelligible to a certain class of readers," but "to a certain other
class . . . incomprehensible."[60] The poem goes on to describe itself similarly. There is always the possibility for poetry to be obscure or "hard,"
with the poetic medium made up of "dim words which obscure" what
it seeks to communicate; at other moments, the same "dim words" can
"[f]lash, lightning-like, with unaccustomed glow." The translated Dante
lyric (*canzone*) that Shelley appended to his "Advertisement" elaborates

on these thoughts of a poem that can be "vocal" and "intelligible" to some, while "incomprehensible" to others:

> My Song, I fear that thou wilt find but few
> Who fitly shall conceive thy reasoning,
> Of such hard matter dost thou entertain;
> Whence, if by misadventure, chance should bring
> Thee to base company (as chance may do),
> Quite unware of what thou dost contain,
> I prithee, comfort thy sweet self again,
> My last delight! tell them that they are dull,
> And bid them own that thou art beautiful.[61]

Dante's *canzone* is particularly appropriate for the poem because it claims that, for select readers (the "few/Who fitly shall conceive thy reasoning"), poetry is indeed a medium insofar as it conveys thoughts and feelings. But for others, because poetry can be *hard*—as Shelley puts it, because a poem can involve "such hard matter"—the poetic medium is only tenuously, or perhaps not at all, a medium, remaining an "incomprehensible" interceding object. These latter readers would remain "quite unaware of what thou ["my song"] dost contain"; like those who cannot appreciate Emily's "music," they would be "deaf to all sweet melody" (6–8). Most importantly, the lyric's addressing of the personified poem as an individual circulating in the social world ("if . . . chance should bring/Thee to base company"), invites one to read the lyric as having additional sociological significance, like *Epipsychidion* itself, and thus implies a striking conceit: just as a "hard" poem might make sense to some while being closed off to others, so an individual can form relationships of mutual understanding (with the "few/Who fitly shall conceive thy reasoning") while encountering indifferent others (those who are "quite unaware of what thou does contain").[62]

We might call this a poetry of ambiversion: the understanding of poetry as communicative and uncommunicative, suggestive of a sociologically informed proposal that this might be a way of negotiating networked life, going back and forth between "extravert and introvert features."[63]

Epipsychidion intimates how poetry may have an inbuilt capacity to transmit or not to transmit, an affective-semantic on/off switch—and, perhaps, the capacity to elicit something between these two poles of contact, perhaps something like Keatsian half-knowledge. And this has implications for the poem's other, sociological concerns about being in a world that feels defined by unprecedented connectedness and, at the same time, by the "interval between us." In other poems too, Shelley figures a poetic mode of interaction. For example, at the start of "The Sensitive-Plant":

> And it opened its fan-like leaves to the light
> And closed them beneath the kisses of night.

"Leaves" elsewhere in Shelley's work stand in for pages and his own writing generally, so his description of the sensitive mimosa plant conjures the materiality of literary works as opened and closed books. But from the perspective of Shelley as poet and media theorist, such lines suggest that literary works can be "open" at some moments to some people, "closed" at other times to or by others. And from the perspective of Shelley as poet and sociologist, such lines suggest that individuals can be "open" at times, and "closed" at other times in the context of densely interconnected social life.

In short, poetry—clear or cloudy, misty, veiled, or dark, and maybe something in between—could model a form of interaction fit for the age of separations, then and perhaps also now. *Epipsychidion* raises the question of how interactions might tend more toward the poetic. It is not quite that Shelley is proposing (or that I am) that literary reading is how society actually works; rather this may be an appropriate way of being in a world of connected-disconnectedness or disconnected-connectedness. Interactions would have the potential of connecting individuals in immersive, intersubjective relations, as in those of poet-audience or "stranger relationality" among readers; such relations involve, but are not finally reducible to, dependencies of exchange, and often surpass them toward a different kind of imagined solidarity.[64] At the same time, individuals would be buffered against the intersubjective encroachments dramatized by *Epipsychidion*, in the same way that mediatedness and the potential for cloudiness, like an opt-out clause, allow readers to curse a work's obscurity and shut the book, or have unintended responses or different responses from other readers, or altogether avoid reading the work—or, as the case may be, leave bottles filled with knowledge or poetry unopened. This latter capacity of ambiversion need not necessarily be reduced to a liberalism of the possessive-individualist kind, and instead points to a poetic-sociological-media theoretical option that is distinct from lamenting networked life, celebrating it, or opting into it ambivalently. In Shelley's case, a vision of this kind would have had to overcome somehow the "dissociation" of pre-disciplinary sociology from poetry that Williams described, and overcome too the norm of communicative clarity in modernity. Neither of these happened. But it is worth appreciating Shelley's attempt—as poet and sociologist and media theorist—at imagining a different basis for sociality. If not quite summed up by a motto like "good 'figured curtain[s]' make good neighbors," or a life of allegory, then a poetry of ambiversion for networked life: one can opt in and out, tune in and out, be open or closed.

It cheered mild Spenser, called from Faery-land
To struggle through dark ways.

William Wordsworth, "Scorn not the Sonnet"

We could posit a desire for communication which is so strong, so idealistic and
hence so frustrated, that it becomes inevitably a dream-state.

Geoffrey Hartman, "I. A. Richards and the Dream of Communication"

4   KEATS'S WAYS

The Dark Passages of Mediation and Giving Up Hyperion

Hyperion: A Dream of Communication

In John Keats's journal letter of December 1818–January 1819 to George
and Georgiana (his brother and sister-in-law) in Kentucky, written on the
cusp of what will come to be hailed as his *annus mirabilis*, he offers his
initial thoughts on the recent death of their brother Tom and then meanders into an arresting thought experiment:

> [S]ometimes I fancy an immense separation, and sometimes, as at
> present, a direct communication of spirit with you. . . . Now the rea-
> son why I do not feel at the present moment so far from you is that I
> rememb[er] your Ways and Manners and actions; I known you man-
> ner of thinking, you manner of feeling [sic]: I know what shape your
> joy or your sorrow w[ou]ld take, I know the manner of you walking,
> standing, sauntering, sitting down, laugh[ing,] punning, and evey [sic]
> action so truly that you seem near to me. You will rem[em]ber me in
> the same manner—and the more when I tell you that I shall read a

passage of Shakspeare [sic] every Sunday at ten o Clock—you read one [a]t the same time and we shall be as near each other as blind bodies can be in the same room.[1]

His letter had begun by assuring George and Georgiana that, in the wake of Tom's death, he has "scarce a doubt of immortality of some nature of [or] other" (*Letters*, 2:4). Nor has he any doubt that souls in the afterlife engage in unmediated communication with each other: "That will be one of the grandeurs of immortality—there will be no space and consequently the only commerce between spirits will be by their intelligence of each other—when they will completely understand each other" (*Letters*, 2:5). "Commerce" or communication in immortality would be more like angelic apprehension—in Miltonic terms, more immediately "intuitive" than "discursive," a conceptual gradation Keats knew well and had underlined in his copy of *Paradise Lost*.[2] But in the intriguing thought experiment that follows, Keats transposes the ease of immortal interaction to the real world; he imagines a situation whereby he and his correspondents might achieve a similar kind of instantaneous, reciprocal "intelligence of each other." Because each party possesses an abundant capacity for sympathetic imagination ("I known . . . you manner of feeling" [sic]), if they were to engage in a coordinated reading of Shakespeare, they would establish an intimate transatlantic connection and overcome the "immense separation" between London and Kentucky. Remembering the name of the ship George and Georgiana took to America six months earlier, the *Telegraph*—which alludes to the late eighteenth-century semaphoric communications technology also known as optical telegraphy—while looking ahead to Mark Twain's 1891 satirical treatment of its electric successor, one might name this scene "mental telegraphy." One might even be tempted to call Keats's scenario Shakespearean Skype. His proposal of synchronized reading raises the same question about time difference that the railways made newly urgent in the early nineteenth century, and which lives on in the scheduling of today's planned mediated interactions: "ten o Clock" in whose time zone?[3]

But even as Keats indulges in this fantasy of instantaneous communication, he intimates its counterfactual nature and the obstacles to true contact. Note his final simile: he declines to liken his scenario to sighted individuals each located in far-flung places and hence invisible to one another. That would be the more appropriate simile for the situation he narrates. That would also be a fitting, reflexive image for the act of postal correspondence in which he is participating; as Charles Lamb confesses in "Distant Correspondents" to his addressee in Australia, "I cannot image to myself whereabout you are."[4] Instead, Keats scribbles off the converse simile of "blind bodies . . . in the same room," as though to register, within his own fantasy, a sense that an ineluctable condition of isolation predominates even when individuals are as closely joined as two bodies in the same room, to say nothing of when they are on different continents. Space might be surmountable with sympathy or technology, but subjectivity is not. Keats's simile seems to anticipate "the double logic" of "remediation," serving as a reminder that the intimacy afforded by a mediated encounter is nevertheless counterbalanced by the interposing distance and the mediation(s) it makes necessary.[5]

The discussion to follow takes this thought experiment—a fantasy of rapid communication at a distance, offset by a heightened sense of the difficulties of mutual understanding—to be a paradigmatic rather than a momentary preoccupation for Keats. I offer an overarching claim about Keats and communication in order to frame a hypothesis about *Hyperion*.[6] Communication and communications media remain a significant, although still largely unremarked, concern of Keats's poetry and letters.[7] The pertinacity with which Keats strives to align himself with the long-standing media of poetry and the book may be responsible for the lack of sustained scholarly commentary on his relation to the larger ecology of contemporaneous means of communication. Yet his letter to his brother and sister-in-law captures him relying on myriad ways—residual, dominant, and emergent—to imagine contact at a distance: he mentions spiritual communication, sympathy, and literature (Shakespeare), while ships, the practice of letter writing itself, optical telegraphy, and perhaps even electric telegraphy (in prototype since 1753) lurk just outside the letter's margins.[8] Reminiscent of the diverse sources that make up the thickly allusive texture of his verse, Keats's letter offers a mixture of media and modes of communication, not solely "high piled books" or poetry ("When I have fears that I may cease to be," 3). But in this manner, his letter suggests a blurry, heterogeneous sense of media change as it is under way, in the process of unfolding. Newer media do not "displace older systems with decisive suddenness," David Thorburn and Henry Jenkins observe as they define "media transition" as an "accretive, gradual process."[9] Keats's poetry can be read from the perspective of media transition, and I will be drawing into relation, uneasy relation, his figurations of both the established textual medium and the incipient logic of telecommunication. Or, put in visual terms, this discussion hopes to take Joseph Severn's familiar 1821 portrait of Keats, indoors, hunched over and immersed in deep reading, and superimpose upon it an image of Romantic-era Britain enmeshed in increasingly far-reaching domestic and global communication and transportation networks.[10] In the introduction, I noted that Wordsworth did not fail to sense his era's connected condition, and he wrote with equal parts worry and prescience in his "Preface" to *Lyrical Ballads* (1800) of the "rapid communication of intelligence"; neither did De Quincey, who, echoing Wordsworth, depicts the "rapid transmission of intelligence" of postal tidings in "The English Mail-Coach." Keats, too, beyond his epistolary fantasy of the "commerce" of "intelligence," harbors a conflicted concern with the communication trends of his time, and the "society of flows" then taking shape.[11]

His letter to George and Georgiana contemplates communication in immortality, and his *Hyperion* fragments, for example and most prominently, similarly inquire how immortals communicate between themselves. Through *Hyperion* and his letter, in treating otherworldly communication, Keats points to the limits of human communication: there is only so much one person can know about another person, only a certain extent to which thoughts and feelings can ever be said to be "exchanged" between people—a notion thrown into high relief by the immediate, "intuitive" thought transfer that is reserved as one of the "grandeurs of immortality," the privilege of only angels and gods. But *Hyperion* involves more than that, more than the letter offers. The poem is also about the mortal-immortal relation: the degree to which immortal events, experiences, and sensations can or cannot be communicated to mortals, and hence the important role of mediators, like the narrator in "Hyperion," Moneta in "The Fall," and Keats himself as a re-teller to us mortal readers of violent immortal succession from the Titans to the Olympians. The fragments pit the problem of "mediation" in its most fundamental sense—"a process whereby two different realms, persons, objects, or terms are brought into relation," in this case, nothing less than the process of relating the separate realms of gods and mortals—against the fantasy of instantaneous communication.[12] What we learn from *Hyperion* is that mediation cannot be solved by communications media, and that inevitable impediments to communication only heighten the desire for a perfect, paradoxically immediate medium that could bridge the separateness that defines mediation.

I suggest that this has something to do with why Keats gives up, or gives up on, "Hyperion" and "The Fall." *Gives up* alludes to Keats's own comments on abandoning the epic ("I have given up Hyperion—there were too many Miltonic inversions in it. . . . I wish to give myself up to other sensations" [*Letters*, 2:167]). But rather than emphasizing Keats's renunciation of Miltonic style, I wish to focus on the meaningfulness of the fragments precisely because of the unfinished form in which Keats offers or gives them up. Readers familiar with the poems will recall that Keats, with fine suddenness, aborts his first essay at epic form during Apollo's deification scene (the beginning of which is on the left in the following quotation), and abandons his second attempt not long after the speaker of "The Fall" gains access to Moneta's brain (below in the following):

> "[Y]et I can read
> A wondrous lesson in thy silent face:
> Knowledge enormous makes a God of me.
> Names, deeds, gray legends, dire events, rebellions,
> Majesties, sovran voices, agonies,
> Creations and destroyings, all at once
> Pour into the wide hollows of my brain."
> ("Hyperion," 3.111-17)

I ached to see what things the hollow brain
Behind enwombed: what high tragedy
In the dark secret chambers of her skull
Was acting.

. . .

"Let me behold, according as thou said'st
What in thy brain so ferments to and fro."—
No sooner had this conjuration pass'd
My devout lips, than side by side we stood . . .
("The Fall," I.276–92)

With remarkable fidelity, these scenes enact the instantaneous access
to another's "thinking" and "feeling" about which Keats had fantasized
in his letter, which he composed as he worked on *Hyperion*. In the first
instance, Apollo reads Mnemosyne's face, and that leads to the instant
transmission—the "at once/Pour[ing]"—of her knowledge from her brain
to his ("Names, deeds, gray legends, dire events, rebellions . . . "). In the
second, "The Fall" employs virtually the same operation, though with the
quest romance speaker "pouring" himself into Moneta's "hollow brain"
rather than receiving its information. These pendant scenes never diminish in their capacity to surprise or confound. Several analyses of *Hyperion*,
predating mine, describe the fragments with recourse to medial vocabulary: Geoffrey Hartman and, more recently, Rei Terada characterize *Hyperion* in cinematic terms, while Charles Rzepka's reading of Keats's career
links "The Fall" and Keats's overall maturation with his self-figuration
as an impresario overseeing, with theatrical capability, a production of
epic.[13] The recursive structure of "The Fall" courts interpretations reliant
on ideas associated with remediation (that is, the later fragment screens,
remakes, or stages the earlier one). I dwell quite differently on these scenes
of thought-transfer-like transmission and their relation to Keats's habitual way throughout his oeuvre of depicting communication and modeling
it poetically, that is, in the medium of poetry.

  This chapter hypothesizes that such dramatizations of, in a phrase
from Keats's letter, "direct communication" in *Hyperion* grate against
Keats's career-long devotion to figures of slow, perplexed communication,

to the difficult processes of mediation and reading alike; that is, the wish for immediacy comes up against the problem of mediation. There are two competing logics of communication at work in Keats's poetry and his letters, and I identify them, taking my cue from Keats's writing, as *pouring* versus *dark passages*. The first, pouring, is exemplified by the scenes in *Hyperion* just quoted, when Keats depicts the comparatively fast and unmediated transmission of knowledge between characters. Stopping short of performing a reading that claims a direct link between the communication technology of telegraphy and Keats, I instead understand *Hyperion*, like his letter to George and Georgiana, as placing and dating him within nineteenth-century British *tele-culture*—Nicholas Royle's term for the cultural fascination with the possibilities of relatively quick communication at a distance, and the often muddled or syncretic mixture of beliefs concerning communication that these possibilities entailed.[14] Tele-culture is a good example of how communication fantasies depend not only or primarily on the medium or the technology, but rather on the desire for rapid communication: indeed, tele-culture can be said to be in mutually reinforcing relations with the New Rhetorical fantasy of "easy" and clear communication (discussed in this book's introduction), the discourse of sympathy, and perhaps too the quasi-science of mesmeric contact at a distance.[15] Moreover, as we have seen with reference to shorthand in Chapter Two, it matters little how rapidly the communication technology actually operates: the *wish* for speed and immediacy, as much as (or rather than) the reality, fuels the rhetoric. In practice, early semaphores relayed encoded signals for single letters, words, or phrases at a time between towers, and a codebook was necessary for decoding the telegraphic signals back into those letters, words, or phrases.[16] But tele-culture—and those immersed in it, including the Romantic poets—tended to celebrate mostly the telegraph's ability to send information instantaneously rather than the slowness associated with the labor of encoding and decoding: thus the "telegraphic imagery" that Celeste Langan and Maureen N. McLane identify in Shelley's "Ode to Liberty" ("Liberty/From heart to heart, from tower to tower, o'er Spain, /Scattering contagious fire into the sky,/Gleamed"), and Coleridge's use of the telegraph as a metaphor for immediacy in a notebook entry that reminds him, "forget not to observe what a vast number of incidents the masts & sails of a Ship can represent, a sort of natural Telegraph."[17] In short, the telegraph was remarkably fast and slow, but the discourse around telegraphy tended to emphasize the former.

In contrast to pouring, and against such rhetoric of telegraphic speed, the idea of "dark passages" indicates Keats's commitment to halting, meandering, and darkling reading and the forms of communication that encourage or require them. Such communication includes the necessarily figured or analogized way that immortal experience must be descriptively mediated to mortals ("Some mourning words, which in our feeble tongue/Would come in these like accents" ["Hyperion," 1.49–50]), but also includes, for Keats, the linguistic style defining *poetry* itself. More often than not, when Keats thinks about a medium, he understands it on the analogy of the "opaque element" of textuality ("Hyperion," 2.23). I organize my explanation of this logic of communication around classical rhetoric's concept of *ductus*, which envisions the frequently laborious passage, or "way," through the textual medium. While almost certainly unfamiliar to Keats, the concept, as heuristic, reveals how he typically understands the difficulties of mediation in terms of literary communication, a process that for Keats involves "repressing haste" ("The Fall," 1.94)—a process that is therefore both antithetical to, and yet inextricable from, the dream of communication.

A reading along these lines, of Keats's negotiation of slow reading and quick transmission, can open new avenues of inquiry into his poetry. It complements the ongoing program of situating Keats in history (and especially politics) that has occupied Keatsian scholarship from early New Historicist polemics of the late 1970s and the 1980s to a recent special issue of *Studies in Romanticism*.[18] Heeding Lisa Gitelman's reminder that history is always mediated as well as stored in media, while recalling Keats's own interest in how and if "melodious utterance" can be "save[d]" ("The Fall," 1.6, 9), we might ask: What can we learn from how Keats's interceding imagination makes sense of the communicative flows crisscrossing and shaping his world?[19] Hence, although T. S. Eliot concluded from Keats's letters that, in comparison to Shelley, "Keats has no theory,"

I hope to show that "ways" of reading and communicating are for Keats something like a theory insofar as they are the means by which he makes his world intelligible to himself, and finally to us.[20] But as my hypothesis has it, even though each of the *Hyperion* poems acts out a scene of nearly instantaneous communicative transfer, these scenes are finally dissonant with Keats's commitment to the laborious ways of reading, and render further composition impossible.

Dark Passages: The *Ductus* of Keats's Imagination

Keats's readers have long noticed and theorized the ornate quality of his verse, its overt displays of figuration and refusals of referential language—in short, its poeticity. His professed ethos of "Negative Capability" (*Letters*, 1:193) and the corollary poetic effect of ambiguity made Keats a perfect case for William Empson's culminating seventh type of ambiguity, and innumerable formalist readings thereafter.[21] Critics continue to address these qualities of his poetry, variously referring to its "complexity," "indeterminacy," and "Keatsian solecism."[22] Meanwhile, other readers, from Marjorie Levinson to James Chandler, have explicated the social and political inflections of Keats's early reception and its influence on his maturer style. Chandler, for example, discusses the Cockney concept of "smokeability"—a susceptibility to being easily understood and/or mocked—and reminds us that "we must not fail to recognize the extent to which Keats's sensitivity to being 'smoked' by the reviewing establishment contributed to the hermeneutic density for which he is now revered."[23]

At the same time, Keats's poetry, as Andrew Bennett argues, anticipates and extensively prefigures those densities, complexities, and indeterminacies met by his readers.[24] I also examine what Bennett calls the "figures of reading" in Keats's poetry, but with particular attention to his recurrent figurations of the space of the textual medium: a text imagined in spatial terms, or a space imagined in textual terms, within which one makes one's way—slowly, with difficulty, and often in darkness. In demonstrating Keats's reliance on these figures, I heuristically call on the term *ductus*, which refers to "the con*duct* of a thinking mind on its way through a composition."[25] It is true that figurations of a peripatetic subject who wanders and struggles through a text can be accounted for in several ways. The idea of a textual pathway can be traced to certain genres and modes (epic, romance, allegory), themes (progress, pilgrimage, exile), and perhaps even to the trajectory of narrative itself, while the prizing of obscurity and difficulty is surely colored by the discourse of sublimity.[26] And by Levinson's reading, for example, such thematizations of textual travel, and the irony of lines like "Much have I travell'd in the realms of gold" ("On First Looking into Chapman's Homer"), point to the socioeconomic fact of Keats's actual inexperience in travel, his textually mediated, second-hand experience.[27] Complementing rather than discounting these other literary and social valences, I advance the notion of *ductus* for a couple of reasons. First, it directs us to the deep origins, in scriptural reading, of tropes associated with a course through a textual space made difficult or "dark" by figuration. These tropes circulate implicitly in Keats's writing, but come to the surface when he alludes directly to the hermeneutic tradition in his "life of Allegory" letter, to which I will shortly return. Second, *ductus* helps to describe how Keats figures the process of mediated communication: he often imagines an encumbered tour through some kind of textual channel, as though traveling through the medium itself.

According to Mary Carruthers, the concept of *ductus* was first defined in a textbook by the fourth-century Latin rhetorician Fortunatianus, where it is conceived as the "flow" or movement of a composition, especially "the way that a composition guides a person to its various goals" (78). *Ductus* thus originated as a technical term with specific reference to the rhetorical "disposition" or structural organization of an argument. But *ductus* also pertained more broadly to the acts of reading and imagination that took place in the context of medieval monastic meditation. Fortunatianus's contemporary, Augustine, in *De doctrina Christiana*, depicts meditative prayer as a route taken by the meditator through the scriptures.[28] Moreover, when meditators visualized making their way through the Bible, they would stop and puzzle over highly allegorical or figurative, that is, dark, places. These difficult ornaments and passages were mentally taxing, but they were for this same reason beneficial: highly allegorical spots served a mnemonic function (that is, they were memorable) and counteracted the very real problem of boredom, and acted as sites for mental expatiation and meditative-interpretive creativity. "All figurative language can function for a reader in this way," Carruthers explains, but "the 'difficult tropes' and schemes of the Bible were particularly important, what Augustine called *obscuritas utilis et salubris*, 'productive and health-giving difficulty'" (116). *Ductus* evokes a journey through a text, within which one encounters obscure, but also intellectually salutary, places.

The diffusion into secular literature of tropes deriving from scriptural reading and its difficult ornaments is a vast and complex story in its own right.[29] Although Keats probably never looked into or sat down to read Fortunatianus, he was likely familiar with Augustine and could have absorbed ideas about dark figures through "the revival of interest in monasticism in the nineteenth century" identified by Peter Manning, which centered on the Reverend Thomas Dudley Fosbrooke's publications about monks; Keats's comment to Shelley that "My Imagination is a monastery and I am its Monk" (*Letters*, 2:323) suggests some degree of his interest in this revival.[30] In any case, Keats had ready access to figures associated with difficult textual paths via the English literary tradition; Paul de Man's observation that "we are reading the work of a man whose experience is mainly literary" is germane in this instance too.[31] A likely source is Spenser's own "darke conceit," *The Faerie Queene*.[32] In the Proem to Book 6, for instance, Spenser describes the "waies" through the "delightfull land of Faery," where "waies" refers in part to the narrative of the allegory itself. Spenser describes this "waie" as "tedious travell," and "travell" can be read simultaneously as travel and travail.[33] That is to say, the phrase likens the course through the poem to tiresome movement and tiresome work in a manner consonant with the notion of *ductus* and the way one makes through a dark text; the general association between Spenser and "dark ways" can be glimpsed not only in Keats, but in Wordsworth's allusion to the same in "Scorn not the Sonnet."[34] Following Spenser closely, Keats uses the "ways" trope in *Endymion* during a similarly self-reflexive moment, even activating the same travel-travail pun. Endymion says:

> And when 'tis his,
> After long toil and travelling, to miss
> The kernel of his hopes, how more than vile:
> Yet, for him there's refreshment even in toil . . . (2.144–47)

Such mentions of toilsome travel in the poem, pointing self-consciously to the unfolding narrative and the phenomenon of reading the poem, are pervasive in *Endymion*. Bennett explains that there is in the poem a "significant homology between physical wandering or disordered space on the one hand, and imaginative or mental wondering or confusion on the other." In other words, Endymion's circuitous journey parallels the "wondering, amazement, and bewilderment [caused] by the confusing and dilated organization of the poem." *Endymion*'s readers, no less than Endymion himself, can be described using the dead metaphor of being "lost."[35] Diverging now from Bennett's reading, I would reframe these figures of textual travel not only as proleptic figures through which Keats anticipates how his readers will experience his poetry, but also as clues to how he imagines things and people moving through space more fundamentally—how he envisions "ways" in general. In his letter on "The vale of Soul-making," he formulates nothing less than the world he inhabits as "the medium of a world like this" or "an Elemental space" featuring "Pains and troubles," through which one struggles and wends, just as a child haltingly proceeds through a text in learning to read (*Letters*, 2:102). And these thoughts flow into the sonnet ("On Fame") copied out in the same letter and its opening figure of "Life's book" (*Letters*, 2:104). It seems that when Keats attempts to visualize his own life or the world he lives in, his mind turns to the idea of a medium, and when he thinks about a medium, he visualizes texts, often difficult ones.

Keats's well-known passage about a "life of Allegory" alludes explicitly to traditional conceptions of obscure, allegorical language, and likens once again the difficulties encountered in the course of one's life to the difficulties of figurative language met by a reader progressing through a text:

> [T]hey are very shallow people who take every thing literal[.] A Man's life of any worth is a continual allegory—and very few eyes can see the Mystery of his life—a life like the scriptures, figurative—which such people can no more make out than they can the hebrew Bible. Lord Byron cuts a figure—but he is not figurative—Shakspeare [sic] led a life of Allegory; his works are the comments on it— (*Letters*, 2:67)

Because the letter is so familiar, it is useful to parse the series of categorical, binary distinctions that Keats makes:

"life of any worth"—a worthless life
Allegorical—"literal"
"Mystery," obscurity—clarity, prominence
Scripture, "hebrew Bible"—non-scriptural writing
non-shallow people—"shallow" people
"figurative"—"cuts a figure"
Shakespeare and Keats—Byron

The main conceit of Keats's letter likens "a life of any worth" to the idea of figurativeness, of which the "Mystery" of scripture is the supreme instance. At first, the metaphor seems puzzling or unpromising since it is not clear why Keats links his idea of the good life to abstract notions such as metaphoricity and allegory. Yet the point of Keats's conceit swims into our ken upon grasping that it hinges on two senses of "obscurity": socioeconomic or social obscurity (as in the "destiny obscure" of Gray's "Elegy"), and the linguistic obscurity associated with allegorical passages of scripture and, eventually, poetic and literary language. The letter attempts to confer the scriptural authority of linguistic obscurity to social obscurity, attempting to recuperate the latter. In so doing, Keats appeals also to the principles of Burkean sublimity, namely its association of obscurity with aesthetic power.[36] But the broader context that renders Keats's conceit intelligible involves the "way" of scripture—littered with dark, allegorical places—that he wants to liken to the course of a middling life featuring its own distresses. By this analogy, semantic clarity and literalness would equate to prominence, "to cut[ting] a figure" (that is, being the opposite of "obscure"). On a personal level for Keats, Byron's aristocratic ease and social prominence are like the ease of clear language—an ease, Keats would say, not without considerable bitterness, indicative of shallowness and productive of "proud bad verse" ("The Fall," 1.208). On a broader intellectual level, Keats justifies the figurative dense-ness of literary language. He repudiates the dominant stylistic ideal of clarity, installed by the New Rhetoric and influencing all writing, literary and otherwise, through Romanticism and beyond—and repudiates too the kind of instantaneous, easy communication about which he fantasizes in the letter to George and Georgiana considered earlier, as well as in the letter considered in the introduction.[37] Against the idea of transparency, Keats's poetic theory foregrounds—and celebrates—the darkness of the poetic medium and linguistic-communicative mediation generally.

From this vantage, it becomes easier to recognize Keats's May 1818 let-ter to John Hamilton Reynolds, where he famously constructs an elaborate analogy of a tour through a "Mansion of Many Apartments" (*Letters*, 1:280), as a variation on his habitual visions of obscure, figurative trails. The tour signifies two processes, each unfolding on a different scale of time. The first process is the advancement of English poetry (the "gregarious advance of intellect" or "a grand march of intellect" [*Letters*, 1:281, 282]) that has forged on between Milton and Wordsworth. The second process recapitu-lates the national tradition of poetry but at the scale of an individual poet's maturation—more specifically, the growth of a poet's mind as plotted by Wordsworth in "Tintern Abbey."[38] These valences are quite clear, but the significance of Keats's peculiar implication that both forms of progress lead to "dark Passages" (*Letters*, 1:281) is less apparent. But read in relation to his thoughts on a "life of Allegory," the dark passages begin to sound less like a hallway and more like the textual "way" that he so often visual-izes. There are precedents in *Endymion*, where he hints at the polysemy of "passage" in order to evoke a mind wandering through a text: Endymion descends into the underworld "Through winding passages, where same-ness breeds/Vexing conceptions of some sudden change" (2.234–36); and later in Book 2, Keats writes again that Endymion "wound/Through a dim passage" (708-9). Glossed in this fashion, Keats's letter implies that poetic development both in an individual and at the level of literary history ideally trends toward dark passages. Unlike Wordsworth, who would take a very different position—that simplicity rather than ornateness of language will prevail, and that seemingly "clear," brief language can actually be *more* puzzling—Keats proposes that the poet's progress and the progress of poetry alike involve the gradual darkening of the poetic-linguistic medium, an increasing metaphoricity. Regarding his stylistic advice to Shelley, "'load every rift' of your subject with ore" (*Letters*, 2:323), one might guess that "ore," in Keats's metaphor, equals metaphor itself.

The "figures of reading" in Keats's poetry are shaped by his premises concerning the dimming of textual "ways" through figuration, which have their own intellectual genealogy traceable to the dark ornaments of scripture. Scenes specifically of puzzled, confused readers in Keats's verse often feature the same dark, encumbered routes that structure the imagery of his letters. "The Eve of Saint Mark" is a good example. Here is Bertha's halted progress through an illuminated book:

> The bells had ceased, the prayers begun,
> And Bertha had not yet half done
> A curious volume, patch'd and torn,
> That all day long, from earliest morn,
> Had taken captive her two eyes
> Among its golden broideries;
> Perplex'd her with a thousand things ... (23-29)

Like a reader paused by, and pausing over, the obscure tropes of scripture, Bertha is "perplex'd"—confused, but also entangled or snagged, as in the original sense of *perplex*—as she reads through her "curious volume."[39] And once again playing with the idea of textual darkness, Keats writes that, "the dusk eve left her dark/Upon the legend of St. Mark" (50-52), where "dark" suggests Bertha's puzzlement as much as the dim reading conditions of dusk. Other scenes from Keats's works come to mind too.[40] Like puzzled Bertha, Porphyro in "The Eve of St. Agnes" first runs into "the old beldame" (90) Angela in the castle, and ends up stumped by her expression: associating Angela with a book, and describing Porphyro's confusion as a failed attempt at reading, Keats narrates, "Porphyro upon her face doth look,/Like puzzled urchin on an aged crone/Who keepeth clos'd a wond'rous riddle-book" (127-30). If capaciously conceived, the category of such moments involving flummoxed readers as well as things that are "hard . . . to understand" ("Lamia," 2.6) in Keats's poetry would even include the inquisitive speaker attempting to parse the Grecian Urn's images and its enigmatic concluding formulation; mythical Argus, appearing in the opening conceit of the Paolo and Francesca sonnet, who is not only "lulled" but also "baffled" (2) by Hermes's story into lapsing from surveillance duty; and in "The Caps and Bells," Crafticant meticulously records bizarre omens and occurrences though their meanings elude him ("Could not conceive what Coralline was at" [672-74]). Keats's poetry and letters obsess over the feel of not to get it.

Pouring: *Hyperion* and the Dead End of Direct Communication

The letters and poems being considered here have a certain consistency when it comes to Keats's positive valuation of dark passages—the rhetorical and literary historical tradition, imagery, figures, and scenarios affiliated with the difficulties of communication, and particularly of reading. By contrast, the *Hyperion* fragments reveal fascinating contradictions and complexities about such matters as immediacy, mediation, and transparent versus obscure language, and suggest that Keats—like the other poets treated in this book—was of at least two minds about communication. As I hypothesized at the start of this chapter, in the case of *Hyperion*, the tension between Keats's different logics of communication ("dark passages" versus tele-culture-inflected "pouring") play a role in his abandonment of his first attempt at the poem and then the second.

Several of *Hyperion*'s characters can be linked to the figurative and thematic array of dark passages, and are therefore consistent with the other characters we have seen similarly portrayed (Argus, Bertha, Crafticant, and company). For example, Saturn's text-based incomprehension of the

Olympian succession in "Hyperion" joins him with Keats's other characters who are perplexed during their dealings with a text. Saturn tells the other Titans that he has studied "that old spirit-leaved book," "pore[d] on Nature's universal scroll," and "read [them] deep" but still cannot find reason for the Titans' overthrow: "No, no-where can unriddle, though I search" (2.133-151). Beyond the central figure of Saturn, the fallen Titans as a whole find themselves in an "opaque element," and even Hyperion, from his position on his "orbed fire" (1.165), "cannot see—but darkness, death and darkness" ("Hyperion," 1.242). Despite or because of the Olympian succession underway, the Titans as a group fit particularly well the profile of the perplexed Keatsian character who finds himself wondering or in darkness, the imagery with which Keats typically figures "deep" reading.

"The Fall" too—recalling the "long toil and travelling" of *Endymion* and the corridors of Keats's "Mansion of Many Apartments" letter—depicts a strenuous progress through a space for that poem's speaker. Put by Moneta through physical and logical trials marked by "patient travail" (1.91) and "toil" (1.92, 121), the speaker says, "slow, heavy, deadly was my pace" (1.129) as he undertakes his "hard task" (1.120). Indeed, the speaker of "The Fall" has little identity other than as a figure defined by his experiences of obscurity and incomprehension: his request to Moneta—"High prophetess . . . purge off,/ . . . my mind's film" (1.145-146)—reveals that his vision is obscured by a "film," as if that film or medium of dense literary language, were a permanent feature clouding his perception. In turn, the speaker himself, as a "dreamer" rather than a "poet" according to Moneta, serves the function of "vex[ing]" the world ("The Fall," 1.202). "The Fall" imagines readers in much the same way, warning us of a toilsome textual journey ahead: "Ye may read who can unwearied pass/Onward from the antichamber of this dream" (1.464-65). *Hyperion*—inspired by the "dark hints" of myth—offers Keats a myth and scope large enough to portray fully the "vex[ing]," dark textual "ways" that image so many kinds of experience for him.[41]

Keats thus attempts the epic genre and the story of theogony not merely or primarily for the sake of proving that he can write in this vein, that he could, like the speaker of "The Fall," "[bear]/the load" (1.389-90) of relating to us this story. Rather, the topos of *accommodation*, a key feature of any narrative presupposing the fundamental incommensurability between immortal experience and communication and that of mortals, makes *Hyperion* an ideal vehicle for continuing to celebrate metaphoricity itself. The Renaissance theory of accommodation upon which Milton drew, and then Keats (drawing on Milton), insisted on allegorical readings of the scriptures rather than "literal misreadings." To recall a phrase from Keats's "life of Allegory" letter, the narration of godly matters necessarily requires "continual allegory" rather than literality.[42] The two fragments frequently treat the problem of accommodation or *commoda verba*, and adhere closely to *Paradise Lost*, as when Raphael describes how he will recount the war in heaven in terms that mortals can understand:

> [W]hat surmounts the reach
> Of human sense I shall delineate so
> By likening spiritual to corporeal forms
> As may express them best.[43]

Immortal experience can be rendered to mortals only through "likening," a comparison of "spiritual" forms to "corporeal" ones. Echoing this and other passages from *Paradise Lost* about accommodation, the *Hyperion* poems comment on the inadequacy of "human sense" for understanding godly sensations, and thereby the necessity of mediators like the narrator in "Hyperion" and Moneta in "The Fall," as well as the necessity of linguistic mediation in the form of similes or conceits that draw on the mortal realm for the closest comparison. The narrator of "Hyperion" says, of Thea, "She spake/ . . . some mourning words, which in our feeble tongue/would come in these like accents." Elsewhere the narrator alludes to the possibility that attempting a "likening" is futile, since sublime, immortal experience cannot really be communicated even via simile: "woe/Too huge for mortal tongue or pen of scribe" (1.159–60). Likewise, in the "The Fall," the ongoing dialogue between the speaker and Moneta is colored by the difference between mortal and godly understanding. As Moneta elaborates on the nature of this difference, and the consequent need for immortal-to-mortal translation through figuration, she reminds the speaker:

> Mortal, that thou may'st understand aright,
> I humanize my sayings to thine ear,
> Making companions of earthly things . . . ("The Fall," 2.1–3)

Humans cannot upwardly grasp immortal information without the benefit of "humanize[d] . . . sayings," without "like accents." In contrast, immortals can downwardly access (or, we might recall, "smoke" in Cockney slang) mortal thoughts and feelings. Apollo, for example, tells us as much when he asks of Mnemosyne, "Why should I tell thee what thou so well seest?" ("Hyperion," 3.84).

Yet Keats's devotion to the imperative of metaphoric accommodation in both "Hyperion" and "The Fall" can also strike one as excessive, even contradictory. It should make a difference to the poems' treatment of mediation that Saturn and his fellow Titans have been stripped of their immortality: "for Fate/Had pour'd a mortal oil upon his head,/A disanointing poison" ("Hyperion," 2.96–98). Reading these lines, Maureen N. McLane observes, in a brilliant discussion of *Hyperion*, that Keats introduces the peculiar, paradoxical idea that gods can be "disanointed": immortals are transformed into, and reduced to the state of, mortals.[44] That being the case, does the experience of "disanointed" immortals still require "humanize[d] . . . sayings" for mortal understanding—and if so, how much? Would not the required "humanize[d] . . . sayings" be of a lesser degree, since these immortals have painfully fallen into mortality? Going by the *Hyperion* poems, one feels that Keats is not entirely sure. At the same time that the dark passages thematized in his other poems and letters persevere into the fragments—most notably around their insistence on the need for metaphorical mediation—*Hyperion* features several occasions where immortal sensations appear entirely proportionate to mortality. We see glimpses, in other words, of a fantasy of immediate comprehension without the need for figurative mediation. Immediately after describing Saturn's "disanointing," the narrator of "Hyperion" describes Saturn's pain with a simile—"As with us mortal men" ("Hyperion," 2.101)—which at first reads like the fragments' other likenings for the benefit of mortal comprehension. Except, in this case, readers have just been reminded than Saturn is now in fact "with us mortal men," and stripped of his power. In this instance, the figure reads more like a literal statement of fact than a figure functioning to convey the dimensions of immortal experience. Again, when Keats describes Hyperion's perception of a series of befuddling omens, his use of the word "or" seems not only to be differentiating but also equating the soon-to-be "disanointed" immortal and the condition of perplexed, confused mortality: "Unseen before by Gods or wondering men" ("Hyperion," 1.183), and "Not heard before by Gods or wondering men" (1.185). Gods and wondering men: these begin to sound less like distinct states of being and more like interchangeable roles given the poem's ongoing depiction of the gods as confused and astonished.

Oceanus's speech to his fellow Titans also marks a difference from Keats's previous commitment to dark passages, reversing Keats's priorities as well as the teleology of poetic maturation and literary history that he so memorably imagined in the "Mansion of Many Apartments" letter:

"As Heaven and Earth are fairer, fairer far
Than Chaos and blank Darkness, though once chiefs:
And as we show beyond that Heaven and Earth
In form and shape compact and beautiful,
In will, in action free, companionship,
And thousand other signs of purer life;
So on our heels a fresh perfection treads,
A power more strong in beauty, born of us
And fated to excel us, as we pass
In glory that old Darkness." ("Hyperion," 2.206–215)

In Keats's letter, the career arc of a single poet and the progress of poetry alike led to "dark passages," a positive stylistic quality defined by figuration and distinguishable from the ideal and norm of perspicuity exemplified by literal language. But Oceanus's creation myth narrates the opposite trajectory, where darkness gradually yields to lightness and greater beauty: "blank Darkness" has given way to the creation of "Heaven and Earth" and "light" ("Hyperion," 2.195), which first led to the Titans, and which now leads to the "fresh perfection" and "beauty" of the Olympians; the Olympians will "excel" the Titans in the same way that the Titans surpassed "in glory that old Darkness." True, darkness is the original condition for creation ("From chaos and parental darkness came/Light" [2.191–92]). But what is of greater significance is that Keats's signature for literary and communicative difficulty has become a passing phase, "that old Darkness," fated to give way to light. At moments like this, *Hyperion* raises a seemingly basic yet nagging, mystifying question—the kind that could be considered representative of "uncritical" rather than "critical" reading, yet, like most supposedly uncritical questions, not so easy to answer.[45] Whose side is Keats on? Apollo the ascendant poet figure, the as yet unfallen Hyperion, defeated yet majestic Saturn or one of his peers, the dreamer-narrator "favored for unworthiness" in "The Fall" (1.182), or another character? Some, none, or all of the above? Or, to ask a related question about the Olympian overthrow of the Titans: Whom are *we* to sympathize with? Which is the right side of history, lightness or "that old Darkness"? In the context of Keats's tropology, certain passages of *Hyperion* identify with the usurped, "darkness"-dwelling Titans ("The Fall," 1.463), in the way Keats's other writings prepare us to expect. Yet other passages, like this one, allegorize the inevitable emergence of a "purer," lighter, perhaps more literal, literary style—an Olympian clarity that will leave behind, and "excel," Keats's favored dark passages.

Keats's earlier poetry and letters show him relying on a cluster of figures deriving from scriptural obscurity, and remaining mostly tied to textual media, encompassing language, poetry, writing, and books: from the linguistic darkness of Bertha's book to the volume itself, from "charactery" to the "high piled books" that contains it ("When I have fears that I may cease to be," 3). But the *Hyperion* poems set out from the assumption that texts are but one subset of a larger, diverse category of media, and the deep reading of difficult texts only one form of engagement with a remote (authorial) entity within the broader phenomenon of communication. Such recognitions clear the way for the *Hyperion* project's comparative reflections on different kinds of communication. The most apparent expressions of these concerns appear at the start of each fragment. "Hyperion" begins memorably with a series of ephemeral communications: oral communications ("As if the ebbing air had but one wave;/So came these words and went" [1.78–79]) as well as those "voiceless," or gestural, ones ("the Naiad 'mid her reeds/Press'd her cold finger closer to her lips" [1.11–14]) that Keats in "Lamia" memorably names "other speech."[46] "The Fall" starts off as if reflecting on the earlier version of the poem, by weighing the materiality and durability of different types of communication. "The Fall" describes those ephemeral communications treated in "Hyperion" ("melodious utterance" that will only "live, dream, and die") and compares them to written or printed "Poesy" that "can save/Imagination" (1.6–10). Like Wordsworth's reflections on inscription across media—inscriptions molded by bureaucratic form on paper, parchment, vellum, and in the case of epitaphs, stone—Keats's thinking stresses the materiality of poetry on "vellum of wild Indian leaf" ("The Fall," 1.5).[47] And, as Coleridge ponders theories of shorthand and transcription, Keats invokes manuscript culture, mentioning "this warm scribe, my hand" ("The Fall," 1.18). More than his other works, then, Hyperion shows Keats moving across a range of communicative media. His focus here is on certain organic media (such as vellum), handwriting, and oral and gestural communications, rather than on the print or bibliographic culture of his time. But this focus is due not to an atavistic impulse on Keats's part but to a deep interest in the fantasies of contact, transmission, and storage that drive the act of communication across diverse media and communication practices. Hyperion, in short, reveals his fascination with the dream of communication.

Above all, in Hyperion, Keats's commitment to dark passages, deep reading, and the difficult process of mediation confronts not only a desire to equate wondering gods with wondering men (thus obviating the need for mediating figures) and to imagine a world moving further and further away from "that old Darkness," but also a particularly intense expression of the dream of communication: the fantasy of instantaneous contact at a distance. Keats's letter to George and Georgiana—which imagines an immediate communication of intelligence across great distance, likely informed by contemporaneous tele-culture—allows us to reframe Hyperion's depictions of communication between fellow immortals as a kind of wish fulfillment. The poems, as we have seen, are oftentimes preoccupied with the perplexed reading and mediation necessary for the mortal comprehension of immortal experience. At these moments, the fragments dramatize the insight of Dante—whose (Englished) style inspired Keats as he wrote "The Fall"—that humans cannot "enter into each other's minds by means of spiritual reflection, as the angels do, because the human spirit is so weighed down by the heaviness and density of the mortal body."[48] One might add to Dante's comment, in the context of *Hyperion*, that humans also cannot enter into each other's minds because of the density and darkness of the media through which human communications must wind their way. But against this reality, *Hyperion* also discloses Keats's fascination with how readily gods can get in touch, a fascination that is simultaneously, and at root, a fantasy of human communication covering such distances with such speed.

After Moneta explains to the speaker of "The Fall" that she speaks in "humanize[d] . . . sayings" for the sake of his mortal understanding, she goes on to say what immortal events would sound like to mortals without the benefit of accommodation:

> . . . [T]hou might'st better listen to the wind,
> Whose language is to thee a barren noise,
> Though it blows legend-laden through the trees. (2.4–6)

Moneta's condescension confirms that immortal experiences without mediation would be like "barren noise," like meaningless sound, to human ears. But her figure also intimates, because it describes the "wind" as carrying information ("legend[s]"), that immortal "language," like wind, blows through the air carrying content. In a striking parallel with the telecultural fantasies of Keats's time, the *Hyperion* poems imagine immortal information flowing freely through the air, in an immaterial and unrestrained manner; immortals engage in a kind of communication that requires no medium. It is as though gods, who are fitted with a "giant nerve" ("Hyperion" 1.175), can transmit and receive sensations, intuitions, and information across distances with great speed. Hyperion, for example, senses that usurpation has taken place, and intuits his own impending overthrow despite his remoteness from the already fallen Titans: "Why do I know ye? . . . Saturn is fallen, am I too to fall?" (1.231–34).

The two most memorable dramatizations of instantaneous, immaterial thought transfer are, of course, the exchanges between Apollo and Mnemosyne in "Hyperion" and between the speaker and Moneta in "The Fall." When Keats aborts "Hyperion," the poem is in the middle of a scene of instantaneous, unmediated communication. About to be deified, Apollo finds he can "read / A wondrous lesson in [Mnemosyne's] face," which leads to the "pour[ing]" of information into his brain: "Names, deeds, gray legends, dire events, rebellions." Like Moneta's depiction of immortal communication at a distance—"legend[s]" covering distance with the speed of wind—Apollo's deification too involves the immediate transmission of "legends" (among other things) from Mnemosyne into his "brain." Similarly, in "The Fall," the speaker is granted his request to be given immediate access to the inside of Moneta's mind—"Let me behold . . . /What in thy brain so ferments to and fro. / No sooner had this conjuration pass'd . . . "—at which point the speaker joins Moneta within a recursive retelling of "Hyperion,"; the speaker's opening description of "The Fall" as a rehearsal ("the dream now purposed to rehearse" [1.16]) is thus quite apt. Like that earlier poem, "The Fall" abruptly ends not long after this scene of "direct communication," suggesting some kind of logical impasse precipitated by the form of the contact gained by the mortal speaker.

If Keats breaks off the *Hyperion* poems after such scenes of unmediated communication, it may be because they are so unlike Keats. These two scenes are the closest to the opposite of himself that Keats ever gets. Although "prophecies" (3.78) have told of Apollo's eventual deification, Apollo, by Keats's description, embodies the defining qualities of befuddled mortality. Much like the speaker of "Ode to a Nightingale," whose "dull brain perplexes and retards" (34), Apollo admits in thoroughly mortal terms that "dark, dark, / And painful oblivion seals my eyes" (3.86–87). In other words, although Apollo will be undergoing a transformation into a god, in the poem—and against the backdrop of Keats's other works—he comes off more as a consummate mortal than candidate for immortality.

It is doubly startling then that Apollo can "read a wondrous lesson" in Mnemosyne's face in order to receive "names, deeds, gray legends, dire events, rebellions" instantaneously and without difficulty, because reading in the Keatsian oeuvre is nearly always a form of "deep" reading through dark passages, and never like the pouring of content from one vessel into another. Far more typical is the experience of Porphyro, who, as we saw, tries to read the old beldame's countenance and "upon her face doth look,/Like puzzled urchin on an aged crone/Who keepeth clos'd a wond'rous riddle-book." After reading this scene of thought transfer devoid of puzzlement, riddle, or resistance in "Hyperion," we would like to ask Keats: What happened to "blind bodies in the same room"?

Just as unlikely is the speaker of "The Fall" reading the "high tragedy" in Moneta's mind and navigating its "dark secret chambers" with an ease Keats typically reserves for the unfettered communicative capacity and understanding of gods. This latter transaction, a mortal given immediate access to the brain of a god, is similarly a dream of communicative contact highly discordant with the dominant logic of mortal communication elsewhere in *Hyperion* as well as across Keats's writings. In any case, one cannot help sensing some confusion in both poems about whether the deification process ought to resemble telegraphic communication at a distance or instantaneous thought transfer. Given Keats's gravitation toward the difficulty of literary reading and mediation rather than immediate transmission, and the priority of dark passages over pouring in his writing, these scenes of contact without the travails of reading are, Keats senses, too easy—a solution too sweet.

I can connect
Nothing with nothing.
> T. S. Eliot, *The Waste Land*

CONCLUSION

COMMUNICATION AND LITERARY COMPETENCE, ANEW

CAN THE CLAIMS OF THIS BOOK come together into a slightly different, broader formulation about poetry, even literary discourse generally? Because literary works are verbal art forms—crafted out of the self-same materials as those by which linguistic communication is being carried out all around us, all the time—every literary work objectifies a negotiation between shared ideals of communication and the artistic impulse to imagine otherwise. This negotiation includes concessions made by literature to communication practices at large: literary works, consciously or not, instantiate social desires about efficient, efficacious communication even when they are defying those same desires and other communicative conventions. In response to these formulations, one might observe that literary works of *all* kinds, not only Romantic poetry, embody to varying degrees this tension between the complex of matters this book calls the "dream of communication" and the literary work's inventiveness (its style, form, diction, and so on). I would agree. It would also be reasonable to say in response to my arguments that there is something potentially radical in the ways literature creatively manipulates the verbal routines and tools of everyday communication, even if or precisely because literary works must always in some measure obey rules of communication (even when the works are engaged in some form of critique). Agreed again. Yet I would nevertheless frame matters in the following way. The degree to which one chooses to emphasize this tension, and how one characterizes it, comes down only to scholarly or pedagogical preference—as this study acknowledged at the outset, "there are other ways to take on" the problems and poems treated herein—but the negotiation I am describing between literary discourse and communication is a fundamental, constituent tension of the literary. The negotiation between the literary work and the world of communication of which it is a part is thus potentially recoverable—should one be interested in doing so—in *any* literary work through the work of close reading and of recovering the relevant era's desires, norms, practices, and infrastructures of communication.[1]

Might we think in terms of communication anew—once more, with a difference—in an era of media? This study as a whole, as with the propositions just given, gives pride of place to "communication," even as it brings into focus communicative media (such as language, writing, poetry, stone, paper, parchment, the telegraph) and their relation to the rather different problem of "mediation" (as seen, for example, between mortals and immortals in *Hyperion*). As the introduction to this book acknowledges, the term *communication* has "the look and ring of a throwback," a certain dorkiness, given the discursive ubiquity today of terms like *media*, *mediation*, and *mediatization*. Media—social media, digital media, the media—are on everyone's tongues and minds. A different feeling clings to the term *communication*, which is more *Cool Hand Luke* than cool, evoking a theme from another time, one encapsulated in that film's well-worn line, "What we've got here is failure to communicate."

Nevertheless, I have tried to maintain a particular emphasis that may be subtle but seems to me significant: the idea that human communication necessarily subsumes or involves media, over the presumption that media imply communication. There are several reasons for this emphasis. The phenomena I have found to be most unexpectedly revelatory for Romantic poetry—hurried handwritten notes-to-self, standardized forms, networked life, and imaginings of telegraphic "pouring" between minds—are best comprehended by *communication*; of course, media play an important part throughout, but so do several other things, most crucially fantasies and practices. The diagram in my introduction depicts the hierarchy I have in mind. Moreover, the collective fascination with "media shift," a topic that understandably continues to attract much attention, has perhaps eclipsed too much the slower and yet equally epochal transformations in communicative ideals that have occurred at the scale of the *longue durée*: for example, the way that communicative style in modernity evolved from the "convention of imperial dress to the convention of the business suit," so to speak—from frills to no-frills.[2] These gradual evolutions in communication—the drive toward brevity and clarity, for example—are differently inflected by different media perhaps, but they nevertheless occur beneath, and persist through, media shifts: the rule of brevity shapes tax forms on vellum, parchment, or paper and in printed and/or handwritten form as much as it does tweets on Twitter. Human communication can be oddly marginalized at the same time that it is arguably called up in any discussion of media. The readings of this book and our own media-centric moment together recommend a reacquaintance with communication.

Walter J. Ong's preference for thinking in terms of "communication" over "media," a theme that occurs across several of his extraordinary works, helps to illustrate what I mean. Looking back over his *Orality and Literacy*, Ong explains that "this book has avoided the term media," because "the term can give a false impression of the nature of verbal communication, and of other human communication as well."[3] I have seen no such need to avoid *media* and related terms—I introduce the idea of *medial difficulty*, and rely much on Carolyn Marvin's notion of "media fantasies"—but Ong's preference remains informative. The "media model," as he calls it, cannot be applied without violence to the special case of linguistic human communication:

> Thinking of a "medium" of communication or of "media" of communication suggests that communication is a pipeline transfer of units of material called "information" from one place to another. . . . This model obviously has something to do with human communication, but, on close inspection, very little, and it distorts the act of communication beyond recognition. . . . Communication is intersubjective. The media model is not. There is no adequate model in the physical universe for this operation of consciousness, which is distinctively human and which signals the capacity of human beings to form true communities wherein person shares with person interiorly, intersubjectively. (172–73)

Even though Ong sharply distinguishes human communication from the media model (which evokes the workings of modern media and information technologies), we know—and Ong knows even better—that verbalization requires some medium or a set of nesting media (such as language, writing, and paper). That is to say, even if "words destroy in-betweenness," words are also always in between us, functioning as a medium and instantiated in media.[4] Ong's real objection is therefore not to the media in the media model, but to the model. This "metaphor" fundamentally misrepresents communication as a "pipeline transfer of units of material called 'information,'" or "cargo" transferred from me to you via some kind of "carrier" or on some "track."[5] One expects Ong to argue that communication aims at, and sometimes achieves, intersubjectivity, "put[ting] me in your consciousness and you in mine."[6] But surprisingly, his argument does not go there. Rather, he argues not (or not only) that intersubjectivity is the aim of communication, but a precondition for it. Ong writes, "I have to be somehow inside the mind of the other in advance [that is, before communication begins] in order to enter with my message, and he or she must be inside my mind" (173): for example, "I can be in touch perhaps through past relationships" (173), thereby engaging in an initial exercise in "intersubjectivity" by remembering previous interactions with a particular interlocutor or others. The "dream" in the dream of communication has a somewhat different connotation for Ong; it is not a delusion, but rather a necessary imaginative projection—like Adam Smith's descriptions of sympathy—that initiates communication and defines it. This view of communication might at first sound overly optimistic—there is no mention of a solipsistic form of idealism—but it is, in fact, part of Ong's broader historical argument. Like the distinction we have seen James W. Carey make between "ritual" and "transmission" views of communication, Ong argues that the medial view of communication is specific to chirographic cultures, imagining as we do the transmission of information to distant (that is, not co-present) addressees, whereas oral cultures viewed communication in more intersubjective, performative, and ritualistic ways. Ong memorably phrases it this way: "Willingness to live with the 'media' model of communication shows chirographic conditioning" (173).

Willingness to live with the media model of communication: one of the main things this book suggests—what we learn about the connected condition from the Romantics—is how not to lose sight of communication while *living with* the dominant media model. Indeed, from the present perspective, it would be reasonable to strengthen Ong's contention: in post-chirographic informational cultures, we inevitably live with the media model, whether or not we are willing. So much so that it is very difficult even to describe human communication without falling back on the media model: we see this in Ong's own need to write about his "message" entering other minds, and literature teachers wincingly hear it every time a student casually refers to a poem's or novel's "message." Yet as I hope to have shown in the foregoing pages, the Romantic poets too found themselves living with the media model of communication, internalizing the logic associated with efficient communications media and technologies. At the same time, they experimented with unintelligibility, tedium, obscurity, figurativeness, and the like, and gave a great deal of thought to the question of communication through poetic expression. If we are to take our cue from them, we too would continue to "live with" the media model, while not presuming that communication is taking place: that is, by not taking communication for granted owing to the fact and ubiquity of media. (Thinking of Ong as well as the previous chapters, one could reinforce the difference between the media model and communication by observing that "social communication" sounds much more redundant than "social media.") This orientation to the connected condition could be called many things. It could be called poetic.

Perhaps a new definition of the poetic suggests itself then. In literary theory, the language paradigm offers an influential definition of literariness. Most influentially, Roman Jakobson in his "Linguistics and Poetics" describes the "poetic" function or literariness as a "focus on the message for its own sake": poetry is distinct from other kinds of linguistic communication because poetry draws attention to the sounds and senses of language itself.[7] This remains for me a valuable definition, and it gets at one way in which literature operates. But as this book has tried to show, the poetic also involves, first, those inexorable norms that determine informational genres and communications (in Jakobson's terms, "referential" communications about "context"), like the norm of brevity that exercised Wordsworth and continues to hold sway today; second, prevailing desiderata associated with media—what Jakobson labels "contact," and describes as the "physical channel" of communication—as in transmission speed or ease of use, matters I have discussed above in connection with Adam Smith's "easy writing," standardized tax forms, and telegraphic "pouring"; and third, closely related desires about a more efficient "code," as we saw in Coleridge's stenographic fantasies pertaining to the inscription and storage of language in real time. That is to say, the poetic is deeply enmeshed with the fantasies and norms that profoundly shape what Jakobson calls "context," "contact," and "code." Now, there are three other pieces of Jakobson's six "factors" or components of communication: the "addresser," the "addressee," and the "message" itself. But if we add to my earlier statements the relatively unexceptionable ideas that all literary works are in one way or another oriented to or cognizant of these three factors—the "addresser" or the author himself or herself, the imagined "addressees" or readers, and the "message" in general, whether it is the work at hand or literary historical consciousness or intertextuality more broadly—we arrive at a different definition of the "poetic." The poetic is a special type of communication that reflects on the *entire* scheme of communicative functions: emotive, conative, referential, phatic, metalingual, and poetic. Literature invites reflection not merely on the "message" itself, but on the dream of communication as a whole. Imagine, then, a recursive version of Jakobson's diagram: a closer look at the "poetic" function reveals nothing other than the diagram again in miniature—and again and again. It is not only the case that literary discourse—a vital literariness—can be discovered beyond the familiar genres of imaginative writing, coloring other occasions of verbal communication: one might think of newspaper headlines—as in the headline, "ITALIAN ASSASSIN BOMB PLOT DISASTER," mulled over by William Empson in *Seven Types of Ambiguity*—or something lyrical uttered at dinner or written in passing in an email.[8] Rather, the world of communication itself can be discovered inside the poetic, since the poetic is always a response to the problem of communication itself. Where Jakobson frames the poetic within the conceptual framework of linguistic communication, we would have the poetic (by this recursion where the poetic also encapsulates communication) as a framework—not the only one, mind you, but a very good one—from which to begin to study human communication.

A difference ought to be discernible between this study and other works that might at first appear similar—for example, literary historical scholarship on print culture, book history, and other kinds of literary media. This book has made it a primary task to demonstrate that Romantic poems look far beyond the media and bibliographical codes associated with literary production itself. The communicative reflexiveness of literary works encompasses nothing less than the dream of communication. Despondent would be the day when neither imaginative genres themselves nor their readers can imagine beyond the categories of print, print culture, or the book, when they cannot look toward the broader social institutions of communication.

If the "literary" encompasses the entire order of communication, what does literature demand of its readers? Setting aside critical thinking, the critique paradigm, and reincarnations of belletristic appreciationism, I would recall the valuable idea of "literary competence" that Jonathan Culler introduces and discusses at length in his *Structuralist Poetics: Structuralism, Linguistics and the Study of Literature*. On the analogy of Noam Chomsky's "linguistic competence," literary competence refers to the *implicit* knowledge possessed by readers about literary discourse—its wealth of operations as well as its conventions—and about how to come up with a written interpretation of a work that can be considered valid by disciplinary norms. In short, literary competence is "what an ideal reader must know implicitly in order to read and interpret works in ways which we consider acceptable, in accordance with the institution of literature."[9] "Competence" sounds off-putting owing to its administrative or corporate associations, but it is in fact a considered, tactical wording. First, competence signals a needful seriousness about the value of literary study as a discipline, that "the time and energy devoted to literary training in schools and universities indicate that the understanding of literature also depends on experience and mastery" (132). Second, and closely related to the first, competence, far from denying "the spontaneous, creative and affective qualities of literature" (140), merely affirms that readings depend on "public" associations as much as private ones, that there exist norms of literary reading, and that there are graduations of interpretive quality (some interpretations may be deemed more compelling or persuasive than others). As Culler puts it, "a work can have a variety of meanings, but not just any meaning whatsoever" (142). Literary competence is, I think, the best name for what the literary curriculum can give to students, and theories of literary competence—which would make explicit the implicit knowledge involved in literary reading and study—are a worthwhile endeavor.

In my view, the digital intensification of the longer connected condition suggests that literary competence today requires an additional emphasis. The literary competence that is taught and learned is ideally made up of not only the important conventions of literature and of literary study but also a heightened awareness of the ideals of efficient, informational verbal communication that everywhere surrounded the literary work, that everywhere surround us. I. A. Richards, thinking in 1935 of media saturation in terms of the greater heterogeneity of language use to which writers and readers were exposed—an "inundation" caused by "extensions of our physical means of communication"—observed that "we all have to swim for ourselves in a verbal medium of mixed quality." Although Richards writes that we each individually "swim for ourselves" through this environment of linguistic-communicative variety, he also notes that we can learn to navigate this world from others: "from the schools, the literary public must take its standards of sensitiveness, acumen, and alertness in reading."[10] Integral to the requisite body of knowledge comprising literary competence, then, would be an awareness that can be cultivated about the "verbal medium of mixed quality" that the literary works in question swam in as well as a self-awareness about the verbal medium that we as readers now swim in—an awareness too of the push and pull between ideals of communication and those of literature, a push and pull that is dramatized by the literary work itself. One must know certain things about *King Lear* in literary and literary historical terms. But one must also approach sitting down to read *King Lear* with a sense of that period's communicative imperatives, which constituted Shakespeare's environment, plus the emails, text messages, social media posts, newspaper websites, and the speech nearby or addressed to us, all of which constitutes our environment, like water for fish. Many discussions of reading in the digital age focus on other, non-literary media that compete for our attention; they lead to pragmatic advice like setting aside one's smartphone during certain forms of reading and similar tasks requiring deep concentration. Nevertheless, literary competence at the present time requires, I think, a deliberateness not about devices alone, but about the varying imperatives, temporalities, rhythms, and qualities of the linguistic communications we swim through. Only one of these is literary, but it is a special case. Literary competence begins with the recognition that literature invites us into a communication without a message, a medium like and unlike other media, and the option to connect (or not to connect) with a feeling like T. S. Eliot's: "I can connect/Nothing with nothing."[11] One can choose to connect with another's frightening, bewildering feeling of disconnectedness, of being lost, and yet, at the same time, have an overwhelming sense of the connectedness and connect-ability of things, when one can connect anything with anything else, which also has the feel of connecting nothing with nothing.

ACKNOWLEDGMENTS

I thank first my main mentors. Cliff Siskin encouraged my work from the very start, and I have learned much from his brilliant brands of provocative farsightedness, argumentation, and difference. John Guillory offered much guidance on poetry, literary history, rhetoric, theories of media and communication, and more, all in a generous manner; his responses to my work and scholarship continue to shape my thinking. I thank Kevis Goodman for the version of Romanticism I know. She changed how I read and teach, and I am also thankful for her wisdom through the final stages of revising my manuscript. Lisa Gitelman and Maureen McLane too gave me generous feedback on my work. They also are big inspirations: from shorthand and standardized forms to the medium of Romantic poetry, their influence is here too.

Charles Mahoney has been a remarkable friend, colleague, and reader of my writing. Alan Liu made this book possible in multiple ways; it has been a trip to go from studying his work on Wordsworth, to talking to him about the digital humanities, to having his generous help in finding a home for this book. I have also learned much from Eugenio Bolongaro, Mary Carruthers, Erik Gray, Ross Hamilton, David C. Hensley, the late Karl Kroeber, Lawrence Lockridge, John Maynard, Karen Newman, Mary Poovey, and James Treadwell. Margaret Breen, Michael Gamer, Patrick Hogan, and Chuck Rzepka have been kind, recent sources of support.

Several close friends have been there for me throughout, especially Sebastien Brion, Ivan Capovski, Cliff Cassidy, Ramsey Chamie, Celia Economides, Tim Eng, Meg Hammond, Cindy Lee, Seth Rudy, Lenora Warren, and Noriko Whyte and the late Carl Schiebler. Deliberations with members of the Re:Enlightenment Project and the Concept Lab stimulated this work at different stages and in direct and indirect ways, and I thank Seth once again, along with Mark Algee-Hewitt, Peter de Bolla, Ryan Heuser, Ewan Jones, Rachael Scarborough King, and Gabriel Recchia.

For various kinds of indispensable feedback or fellowship, I thank Suzanne Barnett, Stephen Behrendt, Marijeta Bozovic, James Brooke-Smith, Andrew Burkett, Dwight Codr, Carrie Crompton and George Elliott, Ashley Cross, Stuart Curran, Hap and Ruth Fairbanks, Jillian Hess, Noel Jackson, Marie and Mihira Jayasekera, Chantal Johnson, Celeste Langan, Tom Mole, Lauren Neefe, Adela Ramos and Christian Gerzso, Brian Rejack, Fred Roden, Shawn Salvant, Greg Semenza, Jeffrey Shoulson, Kate Singer, Chris Washington, and Sarah Winter. I also received smart feedback to segments of this study presented to the 18/19 Group at the University of Colorado Boulder and at the University of Connecticut Humanities Institute, among other venues.

The editors of the Stanford Text Technologies series, Ruth Ahnert and Elaine Treharne, have been very supportive and offered helpful editorial, media historical, and literary historical suggestions on my chapters. Leah Pennywark was a voice of expertise and reassurance, guiding me through the publication process and my multitude of questions with clarity, patience, and friendliness. I am also grateful to Elspeth MacHattie and Jessica Ling for their help during the copyediting and production phases. Finally, this study benefited enormously from a scholarly shade I know only as Reader Two, who made this work better at every step, from proposal to almost-final version. I thank and salute Reader Two, plus the other readers for their valuable responses to my work.

In writing this book, I have relied much on the Boston Library Consortium and the University of Connecticut's Interlibrary Loan Service. As stacks shrink to make way for silliness and as print purchases dwindle, the ILL staff—Joe Natale, Robin Lubatkin, and other reliable staff members—have been the illest: thank you.

Iterations of Chapters 3 and 4, each of them revised and expanded here, initially appeared in the "Multi-Media Romanticisms" volume (November 2016) of the Praxis Series on the Romantic Circles website and in *Studies in Romanticism* (Summer 2014), respectively, and I thank Romantic Circles and the Trustees of Boston University for permission to reprint these pieces. I am also grateful to the University of Connecticut Humanities Institute for giving me a Humanities Book Support Award, which went toward indexing this book.

Most of all, I thank my family: my mother, father, sister, Anna, Bonnie, and Eric. I am especially grateful to my wife Anna and my sister Yuka for being in my life as I worked on this book (and other times besides), and grateful too to my mother, to whom I trace my earliest curiosity about languages and the pleasures of reading.

Introduction

1. I am referring to Keats's poem "Stanzas" ("In drear-nighted December"), in *Keats's Poetry and Prose*, line 21.

2. See Jenkins, Ford, and Green, *Spreadable Media*.

3. De Quincey, "The English Mail-Coach," 190, 183. De Quincey's preference for the mail coach, even though trains "boast of more velocity" (193), is itself a recognizable topos from technological change, an affective attachment to the older technology.

4. De Quincey, "The English Mail-Coach," 202, 190; Wordsworth, "Preface" to *Lyrical Ballads*, 294 (hereafter, "Preface").

5. De Quincey, "The English Mail-Coach," 183; De Quincey, *Collected Writings*, 270.

6. De Quincey, "The English Mail-Coach," 191.

7. Later on, De Quincey himself describes the speed as "ten miles an hour" ("The English Mail-Coach," 204), and this is confirmed by Headrick, *When Information Came of Age*, 188.

8. Here and throughout, I am inspired by Geoffrey Hartman's discussion of "communication compulsion," in Hartman, "I. A. Richards and the Dream of Communication," 32–37.

9. Keats, "The Fall of Hyperion—A Dream," in *Keats's Poetry and Prose*, Canto I, line 198.

10. While the Romantics certainly were, as scholars have rightly characterized them, "media theorists" *avant la lettre*, it is my sense that they congregated most around the dream of communication that was so integral to their craft and

ambitions. For good examples of the argument that Romantic poets were doing media theory, see Langan and McLane, "The Medium of Romantic Poetry," and Burkett, *Romantic Mediations*. In Chapter 3, I take up some of the complexities that ensue from aligning Percy Shelley's poetics with media theory.

11. On Dickens and stenography, see, e.g., Kreilkamp, "Speech on Paper"; and Price, *How to Do Things with Victorian Books*, 94–100.

12. Lamb, "The Superannuated Man," 173.

13. See Guillory, "Genesis of the Media Concept," 339–40; and Elfenbein, *Romanticism and the Rise of English*, 110–11, 124–43.

14. Langan and McLane, "The Medium of Romantic Poetry," 258.

15. Christopher Wordsworth, *Memoirs of William Wordsworth*, 289.

16. Menke, *Telegraphic Realism*, 4.

17. Peters, *Speaking into the Air*, 5.

18. Peters, *Speaking into the Air*, 5.

19. See Gitelman, *Scripts, Grooves, and Writing Machines*, 25. Andrew Piper makes a similar point, but with a focus on books, in Piper, *Dreaming in Books*, 5.

20. Siskin, *The Work of Writing*; and Piper, *Dreaming in Books*, 5–6.

21. Ong, *Orality and Literacy*, 161.

22. Wordsworth, "Preface," 290, 292.

23. Piper, *Dreaming in Books*, 7.

24. On the information state, see Higgs, *The Information State in England*, 64–98.

25. Beniger, *The Control Revolution*, 7.

26. Burke, *Reflections on the Revolution in France*, 80.

27. Wordsworth, *The Excursion*, book 8, line 110. See also Wordsworth's editorials against the Kendal and Windermere railway, in "Kendal and Windermere Railway. Two Letters Re-printed from The Morning Post." For a terrific account of Wordsworth and "systematizations," see Hickey, *Impure Conceits*, 22, inter alia.

28. Taylor, *The Principles of Scientific Management*, 9.

29. McKendrick, "Josiah Wedgwood and Factory Discipline," 41; on the Bentham brothers, see Chapter 2 in this volume; Wordsworth, "Preface," 294.

30. Bentham, *Official Aptitude Maximized, Expense Minimized*, 6.

31. Wordsworth, "Michael," in Wordsworth and Coleridge, *Lyrical Ballads*, lines 131, 134.

32. A particularly relevant example in connection with Wordsworth (and his civil service job, the subject of Chapter 2) is how the bureaucratic genre meant to be the paragon of efficiency, the standardized form, begets "a growth in information to be processed" (Beniger, *The Control Revolution*, 16). See also Guillory, "The

Memo and Modernity," 126n50. Wordsworth's important statements on repetition and tautology can be found in his "Note on 'The Thorn'" (also discussed in Chapter 2), and those on something akin to information overload in his "Preface."

33. Marvin, *When Old Technologies Were New*, 4–7.

34. In place of a literature review, I name some exemplary works: Siskin, *The Work of Writing*; Piper, *Dreaming in Books*; McLane, *Balladeering, Minstrelsy, and the Making of British Romantic Poetry*; Newlyn, *Reading, Writing, and Romanticism: The Anxiety of Reception*; Klancher, *The Making of English Reading Audiences, 1790–1832*; Franta, *Romanticism and the Rise of the Mass Public*; and Altick, *The English Common Reader: A Social History of the Mass Reading Public, 1800–1900*.

35. For cogent arguments on manuscript culture, see Levy, "Austen's Manuscripts and the Publicity of Print"; and Schellenberg, *Literary Coteries and the Making of Modern Print Culture*. A skeptical view of "proliferation" arguments can be found in Elfenbein, *Romanticism and the Rise of English*, 111. On some of the difficulties posed by "print" and "print culture," see Gitelman, *Paper Knowledge*, 7–9.

36. Burkett's *Romantic Mediations* also examines non-literary media technologies (e.g., photography, phonography, moving images). The present study quite differently has as its predominant focus communication fantasies rather than technical media, but it complements Burkett's work for a more basic reason still: the communications media treated here are those contemporaneous with, rather than those post-dating, Romanticism.

37. For a discussion of these concepts, see Chapter 3 in this volume.

38. See, for example, Zielinski, *Deep Time of the Media*.

39. Peters, *The Marvelous Clouds*, 2–3. Also see Chapter 2 in this volume.

40. Peters, *Speaking into the Air*, 10.

41. Carey, *Communication as Culture*, 12–13, 15.

42. Marvin, *When Old Technologies Were New*, 4, 7–8.

43. On this paradox, see the "double logic of remediation," in Bolter and Grusin, *Remediation*, 2–15.

44. Hartman, "I. A. Richards," 35.

45. White, introduction to *The Elements of Style*, xv.

46. Scott, *Seeing Like a State*, 5.

47. Scott, *Seeing Like a State*, 4.

48. Scott, *Seeing Like a State*, 6.

49. Scott, *Seeing Like a State*, 76.

50. Goodman, *Georgic Modernity and British Romanticism*, 22–29. See also Cohen, *Sensible Words*, 1–42.

51. Goodman, *Georgic Modernity*, 26.

52. For an account of Basic English, see Igarashi, "Statistical Analysis at the Birth of Close Reading."

53. Guillory, "Genesis of the Media Concept," 331; Peters, *Speaking into the Air*, 80–81.

54. Peters, *Speaking into the Air*, 80; Guillory, "Genesis of the Media Concept," 331; Williams, "Communication," in *Keywords*, 72.

55. Peters, *Speaking into the Air*, 80.

56. Locke, *Essay Concerning Human Understanding*, 305–06.

57. Locke, *Essay*, 257.

58. Locke, *Essay*, 312.

59. Locke, *Essay*, 315.

60. Guillory, "Genesis of the Media Concept," 334.

61. Howell, *Eighteenth-Century British Logic and Rhetoric*, 541.

62. Guillory, "Genesis of the Media Concept," 338–39; and Guillory, "The Memo and Modernity," 119–20.

63. Smith, *Lectures on Rhetoric and Belles Lettres*, 3, 5, 6.

64. Smith, *Lectures*, 4–7.

65. Hartman, "I. A. Richards," 23.

66. Smith, *Lectures*, 7.

67. Smith, *Lectures*, 7.

68. Locke, *Some Thoughts Concerning Education*, 141–43.

69. Maria Edgeworth and Richard Lovell Edgeworth, *Practical Education*, 1.93. A terrific recent work on Romantic era attention—across disciplinary and discursive realms, including martial vigilance—is Lily Gurton-Wachter's *Watchwords: Romanticism and the Poetics of Attention*.

70. Wordsworth, "The Idiot Boy" (line 169), in Wordsworth and Coleridge, *Lyrical Ballads*.

71. Smith, *Lectures*, 7.

72. Wordsworth, "Preface," 290.

73. Foucault, *Discipline and Punish*, 184.

74. Elfenbein, *Romanticism and the Rise of English*, 6–7

75. In this sense, "norms" are like Émile Durkheim's "social facts." See Durkheim, *The Rules of Sociological Method*, 20–28.

76. Keats, *The Letters of John Keats*, 1:224.

77. Spenser, "The Letter to Raleigh," in *The Faerie Queene*, 224.

78. Nabokov, "The Art of Literature and Commonsense," 372.

79. Nabokov, "The Art of Literature," 371.

80. For media histories of index cards, other kinds of cards, and slips, see Krajewski, *Paper Machines*; and Blair, *Too Much to Know*, 210–17.

81. Felski, *The Limits of Critique*, 1–2. This latest work by Rita Felski develops earlier, and equally perceptive, claims about critique: "Problematizing, interrogating, and subverting are the default options, the deeply grooved patterns of contemporary thought" (Felski, *Uses of Literature*, 2). See also Joseph North, *Literary Criticism*, which offers a welcome challenge to the presumption that the scholarship of the last few decades represents "a political victory for progressives over the relatively conservative criticisms of the mid-century" (7).

82. Felski, *Limits of Critique*, 9.

83. Felski, *Limits of Critique*, 2, 17.

84. Felski, *Limits of Critique*, 8.

85. I take my cue from Geoffrey C. Bowker, Susan Leigh Star, and others who refer to "infrastructural inversion," a method for studying and foregrounding infrastructures, which are otherwise invisible or forgotten until they break down. See, e.g., Bowker and Star, *Sorting Things Out*, 34; and Lampland and Star, "Reckoning with Standards," 17. The normal method seems close to "deflation" too. Oftentimes, deflation implicates those in literary study with interests in media studies, book history, and similar areas. Leah Price describes a "poetics of deflation" as involving, "a dogged or even mulish taste for the mundane, the contingent, and the simpleminded," which "finds its only aesthetic outlet in puns" (*How to Do Things*, 22–23). Chapters 1 and 2 in this volume—on stenography and bureaucracy—make my work consistent with "deflation," yet I prefer the "normal method" because this book does not set out to "deflate" anything else so much as to see how norms of communication play out in non-literary writing practices and then in literary writing.

86. That is to say nothing of the longer history of literary bureaucrats before and after Wordsworth: Chaucer, Spenser, Milton, and Thackeray, to name a few. On "boring things," see Lampland and Star, "Reckoning with Standards," 11. There has been some recent work on Romantic-era administrators, most notably by Jon Klancher. As Klancher astutely puts it, "a larger reason we know so little historically about administration is related to our strong disinclination to consider administrators as cultural 'producers' at all, preferring to think of them instead as bureaucrats, functionaries, or apparatchiks, a picture of the administrator that has an especially strong provenance" (*Transfiguring the Arts and Sciences*, 51). Chapter 2 joins such attempts to study administrators; that the administrative work of so major a poet as Wordsworth has been neglected by scholars testifies to the "disinclination" Klancher describes.

87. Foucault, *Discipline and Punish*, 184.

88. Eliot, "The Metaphysical Poets," 248. There are several studies of modern or contemporary poetic difficulty, including Diepeveen's *The Difficulties of Modernism*; and Altieri and Nace, *The Fate of Difficulty in the Poetry of Our Time*.

89. Richards, *Principles of Literary Criticism*, 274.

90. Reynolds and Wilson, *Scribes and Scholars*, 221–22.

91. Epp, "Coleridge and Romantic Obscurity," 1–6; Christie, "A Recent History of Poetic Difficulty," 544; Fry, "Wordsworth in the 'Rime,'" in *The Rime of the Ancient Mariner*, 322.

92. Steiner, "On Difficulty," 27.

93. Steiner, "On Difficulty," 28.

94. Steiner, "On Difficulty," 33.

95. Steiner, "On Difficulty," 41.

96. Steiner, "On Difficulty," 41–42.

97. Liu, *The Laws of Cool*. See also Paulson, *The Noise of Culture*. William Paulson pursues the "literature-as-noise" metaphor quite far, and though I do not work with this tricky information theory–based conceit, we share some of the same questions.

98. Liu, *The Laws of Cool*, 9.

99. My interest in these other forms may superficially resemble Caroline Levine's arguments in *Forms*, but they are also very distinct from the proposals found in that book, as I explain in Chapter 2.

100. See Levy, "Austen's Manuscripts and the Publicity of Print," and Schellenberg, *Literary Coteries and the Making of Modern Print Culture*.

Chapter 1: Scribble-Scrabble Genius

1. Quotations from Coleridge's poetry and prose (excluding his notebooks), unless otherwise noted, are from *Coleridge's Poetry and Prose: Authoritative Texts, Criticism*, edited by Halmi, Magnuson, and Modiano, and are cited parenthetically in the text: poetry by title and line number(s), and prose by title and page number(s). Quotations from Coleridge's notebooks are from *The Notebooks of Samuel Taylor Coleridge*, and are cited as *Notebooks*, followed by volume and entry numbers.

2. Freud, *The Interpretation of Dreams*, 516–35.

3. Burke, "Why Coleridge?," 163.

4. On the "manifest content" of dreams (as opposed to the "latent content"), see Freud, *The Interpretation of Dreams*, 160–61.

5. My emphasis here on the failure of transcription as much as on forgetting is informed by Ann M. Blair's work on the history of note-taking: Blair demonstrates the enormous significance of note-taking and other writing practices as memory aids from the seventeenth century onward, especially after memory loses the intellectual "primacy of place" it had held since antiquity. Coleridge's misfortune is not only about forgetting, then, but about the interaction of forgetting

and writing-as-memory aid, particularly the act of writing something out with urgency. See Blair, *Too Much to Know*, 75.

6. Erdman, "Coleridge in Lilliput," 33. On Coleridge having "volunteered" the report, see Hessell, *Literary Authors, Parliamentary Reporters*, 89. Hessell clarifies Coleridge's unique role among reporters, a "patchwork" of "reporter, editor, and political correspondent" (75).

7. See Erdman, "Coleridge in Lilliput," 40–62; and Hessell, *Literary Authors*, 61–95. Hessell notes that starting around 1770, "the accepted practice through the 1750s and 1760s of printing bare outlines of the debates now erupted into attempts at comprehensive reports" (62).

8. Pitman, *A History of Shorthand*, 6.

9. As Lisa Gitelman has explained, shorthand script sounds like an unlikely "technology" because of that word's association with "mechanical or electrical" inventions, but grasping shorthand as a technology reveals its similarities with such other historical technologies as the QWERTY keyboard or the VHS cassette: the claims of progress, the multitude of competing inventors, the jostling to become the standard system adopted by bureaucratic, political, and economic organizations (Gitelman, *Scripts, Grooves, and Writing Machines*, 24, 60).

10. On the lifting of the note-taking ban, see Hessell, 64. These longer reports, published initially in pamphlet form before being incorporated into collections like John Debrett's *Parliamentary Register* and William Cobbett's *Parliamentary History*, were usually identified on their pamphlet title pages as capturing "the speech at length," as opposed to being the condensed "substance of the remarks" (see Erdman, "Coleridge in Lilliput," 36–37). On the American context, and the later nineteenth-century transition from "sketches" of congressional proceedings to shorthand-based verbatim transcripts of them, see Gitelman, *Scripts, Grooves, and Writing Machines*, 42–46.

11. Blanchard, *The complete instructor of short hand*, 3. "Kubla Khan" is about three hundred and fifty words long, so Blanchard—were we to believe him—would have been able to take down in shorthand a spoken version of the poem in two and a half minutes. But Coleridge "eagerly" transcribing a dream composition? Who knows.

12. See Hess, "Coleridge's Fly-Catchers: Adapting Commonplace-Book Form"; and Worthen, *The Cambridge Introduction to Samuel Taylor Coleridge*, 41–55.

13. Jackson, *Science and Sensation in Romantic Poetry*, 103–31.

14. Marvin, *When Old Technologies Were New*, 7–8.

15. As Coleridge's notebooks confirm, and as Erdman and Hessell have analyzed in depth, Coleridge took notes of parliamentary speeches as you and I and our students would try to take handwritten notes: not using the scrawls or

abbreviation techniques of shorthand but in fragmentary, idiosyncratically abbreviated longhand English with many lacunae.

16. Langan, "Pathologies of Communication from Coleridge to Schreber," 119–23. The somewhat puzzling exception to this in Coleridge's thinking is his understanding of punctuation, which he conceives of as notations for reading aloud, for recital; he leaves no room in his theory of punctuation for the possibility that these signs might be *logical symbols* for silent reading, which is generally the setting he imagines for the perception and parsing of written notation. See Coleridge, "Punctuation Not Logical but Dramatic."

17. For a shrewd analysis of creative writing and "phonocentrism," see McGurl, *The Program Era: Postwar Fiction and the Rise of Creative Writing*, 234–38.

18. See for example, McLane, *Balladeering, Minstrelsy, and the Making of British Romantic Poetry*, 212–20; Elfenbein, *Romanticism and the Rise of English*, 108–43; and Carlson, *Romantic Marks and Measures*, 129–44. These authors have examined the ways that silent print remediated unsilent speech or orality; their work takes up, among other things, elocution manuals, which visually displayed the sounds of spoken language (e.g., the pronunciation of standard English, emphasis, intonation, and dynamics). Yet as we have seen in connection with "Kubla Khan," and as Langan's aforementioned essay reminds us, Coleridge did not understand his writing as remediating speech; his working assumption was that (in Langan's words) "we may think that which we are incapable of saying" (Langan, "Pathologies of Communication," 127).

19. Williams, Introduction to *Contact*, 17–18.

20. Coleridge, *Lectures 1808–1819*, Vol. I, 195. For a terrific discussion of Coleridge, media and information overload, and the reading public's wish for "instantaneous intelligibility," see Newlyn, *Reading, Writing, and Romanticism*, 39–40.

21. In a recent, persuasive account, Andrew Burkett considers how the disembodied human voice interested both post-Romantic phonography and Romantic poets (Burkett, *Romantic Mediations*, 45–73). Interestingly, the phonograph invented by Edison was named after, and profoundly shaped by, *Phonography*, the widely adopted shorthand system invented by Isaac Pitman decades before, which, as the name suggests, imagined itself as an inscription-based audio recording (Gitelman, *Scripts, Grooves, and Writing Machines*, 24–25). Late eighteenth-century stenography can also be linked to another communications technology, early semaphore telegraphy: there were shorthand systems called "tachygraphy" (from the Greek for "fast" and "writing"), but the first semaphore telegraph, invented by Claude Chappe, was also called "*tachygraphe*" (Standage, *The Victorian Internet: The Remarkable Story of the Telegraph and the Nineteenth Century's On-line Pioneers*, 9). Both shorthand and telegraphy aimed, though in different ways, to

atomize the English language into parts, symbolically translate or encrypt those parts into another semiotic system, and then send them across distances (telegraphy) or record them (shorthand) as rapidly as possible.

22. Perry, "Introduction to *Coleridge's Notebooks*," vii.

23. Klancher, "Transmission Failure," 186–95.

24. Perry, *S. T. Coleridge: Interviews and Recollections*, 149n31.

25. Given shorthand's dependence on rhetorical commonplaces, the difficulty of transcribing Coleridge's speech is consistent with Walter J. Ong's linking of Romanticism and the decline of *loci communes*. See Ong, "Romantic Difference and the Poetics of Technology." If there were speakers whose formulaic speech made them easier to transcribe, there were also those of few words who could be characterized as speaking "stenographically"—a curious inversion where the transcription method defines the speech. De Quincey describes Robert Southey's talk in this way: "the style of his mind naturally prompts him, to adopt a trenchant, pungent, aculeated form of terse, glittering, stenographic sentences" See De Quincey, *Literary Reminiscences*, 2:41.

26. Mendle, "The 'prints' of the Trials: The Nexus of Politics, Religion, Law and Information in Late Seventeenth-Century England," 124.

27. Qtd. in Pitman, *A History of Shorthand*, 4.

28. Lisa Gitelman points out that "before either movies or radio, before phonographs and televisions, making history was unquestionably done on paper by a variety of means. Graphic and legible inscriptions, like still photographs and stenographers' scripts, made history" (Gitelman, *Scripts, Grooves, and Writing Machines*, 24).

29. Orr, "The Blind Spot of History: Logography," 201.

30. Earlier in this same note, he had meant to write "It is worth noting & endeavoring to detect," but miswrote the "to" of the infinitive, resulting in "It is worth noting & endeavoring the detect."

31. A different observation, that "*writing a thing down rids* the mind of it" (*Notebooks*, 1:1388), goes hand in hand with the strategy of distributing the mnemonic burden between mind and notes, and Coleridge is a good example of what Blair calls the early modern "stockpiling approach" to note-taking. See Blair, *Too Much to Know*, 63.

32. See McKusick, *Coleridge's Philosophy of Language*; Robert N. Essick, "Coleridge and the Language of Adam"; and Bewell, "Coleridge and Communication."

33. McKusick, *Coleridge's Philosophy of Language*, 28–31.

34. Paula McDowell, "Defoe's *Essay upon Literature* and Eighteenth-Century Histories of Mediation." See also McLane, *Balladeering, Minstrelsy, and the Making*

of British Romantic Poetry, 215–20, for a reading of Blake's "allegory of poetic mediation."

35. An earlier entry in the same notebook treats "*hieroglyphics* or picture-writing" indifferently and in a different context (*Notebooks*, 2:2402), but in the later entry I think Coleridge is writing a progress narrative of signs.

36. Pitman, *A History of Shorthand*, 6–7; Gitelman, *Scripts, Grooves, and Writing Machines*, 24; Price, *How to Do Things with Books in Victorian Britain*, 96.

37. See Kreilkamp, "Speech on Paper" 14.

38. One exception is Jerome Christensen's helpful discussion of shorthand, in Christensen, *Lord Byron's Strength: Romantic Writing and Commercial Society*, 201–05.

39. Lewis, *An Historical Account of the Rise and Progress of Short Hand*, v–vi. Whereas prior shorthand manuals selectively surveyed previous works in order to claim the superiority of their own new and improved systems, Lewis's *Historical Account* is a first in its aim of comprehensiveness; it discusses, often in depth, at least eighty-seven other systems, and later histories of shorthand, like Pitman's *A History of Shorthand*, heavily rely on and quote from Lewis's history.

40. Lewis, *An Historical Account*, 21. Byron's and Scott's blurbs for "The Lewisian System of Penmanship" are in Lewis's manual, *The Art of Making a Good Pen*, 22.

41. Hessell, *Literary Authors, Parliamentary Reporters*, 64; and Erdman, "Coleridge in Lilliput," 39. Lewis's *Historical Account* also ties the rise of shorthand to "when the privilege of reporting was once admitted" in Parliament" (148). The situation was similar in France, where, as Linda Orr puts it, "stenography culminates with the parallel growth of eighteenth- and nineteenth-century parliamentary institutions." See Orr, "The Blind Spot of History: Logography," 200.

42. Mendle, "The 'prints' of the Trials," 124.

43. The first quotation is from Wordsworth, "Preface of 1815," 30. The quotations in the second instance come from Lewis, *An Historical Account*, pages 18, 8, and 14, respectively.

44. Wordsworth, *The Prelude* (1805) Book 5, line 21; Keats, "The Fall of Hyperion—A Dream," in *Keats's Poetry and Prose*, Canto 1, lines 4–6.

45. Lewis, *An Historical Account*, 16.

46. Despite the bewildering number and kinds of systems, many share features (like having these three kinds of sign) because they derive from, and claim to "improve" upon, a small number of popular previous systems: Mason's aforementioned *A Pen Pluck't from an Eagles Wing: or, The Most Swift, Compendious and Speedy Method of Short-writing* (1672); Thomas Gurney's *Brachygraphy: or, Short-writing Made Easy to the Meanest Capacity* (1752)—this Gurney being the grandfather of the William Brodie Gurney who tried unsuccessfully to take shorthand notes of Coleridge's lectures using the patrimonial system, and this system being the one

learned later by Charles Dickens—John Byrom's *The Universal English Short-hand* (1767); and Samuel Taylor's *An Essay Intended to Establish a Standard for an Universal System of Stenography, or Short Hand Writing* (1786) are among the most influential, much emulated, methods. See Pitman, *A History of Shorthand*, 13. At the same time, it is difficult not to appreciate the obsessive uniqueness of some individual systems. Honore Blanc's French system, *Okygraphie* (1801), for example, involves writing marks—one might say, "notes"—on music notation paper, on and across five staff lines. For a summary of Blanc's system, see Lewis, *Historical Account*, 179–80. On Dickens and stenography, see Kreilkamp, "Speech on Paper"; and Price, *How to Do Things with Books in Victorian Britain*, 94–100.

47. Lewis, *An Historical Account*, 141. From some of the earliest English shorthands—such as Mr. Ratcliff's *A new Art of Short and Swift Writing* (1688), which renders "our daily bread" as "r dly brd"—to Pitman's influential Victorian system, shorthand systems presented themselves as achieving a rationalization of English spelling by offering a more phonetic representation; it comes as no surprise that Pitman was deeply involved in the nineteenth-century spelling reform movement. For more on Ratliff's system, see Lewis, 34. For shorthand and spelling reform, see Gitelman, *Scripts, Grooves, and Writing Machines*, 52–53.

48. Gurney, *Brachygraphy*, 3.

49. Professional parliamentary reporter William Blanchard, in his 1787 shorthand manual, teaches the reader to omit "e"s and "i"s from the middle of words, and to use differently sized loops for other intervening vowels within words. As Blanchard puts it, the surrounding consonant signs and a few loops are "a clue sufficient for all common words in the English tongue." See Blanchard, *The complete instructor of short hand*, 5.

50. Byrom, *The Universal English Short-hand*, 37–38.

51. Gurney, *Brachygraphy*, 20.

52. Lewis, *An Historical Account*, 24.

53. Gurney, *Brachygraphy*, 20.

54. Gurney, *Brachygraphy*, 20. On top of these unwieldy sets of signs—alphabetical, for certain morphemes, and for words and phrases—were an assortment of other rules for abbreviation: rules about the placement of certain diacritical marks around other marks, and the higher or lower positioning of marks relative to the line of writing to represent tenses, conjugations, and so on.

55. Per the *Oxford English Dictionary* (*OED*), a pothook is "a curved or hooked stroke made with the pen, esp. as a component of an unfamiliar or unintelligible script or when learning to write; (also) a crooked character, a scrawl" (s.v. "pot-hook," def. 2); similarly, the *OED* defines a hanger as "a nursery name for the stroke with a double curve . . . one of the elementary forms in

learning to write" (s.v. "hanger," def. 4d). Thus the phrase "pothooks and hangers" denoted the penmanship of children learning to write, although it was also used to describe writing systems using a non-English alphabet, such as Chinese characters, as when Leigh Hunt referred to "some Chinese pothooks and hangers" (qtd. in Kitson, *Forging Romantic China: Sino-British Cultural Exchange 1760–1840*, 178).

56. Price, *How to Do Things with Books in Victorian Britain*, 96.

57. For an explanation of Coleridge's cipher systems, see Kathleen Coburn, "Appendix C: Coleridge's Cryptogram." For a good discussion of the ciphers, see Fulford, *Coleridge's Figurative Language*, 92–101. It is worth noting that not all of Coleridge's ciphers function like shorthand—including those that rely on Greek letters, employ a basic substitution of numbers for letters, or assign each vowel one of four possible signs. These other cipher alphabets do not save time.

58. See Guillory, "Genesis of the Media Concept," 338, for a discussion of this idea in connection with John Wilkins's *An Essay Towards a Real Character, and a Philosophical Language* (1668): "Wilkins's communication at a distance is possible by recourse to the same device—code—that is otherwise the means to *frustrate* communication" or prevent reading by others.

59. Mendle, "The 'prints' of the Trials," 125.

60. Kreilkamp, "Speech on Paper," 15–17.

61. Lewis, *An Historical Account*, 7.

62. See Mitchell, *Blake's Composite Art: A Study of the Illuminated Poetry*, 4–14. As Mitchell points out, "many of Blake's visual images move toward the realm of language, operating as arbitrary signs, emblems, or hieroglyphics" (4).

63. Price, *How to Do Things with Books in Victorian Britain*, 95.

64. Gurney, *Brachygraphy*, 4.

65. Gitelman, *Paper Knowledge*, 134–35; and Cordell, "'Q i-jtb the Raven': Taking Dirty OCR Seriously," 198–99.

66. Cordell, "'Q i-jtb the Raven,'" 193–94.

67. See Elfenbein, *Romanticism and the Rise of English*.

68. As described in note 1, quotations from the 1798 "Rime of the Ancyent Marinere in Seven Parts" and the 1834 "Rime of the Ancient Mariner" are from *Coleridge's Poetry and Prose*; they are cited with the version of the text (1798 or 1834) preceding the line numbers. Coleridge's glosses in the 1834 version are cited by page number.

69. McGann, "The Meaning of the Ancient Mariner."

70. Modiano, *Coleridge and the Concept of Nature*, 15.

71. Modiano, *Coleridge and the Concept of Nature*, 15.

72. Wordsworth, "Note to 'The Ancient Mariner' [from the 1800 edition of *Lyrical Ballads*]," 319.

73. Coleridge, *The Rime of the Ancient Mariner*, illustrated by Alexander Calder. Eight of Calder's illustrations are reproduced in Warren, "A Poem of Pure Imagination (Reconsiderations VI)."

74. For a sustained discussion of page formatting and document design in the Romantic period and before, see Chapter 2 in this volume.

75. Empson, "The Ancient Mariner: An Answer to Warren," 165 (emphasis mine).

76. Warren, "A Poem of Pure Imagination: An Experiment in Reading," 365.

77. Warren, "A Poem of Pure Imagination," 371.

78. Empson at one point describes Warren's reading as a kind of crude associationism incapable of noticing contrasts ("The Ancient Mariner," 168).

79. On hypermediacy, see Bolter and Grusin, *Remediation: Understanding New Media*, 31–44.

80. Eilenberg, *Strange Power of Speech: Wordsworth, Coleridge, and Literary Possession*, 32–33.

81. Ferguson, "Coleridge and the Deluded Reader: 'The Rime of the Ancient Mariner,'" 119.

82. And as Eilenberg observes, the Mariner cries out, "'A sail' for 'a ship' whose sails have rotted away" (*Strange Power of Speech*, 33).

83. Empson, "The Ancient Mariner," 167.

84. Empson, "The Ancient Mariner," 167.

85. Empson, "Introduction to *Coleridge's Verse*," 28.

86. Paul H. Fry describes this form as "the most overdetermined figural recurrence in the poem," and also points to the "barred clouds of 'Dejection' and the fireplace grate of 'Frost at Midnight.'" See Fry, "Wordsworth in the 'Rime,'" 331.

87. Although I think this is coincidental, the shape also resembles the Hebrew *shin* discussed previously.

88. Empson, "Introduction," 50.

89. This image is a detail from Figure 1.1. © The British Library Board. Reprinted with permission of the British Library.

Chapter 2: Wordsworth and Bureaucratic Form

1. Mary Wordsworth, *The Letters of Mary Wordsworth*, 80. According to Mary Moorman's indispensable biography, Wordsworth approached his distributorship with extreme meticulousness. See Moorman, *William Wordsworth*, 249.

2. Byron, *Don Juan*, "Dedication," line 46.

3. [Jeffrey], "Review of *Memorials of a Tour on the Continent*," 450.

4. While Jeffrey and others posit that "the contact of the Stamp-office" had a "bad . . . effect" on Wordsworth ([Jeffrey], Review of *Memorials of a Tour on the Continent*," 456), this characterization is somewhat specious: for one thing,

Jeffrey had been writing politically motivated negative reviews of Wordsworth before the poet's work with the Stamp Office. Regarding the relative neglect of Wordsworth's other job: the biographies of Wordsworth, of course, treat the civil servant position, and Mary Moorman's research is particularly helpful, but there has been very little criticism relating his other career to his poetry. The few exceptions to this neglect include Frey, *British State Romanticism: Authorship, Agency, and Bureaucratic Nationalism,* esp. the Introduction, 1-19, and Chapter 2, "Wordsworth's Establishment Poetics," 54-87; Manning, "Wordsworth at St. Bees: Scandals, Sisterhoods, and Wordsworth's Later Poetry," esp. 291; and Mark Schoenfield's brief but valuable comments in Schoenfield, *The Professional Wordsworth: Law, Labor, and the Poet's Contract,* 241, 247-48.

5. Although there are excellent studies on the general topic of Wordsworth and inscription—e.g., Andrew Bennett's *Wordsworth Writing*—Poovey's *Genres of the Credit Economy* is particularly helpful for this chapter because it relates Wordsworth's views on writing to the broader scriptural economy, to non-literary genres. This is unlike Bennett's aims. See Bennett, *Wordsworth Writing,* 10-12.

6. Poovey, *Genres of the Credit Economy,* 286-99.

7. On paperwork and bureaucracy, see Gitelman, *Paper Knowledge: Toward a Media History of Documents,* 30-32. As James Brooke-Smith has also observed, "institutions are artefacts fashioned from media." See Brooke-Smith, "Classification and Communication in Romantic-era Knowledge Institutions," 240.

8. Burke, *Attitudes toward History,* 2:66-72.

9. As Kramnick and Nersessian point out in their level-headed account, the kind of "form" examined can depend on the inquiry and sought-after explanation; there is no single, true kind of "formal" analysis. If this chapter is more interested in bureaucratic form than in the very familiar units of poetic form, that is because this chapter's concerns—as will become evident—are standardized forms, formulas, formatting, etc., in the context of the interaction between literary and administrative genres. See Kramnick and Nersessian, "Form and Explanation."

10. [Jeffrey], Review of *Memorials of a Tour on the Continent,* 450; "prosy" and "feeble" are also from Jeffrey's review.

11. See Guillory, "The Memo and Modernity," 122-32.

12. Foucault, *Discipline and Punish,* 184.

13. For a recent call to redress the neglect of Romantic-era administrators and bureaucrats—a proposal with which this chapter is clearly sympathetic—see Klancher, *Transfiguring the Arts and Sciences,* 51.

14. Mills, *White Collar: The American Middle Classes,* 235-38.

15. The degree to which the British administrative apparatus was a rationalized bureaucracy in the eighteenth and early nineteenth centuries is debatable. I

am presupposing a quasi-rationalization or a rationalization in process, based on Brewer's *The Sinews of Power: War, Money and the English State, 1688-1783*. Brewer argues that "the board and departments that were either established or revamped in the late seventeenth century were almost all marked by some features which we would describe as 'bureaucratic'" (69); but, then again, "the administrative apparatus of eighteenth-century England" remained "a mixture of medieval and modern institutions" (70) and there persisted sinecurists, pluralists, absent officers whose work was performed by deputies, and various forms of corruption (69–75). There was, in other words, a "compromise between political clientage and administrative efficiency" (75). For slightly different accounts, with relatively stronger emphases on the perseverance of "Old Corruption" and the English *ancien régime*, see Rubinstein, "The End of 'Old Corruption' in Britain 1780–1860"; and David Roberts, "Jeremy Bentham and the Victorian Administrative State." That Wordsworth seems to have strictly separated his distributorship from his poetic career, and that he was so conscientious about his tax collecting work, might be due to his seeking to distinguish his work from the pluralism that was a symptomatic practice of "Old Corruption." See, e.g., Rubinstein, "The End of 'Old Corruption,'" 57.

16. Brewer, *The Sinews of Power*, xvi–xv, 64–87.

17. Brewer, *The Sinews of Power*, xvi; also see Higgs, *The Information State in England*, 31. For a useful work on some of the issues discussed in this chapter—Wordsworth and the "information state"—but reaching different conclusions, see Garrett, *Wordsworth and the Writing of the Nation*, esp. chapters 1 and 2.

18. Blackstone, *Commentaries on the Laws of England*, 1:324.

19. See Mary Wordsworth, *The Letters of Mary Wordsworth*, 80.

20. Wordsworth, *The Letters of William and Dorothy Wordsworth*, Vol. 4, 56–57.

21. On Wordsworth's licensing responsibilities, see Moorman, *William Wordsworth*, 245n1. He was assisted throughout in the accounting work by a clerk whom he hired, John Carter, who also acted during the forty years he worked for the Wordsworth family as gardener, transcriber (including of *The Prelude*), and teacher to the Wordsworth children (Moorman, 245). Wordsworth scholarship awaits a richer biographical account of Carter, a support staff member who facilitated Wordsworth's poetic and bureaucratic work as well as the Wordsworth family's everyday life.

22. See Dowell, *A History of Taxation and Taxes in England*, 285–86; Dagnall, *Creating a Good Impression: Three Hundred Years of The Stamp Office and Stamp Duties*, 1, 11; and Weber, *From Max Weber: Essays in Sociology*, 228. This and all subsequent quotations from *The Excursion* are from Wordsworth, *The Excursion*, edited by Bushell, Butler, and Jaye, and are cited parenthetically in the text by book and line number(s). Quotations from the dedicatory sonnet ("To the Right

Honorable . . . ") are cited by line number; quotations from the "Preface to *The Excursion*" and its "Summary of Contents" are cited by page number.

23. Dagnall, *Creating a Good Impression*, 1-14; Dowell, *A History of Taxation*, 286-96.

24. Qtd. in Dowell, *A History of Taxation*, 296.

25. Dagnall, *Creating a Good Impression*, 15-17; Dowell, *A History of Taxation*, 288-89.

26. Dagnall, *Creating a Good Impression*, 47-49.

27. Moorman, *William Wordsworth*, 249-55.

28. Wordsworth, *The Letters of William and Dorothy Wordsworth*, Vol. 4, 56. Because distributors like Wordsworth earned a percentage of the sales (Moorman, *William Wordsworth*, 246) rather than earning a salary, there is some ambiguity about the extent to which Wordsworth can be considered a bureaucrat in the modern sense. Dagnall, for example, considers distributors as working for, but not employed by, the Stamp Office, because they were not technically full-time workers and they were paid on a poundage basis. See Dagnall, *Creating a Good Impression*, 11, 95. Nonetheless this chapter adopts a view closer to Higgs's in *The Information State in England*, which demonstrates that the state in this epoch was both centralized and decentralized insofar as the tax-collecting and information-gathering operations of the state included a variety of groups, particularly at the local level—e.g., distributors. See also Liu, *Wordsworth: The Sense of History*, 98-99; and Frey, *British State Romanticism*, 55.

29. Wordsworth's bond of office confirms that he did indeed grant licenses to different kinds of vendors, to "Pawnbrokers, Appraisers, Dealers in Thread, Lace, medicines, persons letting to hire Stage Coaches, Diligences," and that he collected duties on "Race Horses [and] Gold and Silver Plate" among other articles (qtd. in Moorman, *William Wordsworth*, 245n1).

30. Dagnall, *Creating a Good Impression*, 23-46; Dowell, *A History of Taxation*, 285-86.

31. See also Schoenfield, *The Professional Wordsworth*, 248-49.

32. This tax was originally inspired by an allusion in Adam Smith's *An Inquiry into the Nature and Causes of the Wealth of Nations* (1776) to an ancient Roman tax on hereditaments. England's then Prime Minister, Lord North, introduced the legacy duty in 1780, and it was expanded in 1796 and subsequent years by North's successor, William Pitt. See Dowell, *A History of Taxation*, 133-35.

33. Gill, *William Wordsworth*, 83-84; See also Liu, *Wordsworth: The Sense of History*, 335. Given the significance of legacies for Wordsworth, one might wish to analogize legacies and literary versions of "inheritance"—the national literary canon (e.g., the "legacies" of Spenser, Shakespeare, Milton) or the deferred

appreciation by a future reading public (a poetic "legacy" for later readers)—both matters of deep concern for Wordsworth, of course, and notable topoi across Romantic literature. Yet the "certain papers called Forms" that Wordsworth processed raise a different question than that of the broad theme of legacies as it appears in Wordsworth's writing, a question more to do with how certain norms of written communication, most starkly exemplified by standardized forms, are met with subtle accommodations and counteractions in his literary writing.

34. This Act is Statute 36 Geo. III., c.52. The legacy duty, although in place since 1780, was easily evaded, either deliberately or through ignorance (one could simply not report the bequest), hence the 1796 Act's provisions. See Lovelass, *An Abstract of, and Observations on, the Statutes Imposing Stamp Duty* [. . .], 10. Before 1796, the legacy duty was a stamp tax only on the paper form, so if no form was completed, no tax was collected; after 1796, the tax was placed on the personal property of the deceased. See also Hanson, *The Acts Relating to Probate, Legacy, and Succession Duties* [. . .], 10–11. After 1802, the Stamp Office sought to remedy the problem of tax evasion by having ecclesiastical registers (which recorded information on wills and administrators) transmitted to them (Hanson, 61–62).

35. Moorman, *William Wordsworth*, 247. Wordsworth also purchased government annuities hinging on the lives of the elderly (i.e., the ages to which they lived); these investments are described in Mitchell and Mitchell, "Wordsworth and the Old Men," 31–52.

36. Lovelass, *An Abstract of, and Observations on, the Statutes Imposing Stamp Duty*, 10.

37. Gitelman, *Paper Knowledge*, 22.

38. Higgs, *The Information State in England*.

39. Wordsworth, *The Letters of William and Dorothy Wordsworth*, Vol. 4, 57.

40. Wordsworth, *The Letters of William and Dorothy Wordsworth*, Vol. 4, 56.

41. Lovelass, *An Abstract of, and Observations on, the Statutes Imposing Stamp Duty*, 24.

42. Wordsworth, *The Letters of William and Dorothy Wordsworth*, Vol. 4, 56.

43. Lovelass, *An Abstract of, and Observations on, the Statutes Imposing Stamp Duty*, 24.

44. Beniger, *The Control Revolution*, 15–16.

45. Scott, *Seeing Like a State*, 4.

46. Foucault, *"Society Must Be Defended,"* 246; see also Scott, *Seeing Like a State*, 80–83.

47. In her rousing recent work *Forms*, Caroline Levine also sets out from the historical fact that "form has never belonged only to the discourse of aesthetics" (2). Yet where Levine calls for an equivalence—a removal of distinctions—between

sociopolitical forms and literary forms, I find it is important to maintain them in in the context of my discussion. It is only by observing the differences between, and the specificities of, social forms (e.g., the arrangements of bodies or spaces) and literary forms (e.g., the arrangements of sounds, words, poetic lines, etc.) that one can observe shadowing forth between the two, and mediating between them, sets of practices in *writing*—one important set is what I am calling *bureaucratic form*. Occupying this mediating position, bureaucratic form, in one direction, has an organizing effect on social form: it is well known that social forms assume and maintain the orderings they do because of bureaucratic form and its orderings, classifications, and standards. One might invoke any number of works in connection with this well-established idea, but among them, I would point to Geoffrey Bowker's and Susan Leigh Star's indispensable *Sorting Things Out* and Scott's aforementioned *Seeing Like a State*. In Scott's words, "the state, of all institutions, is best equipped to insist on treating people according to its schemata, [and] categories that may have begun as . . . artificial inventions . . . can end by becoming categories that organize people's daily experience precisely because they are embedded in state-created institutions that structure that experience" (82–83). That is, social forms are registered—i.e., inscribed and officially filed— and reproduced by bureaucratic form, which finds instantiations in various kinds of identifying documents (e.g., birth certificates, passports) and administrative genres (e.g., the forms one fills out when visiting a doctor's office or when filing one's taxes). As for the effects of bureaucratic form in the other direction, on literary form, that is the substance of this chapter's readings of Wordsworth's literary writings. See also Kramnick and Nersessian, "Form and Explanation."

48. Johnson, *A Dictionary of the English Language.*

49. Eighteenth Century Collections Online, accessed March 13, 2017.

50. Johnson, s.v. "form"

51. Johnson, s.v., "formulary"; *OED*, s.v., "formulary," quotes Johnson (emphasis mine).

52. See also Guillory, "The Memo and Modernity," 127–28.

53. Sinclair, *The Statistical Account of Scotland*, viii (emphasis mine). On Wordsworth and Sinclair, see Glen, "'We Are Seven' in the 1790s."

54. Sinclair, viii–x. Nevertheless, as Mark Salber Phillips has recently stressed, against Sinclair's utilitarian, scientific, information-centric approach, the responses he got back from parish clergy—and what he ended up publishing—created a portrait of "disorderly abundance." See Phillips, *On Historical Distance*, 113.

55. The historian of technical writing, Elizabeth Tebeaux, has argued that early medieval estate accounting manuscripts (ca. 1200), as well as early Exchequer accounts show deliberate strategies of visual-spatial design for the purposes

of ease of use (in a time of very uneven literacy) and standardization, prior even to the early modern commercial practice of double-entry bookkeeping. See Tebeaux, "Visual Texts: Format and the Evolution of English Accounting Texts, 1100–1700."

56. I rely on a helpful series of essays written by members of the Designing Information for Everyday Life, 1815-1914, project at the University of Reading: namely, Paul Stiff, Paul Dobraszczyk, and Mike Esbester.

57. See Esbester, "Taxing Design? Design and Readers in British Tax Forms before 1914," 88. See also Dobraszczyk, "'Give in Your Account': Using and Abusing Victorian Census Forms"; and Stiff, Dobraszczyk, and Esbester, "Designing and Gathering Information: Perspectives on Nineteenth-Century Forms," esp. 65. Aside from my reservation about this group's understanding of forms as facilitating "dialogue"—many forms are not read at all and only filed away for potential later relevance, and many forms seem designed to prevent anything like real "dialogue," since only one side is demanding only certain particulars—I have learned much from the research done by the Designing Information for Everyday Life, 1815-1914, project.

58. See also Guillory, "The Memo and Modernity," 127–28. Guillory observes that modern informational genres like the memo, report, form, etc., depend on graphical arrangement: these written bureaucratic genres do away with classical rhetorical strategies of verbally conveying arrangement and hierarchy in favor of manipulating "the spatial organization of the page" and drawing attention to the structure of the information to be communicated by using headings, indentations, bullet points, and the like.

59. Gitelman, *Paper Knowledge*, 23–24; Stallybrass, "Printing and the Manuscript Revolution," esp. 112; Pamela Neville-Sington, "Press, Politics and Religion," 576.

60. Neville-Sington, "Press, Politics and Religion," 583.

61. Some forms, including those for the British census were also called "schedules." See Dobraszczyk, "'Give in Your Account.'"

62. *OED*, s.v. "form." A useful account by the business historian JoAnne Yates tracks the rise of internal forms in the later nineteenth- and early twentieth-century American corporation (see Yates, *Control through Communication*, 80–85), but the point here is that Wordsworth and his moment's British fiscal-bureaucracy saw a similar rise.

63. See also Mitchell and Mitchell, "Wordsworth and the Old Men," 34, where Wordsworth is, in 1831, referring again to blank forms, this time for the collection of data for an annuities scheme with which he was involved.

64. Stiff, Dobraszczyk, and Esbester, "Designing and Gathering Information," 64.

65. Qtd. in L. J. Hume, "The Development of Industrial Accounting: The Benthams' Contribution," 25.

66. Nersessian, *Utopia, Limited: Romanticism and Adjustment*, 2–9.

67. Curtius, *European Literature and the Latin Middle Ages*, 487–94.

68. See McKendrick, "Josiah Wedgwood and Factory Discipline"; and Thompson, "Time, Work-Discipline, and Industrial Capitalism."

69. All quotations of poems from *Lyrical Ballads* are from Wordsworth and Coleridge, *Lyrical Ballads*, edited by Brett and Jones, and are cited parenthetically in the text by line number(s). Quotations from the "Preface" to *Lyrical Ballads* and "Note on 'The Thorn'" are also from this edition, and are cited by page number.

70. See the introduction to this volume for a discussion of "sauntering" as a type of inattentive reader.

71. Frost, "The Most of It," line 20.

72. White, introduction to *The Elements of Style*, xv.

73. For an interesting thesis that relates poetic concision to the supply and cost of paper during the Romantic period, see Erickson, *The Economy of Literary Form: English Literature and the Industrialization of Publishing*, 19–27. My account may be compatible with Erickson's, although it should be apparent that I am suggesting that brevity in poetry involves several other factors (the New Rhetoric, the consideration of *brevitas*, bureaucratic form, etc.).

74. Hartman, *Wordsworth's Poetry, 1787–1814*, 151.

75. Howell, "Renaissance Rhetoric and Modern Rhetoric," 158–59.

76. Wordsworth, *Essays*, 57. This and subsequent quotations from the three essays are from *Essays upon Epitaphs*, in *The Prose Works of William Wordsworth*, Vol. 2, edited by Owen and Smyser, and are cited parenthetically in the text as *Essays* followed by page number. I refer to all three essays together as *Essays*—although the second and third essays were not published until 1876—acknowledging their thematic continuity and the fact that Wordsworth wrote all three essays in a short time frame. See Owen and Smyser, "Introduction: General" [to *Essays upon Epitaphs*], 45–47.

77. See, e.g., Scodel, *The English Poetic Epitaph: Commemoration and Conflict from Jonson to Wordsworth*, 2.

78. There is also consideration in legal discourse during this era about the relation between documentary writing on paper and writing on stone and other media, in the context of the relative durabilities of different media and the potential for tampering with writing on them. For example, in his *Commentaries on the Laws of England* (1765–1769), William Blackstone notes: "The deed must be *written*, or I presume *printed*; for it may be in any character or any language; but it must be upon paper, or parchment. For if it be written on stone, board, linen, leather, or

the like, it is no deed. Wood or stone may be more durable, and linen less liable to [e]rasures; but writing on paper or parchment unites in itself, more perfectly than any other way, both those desirable qualities: for there is nothing else so durable, and at the same time so little liable to alteration; nothing so secure from alteration, that is at the same time so durable" (Blackstone, *Commentaries*, 2:297).

79. Hartman, "Inscriptions and Romantic Nature Poetry," 31-46; Latour, "Drawing Things Together," 19-68.

80. Nissel, *People Count: A History of the General Register Office*, 2. Beginning with a 1538 injunction by Henry VIII's chief minister, Thomas Cromwell, parochial clergymen were required to record baptisms, weddings, and funerals. Mandated by the state but in practice carried out at the local ecclesiastical level, the registers did not amount to an entirely reliable record of the three particulars they recorded, for reasons ranging from the fact that they did not include information about those who did not belong to the Established Church to the problem of furtive marriages and spotty recordkeeping. From the inception of parish registers, then, various arguments were raised against them. And in 1597 it was mandated that parishes send transcripts of their registers to a diocesan registrar, where information from many parishes was combined in order to be more useful as a larger data set and to ensure that the diocese held a duplicate of local registers in case of fire, floods, or mice. In the later eighteenth century there was a further push toward a national, centralized state registry, which was finally established by law in 1837. See Nissel, 6-11.

81. Foucault, *"Society Must Be Defended,"* 242.

82. Foucault, *"Society Must Be Defended,"* 242-43.

83. See Ferguson, *Pornography*, 18. For a similar line of thinking, see Robert Mitchell, "Biopolitics and Population Aesthetics," which emphasizes how the biopolitical concept of "population" depends on individual idiosyncrasies as much as general statistical similarities.

84. Mitchell, "Biopolitics and Population Aesthetics," 369.

85. Stevens, "Anecdote of Men by the Thousand."

86. Reed, *Wordsworth: The Chronology of the Middle Years, 1800-1815*, 22-25, 683-85; Bushell, Butler, and Jaye, "Eight Stages of *Excursion* Composition," 426-28.

87. On the Wordsworth family's multi-generational ties to the Lowthers, see Manning, "Wordsworth at St. Bees." As Manning urges us to remember, "Wordsworth's revolutionary ardors . . . [are] an aberration from a pattern of family service to the Lowthers" (291).

88. Moorman, *William Wordsworth*, 246-51.

89. Schoenfield, *The Professional Wordsworth*, 247-48.

90. Wordsworth, "Fenwick Note to *The Excursion*," 1222–23.

91. Dowell, *A History of Taxation*, 135.

92. Hickey, *Impure Conceits: Rhetoric and Ideology in Wordsworth's "Excursion,"* 21.

93. See Beniger, *The Control Revolution*.

94. See Goodman, *Georgic Modernity and British Romanticism*, 134.

95. See Phillips, *On Historical Distance*, 97–114.

96. See also Canuel, "Bentham, Utility, and the Romantic Imagination," 506–07.

97. See also Goodman, *Georgic Modernity*, 116; Hickey, *Impure Conceits*, 89–93.

98. Goodman, *Georgic Modernity*, 116.

99. [Jeffrey, Review of *The Excursion* published in the *Edinburgh Review*, October 1807], 40.

100. [Jeffrey, Review of *The Excursion*], 42.

101. Bentham, *Official Aptitude Maximized, Expense Minimized*, 6. Bentham's comment is in the context of his *Constitutional Code*, and its project of making governments more efficient. But the motto can be applied to the Benthamic notion of efficiency in general. It is also of interest that Bentham is credited with coining the very terms *maximize* and *minimize*.

102. Bentham, *Official Aptitude Maximized*, 6.

103. [Jeffrey, Review of *The Excursion*], 39–42.

104. [Jeffrey, Review of *The Excursion*], 39–40.

105. *OED*, s.v. "tl;dr.": "colloq. (orig. and chiefly in electronic communications) (a) int. 'too long; didn't read' (also occasionally 'don't read'); used as a dismissive response to an account, narrative, etc., considered excessively or unnecessarily long, or to introduce a summary of a longer piece of text; (b) adj. designating a short summary of a longer text."

Chapter 3: Shelley amid the Age of Separations

1. Turkle, *Alone Together*, 12.

2. Baym, *Personal Connections in the Digital Age*, 132.

3. Baym, *Personal Connections*, 129.

4. Jagoda, *Network Aesthetics*, 225.

5. Jagoda, *Network Aesthetics*, 224.

6. Beniger, *The Control Revolution*, 7.

7. Siskin and Warner, "This Is Enlightenment," 12.

8. Siskin and Warner, "This Is Enlightenment," 12–15.

9. Ferguson, *An Essay on the History of Civil Society*, 175.

10. Ferguson, *An Essay on the History of Civil Society*, 207.

11. Langan and McLane, "The Medium of Romantic Poetry," 256–57.

12. Williams, "The Romantic Artist," 30.

13. Williams, *Politics and Letters*, 113–15.

14. Gouldner, *The Coming Crisis of Western Sociology*, 358, 332–34. See also Hewitt's *The Possibilities of Society*. It is useful to combine Hewitt's understanding of Romantic "poetic sociology" (Hewitt, ix) (which, she argues, arrives in the wake of the French Revolution, far in advance of sociology's belated discipline formation a century later) with John D. Brewer's argument that pre-sociological discourse—what Mark Salber Phillips calls "the discourse of the social" (*Society and Sentiment*, 18)—emerged in Adam Ferguson's Scottish conjectural history, a key context therefore for Romantic "poetic sociology." See Brewer, "Conjectural History, Sociology and Social Change in Eighteenth Century Scotland."

15. For a contemporary sociological work focused on media, see, e.g., Thompson, *The Media and Modernity: A Social Theory of the Media*.

16. Williams, "The Romantic Artist," 43.

17. Williams, "The Romantic Artist," 47.

18. Williams, "The Romantic Artist," 43.

19. Shelley, *A Defence of Poetry*, 513. Hereafter, all quotations from Shelley's poetry and prose (excluding his correspondence) are from *Shelley's Poetry and Prose: Authoritative Texts, Criticism*, edited by Reiman and Fraistat, and are cited parenthetically in the text by title, book or canto number (when applicable), and line number(s). Quotations from Shelley's letters are from *The Letters of Percy Bysshe Shelley*, and are cited by volume and page numbers.

20. Keach, *Shelley's Style*, 22.

21. Shelley, *A Defence of Poetry*, 531.

22. Shelley, *A Defence of Poetry*, 513.

23. Shelley, *A Defence of Poetry*, 523, 532, 533.

24. Contrary to Raymond Williams, one recalls that Shelley himself was cognizant of his dual commitment to poetry and the social sciences, as well as the fact that poets were "being forced into practical exile": "I consider Poetry very subordinate to moral & political science, & if I were well, certainly I would aspire to the latter" (Shelley, *Letters*, 2:71). On Romantic poets' self-aware and deliberate engagement of moral philosophical discourse, see McLane, *Romanticism and the Human Sciences*, 10–42.

25. Williams, *Marxism and Literature*, 136–40.

26. Williams, *Marxism and Literature*, 140.

27. Williams, *Marxism and Literature*, 141.

28. Shelley, *A Defence of Poetry*, 514.

29. Shelley, *A Defence of Poetry*, 511. At the start of the *Defence*, Shelley

appears to decline taking on this largest of subjects—"let us dismiss those more general considerations which might involve an enquiry into the principles of society itself" (511)—but this is also a disclosure, via paralepsis, of the principal task at hand.

30. St. Clair, *The Reading Nation in the Romantic Period*, 218. To give one example, Steven Goldsmith points out, in *Unbuilding Jerusalem*, that the "internal political dynamics" of *Prometheus Unbound* "are taken to be one and the same as its political effects, by which I mean the way it participates in actual social struggles regarding the relations of power. The limitations of this otherwise valuable approach appear as soon as the liberating impact of the play is made to depend on readers, for indeed Shelley's actual audience was and is very small and remarkably homogeneous" (211n3). This chapter concurs with Goldsmith's argument that Shelley's effects—here I am maintaining poetic-medial-sociological insight—need to be reconstructed in a manner other than one that equates them directly with his works' "internal political dynamics."

31. Warner, *Publics and Counterpublics*, 137.

32. Warner, *Publics and Counterpublics*, 130.

33. The most familiar version of this topos is, of course, found in Wordsworth's "Essay, Supplementary to the Preface," where he writes that "every Author, as far as he is great and at the same time *original*, has had the task of *creating* the taste by which he is to be enjoyed" (80). My discussion's aim is, however, to approach Shelley's difficult style not from the perspective of audiences (present and future), but as a model for sociality in a world that feels highly connected, even too highly connected.

34. See Behrendt, *Shelley and His Audiences*, 143–85.

35. Ferguson, *An Essay on the History of Civil Society*, 24.

36. Ferguson, *An Essay on the History of Civil Society*, 206–07.

37. Brewer, "Conjectural History, Sociology and Social Change in Eighteenth Century Scotland," 17–22. For a concurring account, see Phillips, *Society and Sentiment*, 180–81. Durkheim's concept of "organic solidarity" is discussed later in this chapter.

38. Comte, "Considerations of the Spiritual Power," 211. Comte's study of Ferguson is mentioned by Jones, "Introduction" to *Comte*, xiv.

39. Wordsworth, *Letters of William and Dorothy Wordsworth*, Vol. 3, 375–76.

40. The reference to "the cash nexus and class divisions" comes from Manning, "Wordsworth at St. Bees," 289.

41. Ferguson, *An Essay on the History of Civil Society*, 208.

42. Durkheim, *Division of Labor*, 203, 209.

43. Clifford Siskin too, in *The Work of Writing*, links a communications

development (the proliferation of printed matter in this same period) to an intensification of the drive to specialization in intellectual labor, i.e., division into different kinds of modern professions (104 inter alia).

44. Durkheim, *Division of Labor*, 206.

45. Durkheim, *Rules of Sociological Method*, 92.

46. Durkheim, *Rules of Sociological Method*, 92–93. In his earlier work, *The Division of Labor*, Émile Durkheim makes a similar exception for England: "Yet it may well be that in any given society, a certain division of labor, and in particular the economic division of labor, is very developed, although the segmentary social type is still very strongly pronounced. Indeed, this seems to be the case in England. Large-scale industry and commerce appear to be as developed there as on the Continent, although the 'alveolar' system is still very marked, as is demonstrated both by the autonomy of local life and by the authority preserved by tradition" (221n31).

47. Durkheim's account of "material density" is corroborated by Miranda Burgess's recent work, one aspect of which recovers the period's networks of carriage. I believe there is something close to what Burgess calls "anxiety" in *Epipsychidion*'s troubled image of social agglutination, discussed later in this chapter. See Burgess, "Transport."

48. Wordsworth, "Preface," 294.

49. Wordsworth, "Preface," 294; Smith, *An Inquiry into the Nature and Causes of the Wealth of Nations*, 2:782; see also Chandler, *An Archaeology of Sympathy*, 284.

50. Wordsworth, "Lines Written a Few Miles Above Tintern Abbey . . . ," line 131; Shelley, *The Cenci*, 3.1.277.

51. As P.M.S. Dawson puts it, "Shelley's poetic use of language exploits the ambiguity present in the ordinary usage of 'attraction' (as both the physical force of gravitation and the moral force of love) to suggest that gravitation can be seen as physical manifestation of love, or love as the moral manifestation of gravitation" (Dawson, "'A Sort of Natural Magic,'" 28).

52. Smith, *An Inquiry into the Nature and Causes of the Wealth of Nations*, 1:25.

53. See, e.g., Mitchell, *Sympathy and the State in the Romantic Era*.

54. Durkheim, *Division of Labor*, 50.

55. Durkheim, *Division of Labor*, 50.

56. Shelley, "Advertisement," 392.

57. See Leask, "Shelley's 'Magnetic Ladies': Romantic Mesmerism and the Politics of the Body," 60.

58. Franta, *Romanticism and the Rise of the Mass Public*, 7.

59. Gray, Collins, and Goldsmith, *The Poems of Thomas Gray, William Collins, Oliver Goldsmith*, 157.

60. Shelley, "Advertisement," 392.

61. Shelley, "Advertisement," 393.

62. Shelley, "Advertisement," 393.

63. A popular, self-help book on introversion, Susan Cain's *Quiet: The Power of Introverts in a World That Can't Stop Talking*, also defines someone with a balance between extravert (or "extrovert") and introvert personality qualities as "an ambivert" (14), but much of Cain's work also wishes to imply that introverts are often ambiverts (i.e., they are sometimes extraverted, and not necessarily shy or misanthropic) (11–13).

64. Warner, *Publics and Counterpublics*, 74–75.

Chapter 4: Keats's Ways

1. Keats, *The Letters of John Keats* (2.5). Hereafter, all quotations from Keats's letters are cited parenthetically in the text as *Letters*, with volume and page numbers.

2. Lau, *Keats's Paradise Lost*, 128.

3. Keats presumably means 10 o'clock in his own time zone, and 10 p.m. (which would be the afternoon in Kentucky) rather than 10 a.m. But his wording ("at the same time") is more ambiguous from George's perspective: should George read a passage of Shakespeare at 10 o'clock in his own time zone, or do they need to figure out the time difference so as to be perfectly synchronized? These may appear to be trivial scheduling details, but the significance of Keats's scenario is that such questions about time difference emerge with the possibilities of relatively rapid communication and transportation that his moment was witnessing. See Schivelbusch's classic *The Railway Journey: The Industrialization of Time and Space in the 19th Century*, 42–44, on the gradual standardization, by the various railway lines in Great Britain and the United States, of disparate local times.

4. Lamb, "Distant Correspondents," 96.

5. Bolter and Grusin, *Remediation: Understanding New Media*, 3–15.

6. Throughout this chapter's discussion, *Hyperion* (in italics) refers to both poems at once, as a single literary endeavor. But when referring to one of the *Hyperion* fragments individually, I use "Hyperion" as short for "Hyperion. A Fragment," and "The Fall" as short for "The Fall of Hyperion—A Dream." Quotations from these works and all other poems by Keats are from *Keats's Poetry and Prose: Authoritative Texts, Criticism*, edited by Cox, and are cited parenthetically in the text by title, book or canto number (when applicable), and line number(s).

7. Several recent works on Keats and the topics of communication, media, and book history are of interest here. See Hess, "'This Living Hand': Commonplacing Keats"; Rejack, "Keats on the Sea: The Circulation of Transatlantic Letters"; and Burkett, *Romantic Mediations*, 45–73.

8. More than sixty prototypes of electric telegraphs were attempted between 1753 and 1837, and poetry commenting on electric telegraphy appeared in periodicals throughout. See Standage, *The Victorian Internet*, 18–19.

9. Thorburn and Jenkins, "Introduction: Toward an Aesthetics of Transition," 2–3.

10. Several excellent studies situate the period's literature within a larger, reticulated world, portraying a Romanticism that more and more resembles the flight routes found in the back of in-flight magazines, albeit less densely but nevertheless widely interconnected. See Baucom, *Specters of the Atlantic: Finance Capital, Slavery, and the Philosophy of History*; Burgess, "Transport: Mobility, Anxiety, and the Romantic Poetics of Feeling"; Favret, *War at a Distance: Romanticism and the Making of Modern Wartime*; and Goodman, "'Uncertain Disease': Nostalgia, Pathologies of Motion, Practices of Reading."

11. Wordsworth, "Preface," 294; De Quincey, "The English Mail-Coach," 202. I borrow the term "society of flows" from Armand Mattelart, *The Invention of Communication*.

12. Guillory, "Genesis of the Media Concept," 342.

13. Hartman, "Spectral Symbolism and Authorial Self in Keats's *Hyperion*," 64–66; Terada, "Looking at the Stars Forever," 286; Rzepka, *Self as Mind*, 165–242. For a cinematic reading of Keats's "Lamia," see Orrin Wang's "Coming Attractions: 'Lamia' and Cinematic Sensation."

14. Royle, *Telepathy and Literature: Essays on the Reading Mind*, 4–5. Noel Jackson has also recovered how sentiments, particularly revolutionary feeling, were understood to transfer between individuals on the model of electricity; see Jackson, *Science and Sensation in Romantic Poetry*, 47–51. Miranda Burgess too discusses the circulation of feelings between individuals in "Transport: Mobility, Anxiety, and the Romantic Poetics of Feeling." Both accounts benefit from the sustained analyses and case studies of communicable feeling in Adela Pinch, *Strange Fits of Passion*. On telegraphy in particular, see Richard Menke's *Telegraphic Realism*, and its account of how literature began "imagining itself as a medium and information system in an age of new media" (Menke, 3).

15. On mesmerism, see Winter, *Mesmerized*.

16. Headrick, *When Information Came of Age*, 193–97.

17. Langan and McLane, "The Medium of Romantic Poetry," 257; Coleridge, *Notebooks*, 2:2012.

18. Some early New Historicist readings of Keats include Jerome McGann, "Keats and the Historical Method in Literary Criticism"; and Marjorie Levinson, *Keats's Life of Allegory*. Two special issues of the journal *Studies in Romanticism* are devoted to the question of the relation between Keats and politics. The more recent

one, "Reading Keats, Thinking Politics" (Summer 2011), commemorates an earlier issue edited by Susan Wolfson, "Keats and Politics" (Summer 1986), and contains some nuanced approaches employed today to understand "the political 'thinking' made possible by Keats's poetry" (Rohrbach and Sun, "Reading Keats, Thinking Politics: An Introduction," 231), while revealing the generative influence on such approaches of works like Goodman's *Georgic Modernity and British Romanticism*.

19. Gitelman, *Always Already New*, 20–21, discusses the special relation between history and media.

20. Eliot, "Shelley and Keats," 93.

21. William Empson's reading of the "Ode on Melancholy" sits at the heart of his chapter on the final and severest form of ambiguity. See Empson, *Seven Types of Ambiguity*, 205 and 214–17.

22. I allude, respectively, to the following studies: Stillinger, *Reading The Eve of St. Agnes: The Multiples of Complex Literary Transaction*, 126–28, addresses "complexity"; Simpson, *Romanticism, Nationalism, and the Revolt Against Theory*, 168–71, posits that Keats's rejection of Enlightenment system and method results in a traumatic loss of bearings, as well as in poetic inwardness and "indeterminacy"; and Bennett, *Keats, Narrative and Audience: The Posthumous Life of Writing*, 2ff, reads Keats through the notion of solecism.

23. Chandler, *England in 1819*, 399–400.

24. Bennett, *Keats, Narrative and Audience*, 1–14.

25. Carruthers, *The Craft of Thought*, 77 (emphasis in the original). Hereafter cited parenthetically in the text.

26. See Angus Fletcher's annotation of "[p]rogress, real and ideal," in Fletcher, *Allegory*, 151–57.

27. Levinson, *Keats's Life of Allegory*, 11–15.

28. Augustine describes reading, actually misreading, as a journey: "Anyone with an interpretation of the scriptures that differs from that of the writer is misled, but not because the scriptures are lying. If, as I began by saying, he is misled by an idea of the kind that builds up love, which is the end of the commandment, he is misled in the same way as a walker who leaves his path by mistake but reaches the destination to which the path leads by going through a field. But he must be put right and shown it's more useful not to leave the path, in case the habit of deviating should force him to go astray or even adrift" (Augustine, *On Christian Teaching*, 27). See also Eden, *Hermeneutics and the Rhetorical Tradition*, 53–63, and that work's discussion of Augustine's figurations of reading as a homecoming.

29. The process by which the difficulty or authority of scripture is invoked by certain "secular" literary texts seeking to wield an analogous kind of authority is complex and has already received ample explication. Angus Fletcher offers a

lucid genealogy, from the "difficult ornament" of scripture to eighteenth-century sublimity, in Fletcher, *Allegory*, 233–45. See also Guillory, *Poetic Authority*, viii–x, 21–22; and Ziolkowski, "Theories of Obscurity in the Latin Tradition."

30. Manning, "Wordsworth at St. Bees," 275–76.

31. De Man, "Introduction: The Negative Road," xi.

32. For a sustained discussion of Spenser's influence on Keats, see Kucich, *Keats, Shelley, and Romantic Spenserianism*, 137–239.

33. Spenser, *The Faerie Queene: Book Six and the Mutabilitie Cantos*, Proem, stanza 1, lines 1–7.

34. Wordsworth, "Scorn not the Sonnet," line 11.

35. Bennett, *Keats, Narrative and Audience*, 78–79. For an interesting recent study that situates the idea of travails in Keats within the context of secret societies, see Wunder's *Keats, Hermeticism, and the Secret Societies*. Wunder observes that "Rosicrucian and Masonic texts consistently stressed the struggles man must face to gain wisdom and reach a higher state of spirituality, and both societies maintained that the search itself, the process, was the key. . . . Masonic initiation rites offered to their brethren a process by which they moved in stages called 'grades' to what initiates were told was a purer 'approximation of spiritual essence'" (17).

36. See Burke, *A Philosophical Enquiry into the Origin of Our Ideas of the Sublime and Beautiful and Other Pre-revolutionary Writings*, 102–03, 171–77.

37. In the letter considered in the introduction to this book, Keats seems to celebrate the stylistic principle of clarity. Also see the introduction for a treatment of the New Rhetoric, drawing on Guillory, "The Memo and Modernity," 119–20; Goodman, *Georgic Modernity*, 17–37; and Elfenbein, *Romanticism and the Rise of English*, 144–84.

38. James Chandler has suggested that Wordsworth's ode "Intimations of Immortality [. . .]" anticipates Ernst Haeckel's theory of biological recapitulation (i.e., ontogeny recapitulates phylogeny), and we see the same operation adopted by Keats's Wordsworthian letter (Chandler, "Wordsworth's Great Ode," 137).

39. Such images of entanglement and intricacy are appropriately legion in "Lamia," where Keats most fully explores the etymological and figurative web formed by the idea of perplexity: e.g., "cirque-couchant" (1.46); "gordian" (1.47); "interwreathed" (1.52); "golden brede" (1.158); "twisted braid" (1.186); "tangle[s] . . . in her mesh" (1.295); "to entangle, trammel up and snare" (2.52–53).

40. On these grounds, one might say that Wordsworth's greatest imprint on Keats's poetry is the epitaphic "Halted Traveller" mode, although Keats's specific variation takes the form that I have been reconstructing above as "dark passages." See Geoffrey Hartman's discussion of the "Halted Traveller" in Hartman, *Wordsworth's Poetry, 1787–1814*, 12–13.

41. Richard Woodhouse refers to the "dark hints in the Mythological poets of Greece & Rome" on the basis of which Keats would compose *Hyperion* (see Keats, *Keats's Poetry and Prose*, 476).

42. C. A. Patrides, "Paradise Lost and the Theory of Accommodation," 60.

43. On *commoda verba*, see Eden, *Hermeneutics and the Rhetorical Tradition*, 4; and Milton, *Paradise Lost*, 5.571–574. This example is discussed in Patrides, "Paradise Lost and the Theory of Accommodation," 59–60.

44. McLane, *Romanticism and the Human Sciences*, 203.

45. See Warner, "Uncritical Reading."

46. In "Lamia," in a wonderful simile, Keats compares the "trembling tone" (1.301) of Lamia's whisper to what transpires when "those who, safe together met alone/For the first time through many anguish'd days,/Use other speech than looks" (1.302–04): i.e., when two people can finally exchange words rather than mere glances. "Other speech" thus paradoxically denotes speech, and suggests that Keats understood many different kinds of communication—non-verbal ("looks") and verbal alike—in terms of language ("speech").

47. See Chapter 2 for Wordsworth's ideas on inscription across media.

48. Dante Alighieri, *De Vulgari Eloquentia*, 7.

Conclusion

1. My emphasis throughout on desires—communicative desires and media fantasies shared as cultural ideals and codified as norms—marks a difference from "artifactual" histories of communication (see the introduction) and from Friedrich A. Kittler's brilliant readings of how literature is shaped by "the material and technical resources at its disposal" (Wellbery, foreword to *Discourse Networks 1800/1900*, xiii).

2. Howell, "Renaissance Rhetoric and Modern Rhetoric," 158.

3. Ong, *Orality and Literacy*, 172. Hereafter cited parenthetically in the text. Ong makes similar statements in "The Literate Orality of Popular Culture Today," 290.

4. Ong, "The Literate Orality of Popular Culture Today," 290.

5. Ong, "The Literate Orality of Popular Culture Today," 290.

6. Ong, "The Literate Orality of Popular Culture Today," 290.

7. Jakobson, "Linguistics and Poetics," 69. See also McGann, *The Textual Condition*, 10–11.

8. Empson, *Seven Types of Ambiguity*, 236–37.

9. Culler, *Structuralist Poetics*, 144. Hereafter cited parenthetically in the text.

10. Richards, *Basic in Teaching*, 59–60.

11. Eliot, *The Waste Land*, lines 301–02.

Alighieri, Dante. *De Vulgari Eloquentia.* Translated by Steven Botterill. New York: Cambridge University Press, 1996.

Altick, Richard D. *The English Common Reader: A Social History of the Mass Reading Public, 1800–1900.* Columbus: Ohio State University Press, 1998.

Altieri, Charles, and Nicholas D. Nace. *The Fate of Difficulty in the Poetry of Our Time.* Evanston: Northwestern University Press, 2018.

Augustine. *On Christian Teaching.* Translated by R.P.H. Green. Oxford: Oxford University Press, 1997.

Baucom, Ian. *Specters of the Atlantic: Finance Capital, Slavery, and the Philosophy of History.* Durham: Duke University Press, 2005.

Baym, Nancy K. *Personal Connections in the Digital Age.* Cambridge: Polity Press, 2010.

Behrendt, Stephen C. *Shelley and His Audiences.* Lincoln: University of Nebraska Press, 1989.

Beniger, James R. *The Control Revolution: Technological and Economic Origins of the Information Society.* Cambridge, MA: Harvard University Press, 1986.

Bennett, Andrew. *Keats, Narrative, and Audience: The Posthumous Life of Writing.* Cambridge: Cambridge University Press, 1994.

———. *Wordsworth Writing.* Cambridge: Cambridge University Press, 2007.

Bentham, Jeremy. *Official Aptitude Maximized, Expense Minimized.* Edited by Philip Schofield. Oxford: Clarendon Press, 1993.

Bewell, Alan. "Coleridge and Communication." *Romanticism and Victorianism on the Net* 61 (April 2012). http://doi.org/10.7202/1018598ar.

Blackstone, William. *Commentaries on the Laws of England.* 4 vols. Chicago: University of Chicago Press, 1979.

Blair, Ann M. *Too Much to Know: Managing Scholarly Information before the Modern Age.* New Haven: Yale University Press, 2010.

Blanchard, William Isaac. *The Complete Instructor of Short Hand. Upon Principles Applicable to the European Languages* [. . .]. London: 1787. Eighteenth Century Collections Online (hereafter ECCO).

Bolter, J. David, and Richard A. Grusin. *Remediation: Understanding New Media.* Cambridge, MA: MIT Press, 1999.

Bowker, Geoffrey C., and Susan Leigh Star. *Sorting Things Out: Classification and Its Consequences.* Cambridge, MA: MIT Press, 1999.

Brewer, John. *The Sinews of Power: War, Money, and the English State, 1688–1783.* New York: Knopf, 1989.

Brewer, John D. "Conjectural History, Sociology and Social Change in Eighteenth Century Scotland: Adam Ferguson and the Division of Labor." In *The Making of Scotland: National, Culture and Social Change,* edited by David McCrone, Stephen Kendrick, and Pat Straw, 13–30. Edinburgh: Edinburgh University Press and the British Sociological Association, 1989.

Brooke-Smith, James. "Classification and Communication in Romantic-era Knowledge Institutions." *Nineteenth-Century Contexts* 38, no. 4 (2016): 233–45.

Burgess, Miranda. "Transport: Mobility, Anxiety, and the Romantic Poetics of Feeling." *Studies in Romanticism* 49, no. 2 (Summer, 2010): 229–60.

Burke, Edmund. *A Philosophical Enquiry into the Origin of Our Ideas of the Sublime and Beautiful and Other Pre-revolutionary Writings.* Edited by David Womersley. New York: Penguin, 1998.

———. *Reflections on the Revolution in France.* Edited by L. G. Mitchell. Oxford: Oxford University Press, 1993.

Burke, Kenneth. *Attitudes toward History.* 2 vols. New York: New Republic, 1937.

———. "Why Coleridge?" *The New Republic,* September 13, 1939: 163–64.

Burkett, Andrew. *Romantic Mediations: Media Theory and British Romanticism.* Albany: State University of New York Press, 2016.

Bushell, Sally, James A. Butler, and Michael C. Jaye with the assistance of David Garcia. "Eight Stages of *Excursion* Composition." In *The Excursion* by William Wordsworth, edited by Sally Bushell, James A. Butler, and Michael C. Jaye, with the assistance of David Garcia. 426–28. Ithaca: Cornell University Press, 2007.

Byrom, John. *The Universal English Short-hand* [. . .]. Manchester: Joseph Harrop, 1767. Google eBook. https://books.google.com/books?id=Azg5AAAAMAAJ.

Byron, George Gordon. *Don Juan.* In Lord Byron, *The Major Works,* edited by Jerome J. McGann, 373–879. Oxford: Oxford University Press, 1986.

Cain, Susan. *Quiet: The Power of Introverts in a World That Can't Stop Talking.* New York: Broadway Paperbacks, 2012.

Canuel, Mark. "Bentham, Utility, and the Romantic Imagination." In *Selected Writings: Jeremy Bentham*, edited by Stephen G. Engelmann, 500–19. New Haven: Yale University Press, 2011.

Carey, James W. "A Cultural Approach to Communication." In *Communication as Culture: Essays on Media and Society*, 11–28. London: Routledge, 2009.

Carlson, Julia S. *Romantic Marks and Measures: Wordsworth's Poetry in Fields of Print.* Philadelphia: University of Pennsylvania Press, 2016.

Carruthers, Mary. *The Craft of Thought: Meditation, Rhetoric, and the Making of Images, 400–1200.* Cambridge: Cambridge University Press, 1998.

Chandler, James. *An Archaeology of Sympathy: The Sentimental Mode in Literature and Cinema.* Chicago: University of Chicago Press, 2013.

———. *England in 1819: The Politics of Literary Culture and the Case of Romantic Historicism.* Chicago: University of Chicago Press, 1998.

———. "Wordsworth's Great Ode: Romanticism and the Progress of Poetry." In *The Cambridge Companion to British Romantic Poetry*, edited by James Chandler and Maureen N. McLane, 136–54. Cambridge: Cambridge University Press, 2008.

Christensen, Jerome. *Lord Byron's Strength: Romantic Writing and Commercial Society.* Baltimore: Johns Hopkins University Press, 1993.

Christie, William. "A Recent History of Poetic Difficulty." *ELH* 67, no. 2 (2000): 539–64.

Coburn, Kathleen. "Appendix C: Coleridge's Cryptogram." In *The Notebooks of Samuel Taylor Coleridge*, Vol. 2, Part 2, *Notes*, edited by Kathleen Coburn, 412–15. New York: Pantheon Books, 1957.

Cohen, Murray. *Sensible Words: Linguistic Practice in England, 1640–1785.* Baltimore: Johns Hopkins University Press, 1977.

Coleridge, Samuel Taylor. *Coleridge's Poetry and Prose: Authoritative Texts, Criticism.* Edited by Nicholas Halmi, Paul Magnuson, and Raimonda Modiano. New York: W. W. Norton, 2004.

———. *Lectures 1808–1819: On Literature.* Vol. 1, edited by R. A. Foakes. Princeton: Princeton University Press, 1987.

———. *The Notebooks of Samuel Taylor Coleridge.* Vols. 1 and 2, edited by Kathleen Coburn. New York: Pantheon Books, 1957, 1961. Vol. 3, edited by Kathleen Coburn. Princeton: Princeton University Press, 1973. Vol. 4, edited by Kathleen Coburn and Merton Christensen. Princeton: Princeton University Press, 1990.

————. "Punctuation Not Logical but Dramatic." In *Inquiring Spirit: A New Presentation of Coleridge from His Published and Unpublished Prose Writings*, edited by Kathleen Coburn, 106–10. Toronto: University of Toronto Press, 1979.

————. *The Rime of the Ancient Mariner*. Illustrated by Alexander Calder, with an essay by Robert Penn Warren. New York: Reynal & Hitchcock, 1946.

Comte, Auguste. "Considerations of the Spiritual Power." In *Comte: Early Political Writings*, edited by H. S. Jones, 187–227. Cambridge: Cambridge University Press, 1998.

Cordell, Ryan. "'Q i-jtb the Raven': Taking Dirty OCR Seriously." *Book History* 20, no. 1 (2017): 188–225.

Culler, Jonathan. *Structuralist Poetics: Structuralism, Linguistics, and the Study of Literature*. New York: Routledge, 2002.

Curtius, Ernst Robert. *European Literature and the Latin Middle Ages*. Princeton: Princeton University Press, 1967.

Dagnall, Harry. *Creating a Good Impression: Three Hundred Years of the Stamp Office and Stamp Duties*. London: H.M.S.O., 1994.

Dawson, P. M. S. "'A Sort of Natural Magic': Shelley and Animal Magnetism." *The Keats-Shelley Review* 1, no. 1 (1986): 15–34.

De Man, Paul. "Introduction: The Negative Road." In *John Keats: Selected Poetry*, ix–xxxvi. New York: New American Library, 1966.

De Quincey, Thomas. *The Collected Writings of Thomas De Quincey*. Vol. 1, *Autobiography from 1785–1803*. Edited by David Masson. Edinburgh: Black, 1889.

————. "The English Mail-Coach, or the Glory of Motion." In *Confessions of an English Opium-Eater and Other Writings*, edited by Grevel Lindop, 183–233. Oxford: Oxford University Press, 1998.

————. *Literary Reminiscences; from the Autobiography of an English Opium-Eater*, Vol. 2. Boston: Ticknor, Reed, and Fields, 1851. Google ebook. https://books.google.com/books?id=sodKAAAAYAAJ.

Diepeveen, Leonard. *The Difficulties of Modernism*. New York: Routledge, 2002.

Dobraszczyk, Paul. "'Give in Your Account': Using and Abusing Victorian Census Forms." *Journal of Victorian Culture* 14, no. 1 (2009): 1–25.

Dowell, Stephen. *A History of Taxation and Taxes in England, from the Earliest Times to the Present Day*. Vol. 3, *Direct Taxes and Stamp Duties*. New York: A. M. Kelley, 1965.

Durkheim, Émile. *The Division of Labor in Society*. Edited by Steven Lukes. Translated by W. D. Halls. New York: Free Press, 2014.

————. *The Rules of Sociological Method and Selected Texts on Sociology and its Method*. Edited by Steven Lukes. Translated by W. D. Halls. New York: Free Press, 2014.

Eden, Kathy. *Hermeneutics and the Rhetorical Tradition: Chapters in the Ancient Legacy and Its Humanist Reception.* New Haven: Yale University Press, 1997.

Edgeworth, Maria, and Richard Lovell Edgeworth. *Practical Education.* 2 vols. London: J. Johnson, 1798. ECCO.

Eilenberg, Susan. *Strange Power of Speech: Wordsworth, Coleridge, and Literary Possession.* Oxford: Oxford University Press, 1992.

Elfenbein, Andrew. *Romanticism and the Rise of English.* Stanford: Stanford University Press, 2009.

Eliot, T. S. "The Metaphysical Poets." In *Selected Essays, 1917-1932*, 241-50. New York: Harcourt, Brace, 1932.

———. "Shelley and Keats." In *The Use of Poetry and the Use of Criticism: Studies in the Relation of Criticism to Poetry in England*, 78-94. Cambridge, MA: Harvard University Press, 1961.

———. *The Waste Land.* Edited by Michael North. New York: W. W. Norton, 2000.

Empson, William. "The Ancient Mariner: An Answer to Warren." Edited by John Haffenden. *The Kenyon Review* 15, no.1 (1993): 155-77.

———. Introduction to *Coleridge's Verse: A Selection*, edited by William Empson and David Pirie, 13-100. New York: Schocken Books, 1973.

———. *Seven Types of Ambiguity.* New York: New Directions, 1966.

Epp, Leonard. "Coleridge and Romantic Obscurity." *Literature Compass* 1, no. 1 (2005): 1-6.

Erdman, David V. "Coleridge in Lilliput: The Quality of Parliamentary Reporting in 1800." *Speech Monographs* 27, no. 1 (1960): 33-62.

Erickson, Lee. *The Economy of Literary Form: English Literature and the Industrialization of Publishing, 1800-1850.* Baltimore: Johns Hopkins University Press, 1996.

Esbester, Mike. "Taxing Design? Design and Readers in British Tax Forms before 1914." *Design Issues* 27 no. 3 (2011): 84-97.

Essick, Robert N. "Coleridge and the Language of Adam." In *Coleridge's Biographia Literaria: Text and Meaning*, edited by Frederick Burwick, 62-74. Columbus: Ohio State University Press, 1989.

Favret, Mary. *War at a Distance: Romanticism and the Making of Modern Wartime.* Princeton: Princeton University Press, 2010.

Felski, Rita. *The Limits of Critique.* Chicago: University of Chicago Press, 2015.

———. *Uses of Literature.* Malden: Wiley-Blackwell, 2008.

Ferguson, Adam. *An Essay on the History of Civil Society.* Edited by Fania Oz-Salzberger. Cambridge: Cambridge University Press, 1995.

Ferguson, Frances. "Coleridge and the Deluded Reader: 'The Rime of the Ancient Mariner.'" In *The Rime of the Ancient Mariner*, edited by Paul H. Fry, 113-30. Boston: Bedford/St. Martin's Press, 1999.

———. *Pornography, the Theory: What Utilitarianism Did to Action*. Chicago: University of Chicago Press, 2004.

Fletcher, Angus. *Allegory: The Theory of a Symbolic Mode*. Ithaca: Cornell University Press, 1970.

Foucault, Michel. *Discipline and Punish: The Birth of the Prison*. New York: Vintage Books, 1995.

———. *"Society Must Be Defended": Lectures at the Collège de France, 1975–1976*. Edited by Mauro Bertani and Alessandro Fontana. Translated by David Macey. New York: Picador, 2003.

Franta, Andrew. *Romanticism and the Rise of the Mass Public*. Cambridge: Cambridge University Press, 2007.

Freud, Sigmund. *The Interpretation of Dreams*. Translated and edited by James Strachey. New York: Basic Books, 2010.

Frey, Anne. *British State Romanticism: Authorship, Agency, and Bureaucratic Nationalism*. Stanford: Stanford University Press, 2010.

Frost, Robert. "The Most of It." In *The Poetry of Robert Frost: The Collected Poems, Complete and Unabridged*, edited by Edward Connery Lathem, 338. New York: Henry Holt, 1969.

Fry, Paul H. "Wordsworth in the 'Rime.'" In *The Rime of the Ancient Mariner*, edited by Paul H. Fry, 319–42. Boston: Bedford/St. Martin's, 1999.

Fulford, Tim. *Coleridge's Figurative Language*. New York: St. Martin's Press, 1991.

Garrett, James M. *Wordsworth and the Writing of the Nation*. Aldershot: Ashgate, 2008.

Gill, Stephen. *William Wordsworth: A Life*. Oxford: The Clarendon Press, 1989.

Gitelman, Lisa. *Always Already New: Media, History, and the Data of Culture*. Cambridge, MA: MIT Press, 2008.

———. *Paper Knowledge: Toward a Media History of Documents*. Durham: Duke University Press, 2014.

———. *Scripts, Grooves, and Writing Machines: Representing Technology in the Edison Era*. Stanford: Stanford University Press, 1999.

Glen, Heather. "'We Are Seven' in the 1790s." In *Grasmere 2012: Selected Papers from the Wordsworth Summer Conference*, edited by Richard Gravil, 8–33. Humanities-Ebooks, 2012.

Goldsmith, Steven. *Unbuilding Jerusalem: Apocalypse and Romantic Representation*. Ithaca: Cornell University Press, 1993.

Goodman, Kevis. *Georgic Modernity and British Romanticism: Poetry and the Mediation of History*. Cambridge: Cambridge University Press, 2004.

———. "'Uncertain Disease': Nostalgia, Pathologies of Motion, Practices of Reading." *Studies in Romanticism* 49, no. 2 (Summer 2010): 197–227.

Gouldner, Alvin W. *The Coming Crisis of Western Sociology*. New York: Basic Books, 1970.

Gray, Thomas, William Collins, and Oliver Goldsmith. *The Poems of Thomas Gray, William Collins, Oliver Goldsmith*. Edited by Roger H. Lonsdale. Harlow: Longmans, 1969.

Guillory, John. *Cultural Capital: The Problem of Literary Canon Formation*. Chicago: University of Chicago Press, 1993.

———. "Genesis of the Media Concept." *Critical Inquiry* 36, no. 2 (2010): 321–62.

———. "The Memo and Modernity." *Critical Inquiry* 31, no. 1 (2004): 108–32.

———. *Poetic Authority: Spenser, Milton, and Literary History*. New York: Columbia University Press, 1983.

Gurney, Thomas. *Brachygraphy: or, Short-writing Made Easy to the Meanest Capacity* [. . .]. 1752. ECCO.

Gurton-Wachter, Lily. *Watchwords: Romanticism and the Poetics of Attention*. Stanford: Stanford University Press, 2016.

Hanson, Alfred. *The Acts Relating to Probate, Legacy, and Succession Duties* [. . .]. London: Stevens and Haynes, 1870. Google ebook. https://books.google.com/books?id=K6pDAAAAcAAJ.

Hartman, Geoffrey H. "I. A. Richards and the Dream of Communication." In *The Fate of Reading and Other Essays*, 20–40. Chicago: University of Chicago Press, 1975.

———. "Inscriptions and Romantic Nature Poetry." In *The Unremarkable Wordsworth*, 31–46. Minneapolis: University of Minnesota Press, 1987.

———. "Spectral Symbolism and Authorial Self in Keats's *Hyperion*." In *The Fate of Reading and Other Essays*, 57–73. Chicago: University of Chicago Press, 1975.

———. *Wordsworth's Poetry, 1787–1814*. Cambridge, MA: Harvard University Press, 1987.

Headrick, Daniel R. *When Information Came of Age: Technologies of Knowledge in the Age of Reason and Revolution, 1700–1850*. Oxford: Oxford University Press, 2000.

Hess, Jillian M. "Coleridge's Fly-Catchers: Adapting Commonplace-Book Form." *Journal of the History of Ideas* 73, no. 3 (2012): 463–83.

———. "'This Living Hand': Commonplacing Keats." *The Keats-Shelley Review* 24, no. 1 (2013): 15–21.

Hessell, Nikki. *Literary Authors, Parliamentary Reporters: Johnson, Coleridge, Hazlitt, Dickens*. Cambridge: Cambridge University Press, 2014.

Hewitt, Regina. *The Possibilities of Society: Wordsworth, Coleridge, and the Sociological Viewpoint of English Romanticism*. Albany: State University of New York Press, 1997.

Hickey, Alison. *Impure Conceits: Rhetoric and Ideology in Wordsworth's 'Excursion.'* Stanford: Stanford University Press, 1997.

Higgs, Edward. *The Information State in England: The Central Collection of Information on Citizens since 1500.* Basingstoke: Palgrave Macmillan, 2004.

Howell, Wilbur Samuel. *Eighteenth-Century British Logic and Rhetoric.* Princeton: Princeton University Press, 1971.

———. "Renaissance Rhetoric and Modern Rhetoric: A Study in Change." In *Poetics, Rhetoric, and Logic: Studies in the Basic Disciplines of Criticism,* 141-62. Ithaca: Cornell University Press, 1975.

Hume, L. J. *Bentham and Bureaucracy.* Cambridge: Cambridge University Press, 1981.

———. "The Development of Industrial Accounting: The Benthams' Contribution." *Journal of Accounting Research* 8, no. 1 (1970): 21-33.

Igarashi, Yohei. "Statistical Analysis at the Birth of Close Reading." *New Literary History* 46, no. 3 (2015): 485-504.

Jackson, Noel. *Science and Sensation in Romantic Poetry.* Cambridge: Cambridge University Press, 2011.

Jagoda, Patrick. *Network Aesthetics.* Chicago: University of Chicago Press, 2016.

Jakobson, Roman. "Linguistics and Poetics." In *Language in Literature,* edited by Krystyna Pomorska and Stephen Rudy, 62-94. Cambridge, MA: Harvard University Press, 1987.

[Jeffrey, Francis.] Review of *Memorials of a Tour on the Continent. The Edinburgh Review* 74, art. VIII (November 1822): 449-456. *ProQuest British Periodicals.*

[Jeffrey, Francis, Review of *The Excursion,* published in the *Edinburgh Review,* October 1807]. In John O. Hayden, *Romantic Bards and British Reviewers: A Selected Edition of the Contemporary Reviews of the Works of Wordsworth, Coleridge, Byron, Keats, and Shelley.* Lincoln: University of Nebraska Press, 1971.

Jenkins, Henry, Sam Ford, and Joshua Green. *Spreadable Media: Creating Value and Meaning in a Networked Culture.* New York: NYU Press, 2013.

Johnson, Samuel. *A Dictionary of the English Language* [. . .]. London: J. and P. Knapton; T. and T. Longman; C. Hitch and L. Hawes; A. Millar; and R. and J. Dodsley, 1755. ECCO.

Jones, H. S. Introduction to *Comte: Early Political Writings,* edited by H. S. Jones, vii-xxviii. Cambridge: Cambridge University Press, 1998.

Keach, William. *Shelley's Style.* New York: Methuen, 1984.

Keats, John. *Keats's Poetry and Prose: Authoritative Texts, Criticism.* Edited by Jeffrey N. Cox. New York: W. W. Norton, 2009.

———. *The Letters of John Keats.* 2 vols. Edited by Hyder Edward Rollins. Cambridge, MA: Harvard University Press, 1958.

Kitson, Peter J. *Forging Romantic China: Sino-British Cultural Exchange, 1760–1840*. Cambridge: Cambridge University Press, 2013.

Klancher, Jon P. *The Making of English Reading Audiences, 1790–1832*. Madison: University of Wisconsin Press, 1987.

———. *Transfiguring the Arts and Sciences: Knowledge and Cultural Institutions in the Romantic Age*. Cambridge: Cambridge University Press, 2016.

———. "Transmission Failure." In *Theoretical Issues in Literary History*, edited by David Perkins, 173–95. Cambridge, MA: Harvard University Press, 1991.

Krajewski, Markus. *Paper Machines: About Cards & Catalogs, 1548–1929*. Cambridge, MA: MIT Press, 2011.

Kramnick, Jonathan, and Anahid Nersessian. "Form and Explanation." *Critical Inquiry* 43, no. 3 (2017): 650–69.

Kreilkamp, Ivan. "Speech on Paper: Charles Dickens, Victorian Phonography, and the Reform of Writing." In *Literary Secretaries/Secretarial Culture*, edited by Leah Price and Pamela Thurschwell, 13–31. Aldershot: Ashgate, 2005.

Kucich, Greg. *Keats, Shelley, and Romantic Spenserianism*. University Park: Pennsylvania State University Press, 1991.

Lamb, Charles. "Distant Correspondents." In *The Complete Works and Letters of Charles Lamb*, 93–97. New York: Modern Library, 1935.

———. "The Superannuated Man." In *The Complete Works and Letters of Charles Lamb*, 172–77. New York: Modern Library, 1935.

Lampland, Martha, and Susan Leigh Star. "Reckoning with Standards." In *Standards and their Stories: How Quantifying, Classifying, and Formalizing Practices Shape Everyday Life*, edited by Martha Lampland and Susan Leigh Star, 3–24. Ithaca: Cornell University Press, 2009.

Langan, Celeste. "Pathologies of Communication from Coleridge to Schreber." *South Atlantic Quarterly* 102, no.1 (2003): 117–52.

Langan, Celeste, and Maureen N. McLane. "The Medium of Romantic Poetry." In *The Cambridge Companion to British Romantic Poetry*, edited by James Chandler and Maureen N. McLane, 239–62. Cambridge: Cambridge University Press, 2008.

Latour, Bruno. "Drawing Things Together." In *Representation in Scientific Practice*, edited by Michael Lynch and Steve Woolgar, 19–68. Cambridge, MA: MIT Press, 1990.

Lau, Beth. *Keats's Paradise Lost*. Gainesville: University Press of Florida, 1998.

Leask, Nigel. "Shelley's 'Magnetic Ladies': Romantic Mesmerism and the Politics of the Body." In *Beyond Romanticism: New Approaches to Texts and Contexts, 1780–1832*, edited by Stephen Copley and John Whale, 53–78. London: Routledge, 1992.

Levine, Caroline. *Forms: Whole, Rhythm, Hierarchy, Network*. Princeton: Princeton University Press, 2015.

Levinson, Marjorie. *Keats's Life of Allegory: The Origins of a Style*. Oxford: Blackwell, 1988.

Levy, Michelle. "Austen's Manuscripts and the Publicity of Print." *ELH* 77, no. 4 (2010): 1015–40.

Lewis, James Henry. *The Art of Making a Good Pen* [. . .]. Bristol: 1825. Google eBook. https://books.google.com/books?id=BppcAAAAcAAJ.

———. *An Historical Account of the Rise and Progress of Short Hand* [. . .]. London: Sherwood, Neeley, and Jones, 1816. Google eBook. https://books.google.com /books?id=Og8LAAAAMAAJ.

Liu, Alan. *The Laws of Cool: Knowledge Work and the Culture of Information*. Chicago: University of Chicago Press, 2004.

———. *Wordsworth: The Sense of History*. Stanford: Stanford University Press, 1989.

Locke, John. *An Essay Concerning Human Understanding*. Edited by P. H. Nidditch. Oxford: Oxford University Press, 1979.

———. *Some Thoughts Concerning Education*. London: A. and J. Churchill, 1693. Google eBook. https://books.google.com/books?id=OCUCAAAAQAAJ.

Lovelass, Peter. *An Abstract of, and Observations on, the Statutes Imposing Duty on Administrations, Probates of Wills, Property Disposed of by Will, and Distributable by the Statute of Distributions* [. . .]. London: 1796. ECCO.

Manning, Peter J. "Wordsworth at St. Bees: Scandals, Sisterhoods, and Wordsworth's Later Poetry." In *Reading Romantics*, 273–99. Oxford: Oxford University Press, 1990.

Marvin, Carolyn. *When Old Technologies Were New: Thinking about Electric Communication in the Late Nineteenth Century*. New York: Oxford University Press, 1988.

Mason, William. *A Pen Pluck't from an Eagles Wing*. London: J. Darby, 1672. Early English Books Online.

Mattelart, Armand. *The Invention of Communication*. Translated by Susan Emanuel. Minneapolis: University of Minnesota Press, 1996.

McDowell, Paula. "Defoe's Essay upon Literature and Eighteenth-Century Histories of Mediation." *PMLA* 130, no. 3 (2015): 566–83.

McGann, Jerome J. "Keats and the Historical Method in Literary Criticism." In *The Beauty of Inflections: Literary Investigations in Historical Method and Theory*, 15–65. Oxford: Clarendon Press, 1988.

———. "The Meaning of the Ancient Mariner." *Critical Inquiry* 8, no. 1 (1981): 35–67.

———. *The Textual Condition*. Princeton: Princeton University Press, 1991.

McGurl, Mark. *The Program Era: Postwar Fiction and the Rise of Creative Writing*. Cambridge, MA: Harvard University Press, 2009.

McKendrick, Neil. "Josiah Wedgwood and Factory Discipline." *The Historical Journal* 4, no. 1 (1961): 30–55.

McKusick, James C. *Coleridge's Philosophy of Language*. New Haven: Yale University Press, 1986.

McLane, Maureen N. *Balladeering, Minstrelsy, and the Making of British Romantic Poetry*. Cambridge: Cambridge University Press, 2008.

———. *Romanticism and the Human Sciences: Poetry, Population, and the Discourse of the Species*. Cambridge: Cambridge University Press, 2000.

Mendle, Michael. "The 'prints' of the Trials: The Nexus of Politics, Religion, Law and Information in Late Seventeenth-Century England." In *Fear, Exclusion and Revolution: Roger Morrice and Britain in the 1680s*, edited by Jason McElligott, 123–37. Aldershot: Ashgate, 2006.

Menke, Richard. *Telegraphic Realism: Victorian Fiction and Other Information Systems*. Stanford: Stanford University Press, 2008.

Mills, C. Wright. *White Collar: The American Middle Classes*. New York: Oxford University Press, 1956.

Milton, John. *Paradise Lost*. Edited by David Scott Kastan. Indianapolis: Hackett, 2005.

Mitchell, Charlotte, and Charles Mitchell. "Wordsworth and the Old Men." *The Journal of Legal History* 25, no. 1 (2004): 31–52.

Mitchell, Robert. "Biopolitics and Population Aesthetics." *South Atlantic Quarterly* 115, no. 2 (2016): 367–98.

———. *Sympathy and the State in the Romantic Era: Systems, State Finance, and the Shadows of Futurity*. London: Routledge, 2007.

Mitchell, W. J. T. *Blake's Composite Art: A Study of the Illuminated Poetry*. Princeton: Princeton University Press, 1978.

Modiano, Raimonda. *Coleridge and the Concept of Nature*. London: Macmillan, 1985.

Moorman, Mary. *William Wordsworth: The Later Years 1803–1850*. London: Oxford University Press, 1965.

Nabokov, Vladimir. "The Art of Literature and Commonsense." In *Lectures on Literature*, edited by Fredson Bowers, 371–80. San Diego: Harcourt, 1982.

Nersessian, Anahid. *Utopia, Limited: Romanticism and Adjustment*. Cambridge, MA: Harvard University Press, 2015.

Neville-Sington, Pamela. "Press, Politics and Religion." In *The Cambridge History of the Book in Britain*, Vol. 3, *1400–1557*, edited by Lotte Hellinga and J. B. Trapp, 575–607. Cambridge: Cambridge University Press, 1999.

Newlyn, Lucy. *Reading, Writing, and Romanticism: The Anxiety of Reception.* Oxford: Oxford University Press, 2000.

North, Joseph. *Literary Criticism: A Concise Political History.* Cambridge, MA: Harvard University Press, 2017.

Nissel, Muriel. *People Count: A History of the General Register Office.* London: H.M.S.O., 1987.

Ong, Walter J. "The Literate Orality of Popular Culture Today." In *Rhetoric, Romance, and Technology; Studies in the Interaction of Expression and Culture*, 284–303. Ithaca: Cornell University Press, 1971.

———. *Orality and Literacy: The Technologizing of the Word.* New York: Routledge, 2002.

———. "Romantic Difference and the Poetics of Technology." In *Rhetoric, Romance, and Technology; Studies in the Interaction of Expression and Culture*, 255–83. Ithaca: Cornell University Press, 1971.

Orr, Linda. "The Blind Spot of History: Logography." *Yale French Studies* 73 (1987): 190–214.

Owen, W. J. B., and Jane Worthington Smyser. "Introduction: General" [to *Essays upon Epitaphs*]. In *The Prose Works of William Wordsworth*, Vol. 2, edited by W. J. B. Owen and Jane Worthington Smyser, 45–47. Oxford: Clarendon Press, 1974.

Oxford English Dictionary Online. 2nd ed.

Patrides, C. A. "Paradise Lost and the Theory of Accommodation." *Texas Studies in Literature and Language* 5, no. 1 (Spring 1963): 58–63.

Paulson, William R. *The Noise of Culture: Literary Texts in a World of Information.* Ithaca: Cornell University Press, 1988.

Perry, Seamus. Introduction to *Coleridge's Notebooks: A Selection*, vii–xiv. Oxford: Oxford University Press, 2002.

———. *S. T. Coleridge: Interviews and Recollections.* Basingstoke: Palgrave, 2000.

Peters, John Durham. *The Marvelous Clouds: Toward a Philosophy of Elemental Media.* Chicago: University of Chicago Press, 2016.

———. *Speaking into the Air: A History of the Idea of Communication.* Chicago: University of Chicago Press, 1999.

Phillips, Mark Salber. *On Historical Distance.* New Haven: Yale University Press, 2015.

———. *Society and Sentiment: Genres of Historiographical Writing in Britain, 1740–1820.* Princeton: Princeton University Press, 2000.

Pinch, Adela. *Strange Fits of Passion: Epistemologies of Emotion, Hume to Austen.* Stanford: Stanford University Press, 1996.

Piper, Andrew. *Dreaming in Books: The Making of the Bibliographic Imagination in the Romantic Age.* Chicago: University of Chicago Press, 2009.

Pitman, Isaac. *A History of Shorthand*. London: I. Pitman & Sons, 1891.

Poovey, Mary. *Genres of the Credit Economy: Mediating Value in Eighteenth- and Nineteenth-Century Britain*. Chicago: University of Chicago Press, 2008.

Price, Leah. *How to Do Things with Books in Victorian Britain*. Princeton: Princeton University Press, 2012.

Reed, Mark L. *Wordsworth: The Chronology of the Middle Years, 1800–1815*. Cambridge, MA: Harvard University Press, 1975.

Rejack, Brian. "Keats on the Sea: The Circulation of Transatlantic Letters." Paper presented at "Romantic Discontents," the 24th Annual Conference of the North American Society for the Study of Romanticism, University of California, Berkeley, 11 August 2016.

Reynolds, L. D., and Nigel Guy Wilson. *Scribes and Scholars: A Guide to the Transmission of Greek and Latin Literature*. London: Oxford University Press, 1968.

Richards, I. A. *Basic in Teaching: East and West*. London: Kegan Paul, Trench, Trubner, 1935.

———. *Principles of Literary Criticism*. New York: Routledge, 2001.

Roberts, David. "Jeremy Bentham and the Victorian Administrative State." *Victorian Studies* 2, no. 3 (1959): 193–210.

Rohrbach, Emily, and Emily Sun. "Reading Keats, Thinking Politics: An Introduction." In "Reading Keats, Thinking Politics," special issue, *Studies in Romanticism* 50, no. 2 (Summer 2011): 229–37.

Royle, Nicholas. *Telepathy and Literature: Essays on the Reading Mind*. Oxford: Blackwell, 1991.

Rubinstein, W. D. "The End of "Old Corruption" in Britain 1780–1860." *Past & Present* 101 (1983): 55–86.

Rzepka, Charles. *Self as Mind: Vision and Identity in Wordsworth, Coleridge, and Keats*. Cambridge, MA: Harvard University Press, 1986.

Schellenberg, Betty A. *Literary Coteries and the Making of Modern Print Culture, 1740–1790*. Cambridge: Cambridge University Press, 2016.

Schivelbusch, Wolfgang. *The Railway Journey: The Industrialization of Time and Space in the 19th Century*. Berkeley: University of California Press, 1986.

Schoenfield, Mark K. *The Professional Wordsworth: Law, Labor, and the Poet's Contract*. Athens: University of Georgia Press, 1996.

Scodel, Joshua. *The English Poetic Epitaph: Commemoration and Conflict from Jonson to Wordsworth*. Ithaca: Cornell University Press, 1991.

Scott, James C. *Seeing Like a State: How Certain Schemes to Improve the Human Condition Have Failed*. New Haven: Yale University Press, 1998.

Shelley, Percy Bysshe. *The Letters of Percy Bysshe Shelley*. 2 vols. Edited by Frederick L. Jones. Oxford: Clarendon Press, 1964.

———. *Shelley's Poetry and Prose: Authoritative Texts, Criticism*. Edited by Donald H. Reiman and Neil Fraistat. New York: W. W. Norton, 2002.

Simpson, David. *Romanticism, Nationalism, and the Revolt Against Theory*. Chicago: Univsersity of Chicago Press, 1993.

Sinclair, John. *The Statistical Account of Scotland. Drawn Up from the Communications of the Ministers of the Different Parishes*. Vol. 1. Edinburgh: William Creech, 1791. ECCO.

Siskin, Clifford. *The Work of Writing: Literature and Social Change in Britain, 1700–1830*. Baltimore: Johns Hopkins University Press, 1998.

Siskin, Clifford, and William Warner. "This Is Enlightenment: An Invitation in the Form of an Argument." In *This Is Enlightenment*. Edited by Clifford Siskin and William Warner, 1–36. Chicago: University of Chicago Press, 2010.

Smith, Adam. *An Inquiry into the Nature and Causes of the Wealth of Nations*. Edited by R. H. Campbell and A. S. Skinner. Indianapolis: Liberty Fund, 1981.

———. *Lectures on Rhetoric and Belles Lettres*. Edited by J. C. Bryce. Indianapolis: Liberty Fund, 2007.

Spenser, Edmund. *The Faerie Queene: Book Six and the Mutabilitie Cantos*. Edited by Andrew Hadfield and Abraham Stoll. Indianapolis: Hackett, 2007.

———. "The Letter to Raleigh." In *The Faerie Queene: Book Six and the Mutabilitie Cantos*, edited by Andrew Hadfield and Abraham Stoll, 223–226. Indianapolis: Hackett, 2007.

St. Clair, William. *The Reading Nation in the Romantic Period*. Cambridge: Cambridge University Press, 2004.

Stallybrass, Peter. "Printing and the Manuscript Revolution." In *Explorations in Communication and History*, edited by Barbie Zelizer, 111–18. London: Routledge, 2008.

Standage, Tom. *The Victorian Internet: The Remarkable Story of the Telegraph and the Nineteenth Century's On-line Pioneers*. New York: Bloomsbury, 2014.

Steiner, George. "On Difficulty." In *On Difficulty and Other Essays*, 18–47. New York: Oxford University Press, 1978.

Stevens, Wallace. "Anecdote of Men by the Thousand." In *Wallace Stevens: Selected Poems*, edited by John N. Serio, 35. New York: Knopf, 2015.

Stiff, Paul, Paul Dobraszczyk, and Mike Esbester. "Designing and Gathering Information: Perspectives on Nineteenth-Century Forms." In *Information History in the Modern World: Histories of the Information Age*, edited by Toni Willer, 57–88. Basingstoke: Palgrave Macmillan, 2011.

Stillinger, Jack. *Reading The Eve of St. Agnes: The Multiples of Complex Literary Transaction*. Oxford: Oxford University Press, 1999.

Taylor, Frederick Winslow. *The Principles of Scientific Management*. New York: W. W. Norton, 1967.

Taylor, Samuel. *An Essay Intended to Establish a Standard for an Universal System of Stenography, or Short Hand Writing.* London: J. Bell, 1786. ECCO.

Tebeaux, Elizabeth. "Visual Texts: Format and the Evolution of English Accounting Texts, 1100–1700." *Journal of Technical Writing and Communication* 30, no. 4 (2000): 307–41.

Terada, Rei. "Looking at the Stars Forever." *Studies in Romanticism* 50, no. 2 (Summer 2011): 275–309.

Thompson, E. P. "Time, Work-Discipline, and Industrial Capitalism." *Past & Present* 38 (1967): 56–97.

Thompson, John B. *The Media and Modernity: A Social Theory of the Media.* Stanford: Stanford University Press, 1995.

Thorburn, David, and Henry Jenkins. "Introduction: Toward an Aesthetics of Transition." In *Rethinking Media Change: The Aesthetics of Transition*, edited by David Thorburn and Henry Jenkins, 1–16. Cambridge, MA: MIT Press, 2003.

Turkle, Sherry. *Alone Together: Why We Expect More from Technology and Less from Each Other.* New York: Basic Books, 2012.

Wang, Orrin N. C. "Coming Attractions: 'Lamia' and Cinematic Sensation." *Studies in Romanticism* 42, no. 4 (Winter 2003): 461–500.

Warner, Michael. *Publics and Counterpublics.* New York: Zone Books, 2005.

———. "Uncritical Reading." In *Polemic: Critical or Uncritical*, edited by Jane Gallop, 13–38. New York: Routledge, 2004.

Warren, Robert Penn. "A Poem of Pure Imagination: An Experiment in Reading." In *New and Selected Essays*, 335–99. New York: Random House, 1989.

———. "A Poem of Pure Imagination (Reconsiderations IV)." *The Kenyon Review* 8, no. 3 (1946): 391–427.

Weber, Max. *From Max Weber: Essays in Sociology.* Translated and edited by H. H. Gerth and C. Wright Mills. London: Routledge, 2009.

Wellbery, David E. Foreword to *Discourse Networks 1800/1900*, by Friedrich A. Kittler, vii–xxxiii. Translated by Michael Metteer, with Chris Cullens. Stanford: Stanford University Press, 1990.

White, E. B. Introduction to *The Elements of Style*, by William Strunk and E. B. White, xiii–xviii. New York: Longman, 2000.

Williams, Raymond. "Communication." In *Keywords: A Vocabulary of Culture and Society.* New York: Oxford University Press, 1985.

———. Introduction to *Contact: Human Communication and its History*, edited by Raymond Williams, 8–20. New York: Thames and Hudson, 1981.

———. *Marxism and Literature.* Oxford: Oxford University Press, 1977.

———. *Politics and Letters: Interviews with New Left Review.* London: Verso Books, 2015.

———. "The Romantic Artist." In *Culture and Society, 1780–1950*, 30–48. New York: Columbia University Press, 1983.

Winter, Alison. *Mesmerized: Powers of Mind in Victorian Britain*. Chicago: University of Chicago Press, 1998.

Wordsworth, Christopher. *Memoirs of William Wordsworth, Poet-Laureate, D.C.L.* Vol. II. London: E. Moxon, 1851. Google eBook. https://books.google.com /books?id=x_AsAAAAYAAJ.

Wordsworth, Mary. *The Letters of Mary Wordsworth, 1800–1855*. Edited by Mary Elizabeth Burton. Oxford: Clarendon Press, 1958.

Wordsworth, William. "Essay, Supplementary to the Preface." In *The Prose Works of William Wordsworth*, Vol. 3, edited by W. J. B. Owen and Jane Worthington Smyser, 62–84. Oxford: Clarendon Press, 1974.

———. "Essays Upon Epitaphs." In *The Prose Works of William Wordsworth*, Vol. 2, edited by W. J. B. Owen and Jane Worthington Smyser, 49–96. Oxford: Clarendon Press, 1974.

———. *The Excursion*. Edited by Sally Bushell, James A. Butler, and Michael C. Jaye, with the assistance of David Garcia. Ithaca: Cornell University Press, 2007.

———. "Fenwick Note to *The Excursion*." In *The Excursion*, edited by Sally Bushell, James A. Butler, and Michael C. Jaye, with the assistance of David Garcia, 1214–24. Ithaca: Cornell University Press, 2007.

———. "Kendal and Windermere Railway. Two Letters Re-printed from The Morning Post." In *The Prose Works of William Wordsworth*, Vol. 3, edited by W. J. B. Owen and Jane Worthington Smyser, 337–56. Oxford: Clarendon Press, 1974.

———. "Lines Written a Few Miles above Tintern Abbey [. . .]." In William Wordsworth and Samuel Taylor Coleridge, *Lyrical Ballads*, edited by R. L. Brett and A. R. Jones, 156–61. London: Routledge, 2005.

———. "Note on 'The Thorn'" In William Wordsworth and Samuel Taylor Coleridge, *Lyrical Ballads*, edited by R. L. Brett and A. R. Jones, 331–34. New York: Routledge, 2005.

———. "Note to 'The Ancient Mariner' [from the 1800 Edition of *Lyrical Ballads*]." In William Wordsworth and Samuel Taylor Coleridge, *Lyrical Ballads*, edited by R. L. Brett and A. R. Jones, 318–19. New York: Routledge, 2005.

———. "Preface." In William Wordsworth and Samuel Taylor Coleridge, *Lyrical Ballads*, edited by R. L. Brett and A. R. Jones, 286–314. New York: Routledge, 2005.

———. "Preface of 1815." In *The Prose Works of William Wordsworth*, Vol. 3, edited by W. J. B. Owen and Jane Worthington Smyser, 26–40. Oxford: Clarendon Press, 1974.

———. *The Prelude, 1799, 1805, 1850: Authoritative Texts, Context and Reception, Recent Critical Essays*. Edited by Jonathan Wordsworth, M. H. Abrams, and Stephen Gill. New York: W. W. Norton, 1979.

———. "Scorn not the Sonnet." In *Wordsworth's Poetry and Prose*, edited by Nicholas Halmi, 550. New York: W. W. Norton, 2014.

Wordsworth, William, and Dorothy Wordsworth. *The Letters of William and Dorothy Wordsworth*. Vol. 3, *The Middle Years*, Part 2, *1812–1820*. 2nd ed. Edited by Ernest De Selincourt. Revised by Mary Moorman and Alan G. Hill. Oxford: Clarendon Press, 1970.

———. *The Letters of William and Dorothy Wordsworth*. Vol. 4, *The Later Years*, Part 1, *1821–1828*. 2nd ed. Edited by Ernest De Selincourt. Revised, Arranged, and Edited by Alan G. Hill. Oxford: Clarendon Press, 1978.

Wordsworth, William, and Samuel Taylor Coleridge. *Lyrical Ballads*. Edited by R. L. Brett and A. R. Jones. London: Routledge, 2005.

Worthen, John. *The Cambridge Introduction to Samuel Taylor Coleridge*. Cambridge: Cambridge University Press, 2010.

Wunder, Jennifer N. *Keats, Hermeticism, and the Secret Societies*. Hampshire: Ashgate, 2008.

Yates, JoAnne. *Control through Communication: The Rise of System in American Management*. Baltimore: Johns Hopkins University Press, 1989.

Zielinski, Siegfried. *Deep Time of the Media: Toward an Archaeology of Hearing and Seeing by Technical Means*. Cambridge, MA: MIT Press, 2006.

Ziolkowski, Jan M. "Theories of Obscurity in the Latin Tradition." *Mediaevalia* 19 (1996): 101–70.

Page numbers in italics refer to illustrations.